THE GENERATIONS
OF HEAVEN AND EARTH

THE GENERATIONS OF HEAVEN AND EARTH

Adam, the Ancient World, and Biblical Theology

JON GARVEY

 CASCADE *Books* · Eugene, Oregon

THE GENERATIONS OF HEAVEN AND EARTH
Adam, the Ancient World, and Biblical Theology

Cascade Books
An Imprint of Wipf and Stock Publishers
199 W. 8th Ave., Suite 3
Eugene, OR 97401

www.wipfandstock.com

PAPERBACK ISBN: 978-1-5326-8165-3
HARDCOVER ISBN: 978-1-5326-8166-0
EBOOK ISBN: 978-1-5326-8167-7

Cataloguing-in-Publication data:

Names: Garvey, Jon, author.

Title: The generations of heaven and earth : Adam, the ancient world, and biblical theology / Jon Garvey.

Description: Eugene, OR: Cascade Books, 2020. | Includes bibliographical references and index.

Identifiers: ISBN 978-1-5326-8165-3 (paperback) | ISBN 978-1-5326-8166-0 (hardcover) | ISBN 978-1-5326-8167-7 (ebook)

Subjects: LCSH: Adam (Biblical figure). | Theological anthropology—Christianity. | Human beings—Origin.

Classification: BT701.3 .G50 2020 (paperback) | CALL NUMBER (ebook)

Manufactured in the U.S.A.   01/13/20

To Edie, Emma, Isabel, Martha, and Skye,
Daughters of Eve,
and perhaps one day universal genealogical ancestors.

CONTENTS

LIST OF FIGURES AND TABLES

PREFACE

THIS BOOK IS INTENDED to complement the work of MD and computational biologist Joshua Swamidass, recently published in book form under the title *The Genealogical Adam and Eve.*[1] Genealogical Adam is a new interpretive paradigm for the early chapters of Genesis that is based on recent discoveries in the scientific study of genealogy. It has been attracting much positive attention in the last couple of years from those of diverse positions in the Christian "origins discussion," and people in a wide range of theological traditions ranging from Orthodox and Roman Catholic to Evangelical—and perhaps surprisingly, those interested even include atheists.

Briefly, its scientific claim is that a historical couple living in the Ancient Near East, amongst an existing human population, at any time plausibly matching the biblical account, would *almost certainly* be common ancestors of everyone living in the world today, and indeed in the world to which the universal gospel came at the time of Jesus.

Thus it preserves all the historical theological doctrines based on the Genesis account, whilst simultaneously affirming the reliability of the new information we have gained over recent centuries about human history.

Such information, discovered through a whole range of sciences like geology, astronomy, archaeology, anthropology, linguistics, paleontology, and, more recently, genetics, challenged first of all the prevailing assumption that the cosmos was created in one week just six thousand years ago. But as evidence also seemed to build against the traditional teaching that mankind arose from a single specially created couple at that relatively recent time, we have seen, over a number of generations now, a tendency to allegorize Adam or to deny his existence altogether. It has even become

1. Swamidass, *Genealogical Adam and Eve.*

fashionable to regard broadly historical understandings of the first couple as crude and literalistic, thus making a theological virtue of a necessity that actually arose from science, not revelation.

This has all had a profound effect on the most basic Christian teachings, from the doctrine of creation[2] to original sin and the whole concept of salvation history. It has even affected the doctrine of God, in ways that it is beyond my scope to unpack here. If Genealogical Adam is valid, we will need to relearn teachings that have become marginalized by what turns out to have been misleading science, because it was incomplete and focused on the wrong things.

Even amongst those of a more conservative bent, the undeniable existence of widespread and culturally sophisticated humans for many millennia has sometimes led to their pushing Adam back in time to the Paleolithic, and thus as far outside history, properly understood, as the allegorizers do. The date for Adam thus estimated has to become earlier each year, as more discoveries are made about the artistic, technological, linguistic, and perhaps spiritual capacities of Neanderthals, Denisovans, and even earlier than them, *Homo erectus*. Furthermore, evidence of widespread hybridization with these earlier hominins has blurred any understanding of what "human" might mean in biblical terms, if Adam and Eve must predate them. Genealogical Adam allows Adam to exist when the Bible (if all too approximately) says he did, and encourages us to seek a clearer theological understanding of what it means to be human.

I will give only a brief account of Genealogical Adam in the Introduction, and I refer you to Swamidass's definitive treatment of the science to gain a fuller understanding. You will gain much less from this book if you have not read Joshua's.

My own aim here is ambitious in another way than science-faith *rapprochement*. Whereas Genealogical Adam has been presented by Swamidass (and by a very few others before he took it up) as a plausible *possibility* for resolving the tensions between Scripture and science,[3] I have become increasingly convinced that it might better be regarded as the rediscovery, after very many centuries, of an assumption that was obvious to the Bible writers and their original audience. In other words, I consider it likely that Genesis was written in full knowledge that Adam

---

2. See my reevaluation of creation doctrine in Garvey, *God's Good Earth*.

3. "I am a scientist. In the spirit of science, I am curious about the question of Adam and Eve. Questions are far more interesting than the settled answers." Swamidass, *Genealogical Adam and Eve*, 23.

and Eve were called *out of* and *for the sake of* an existing and widespread mankind.

That the Bible writers thought a lot about genealogy is evident from both Old and New Testaments. We underestimate it and misunderstand it, for the same reason that it has been confidently stated for so many years that science has disproven a historical Adam: we have got used, largely because of evolutionary theory, to thinking *genetically*, rather than *genealogically*. We see individual lines of descent where the ancients saw swirling rivers. We see a neat tree of life, whereas perhaps ancient people saw a pudding being stirred.

My contention is that Genealogical Adam is not just another "concordist" theory, attempting to find a fix for the incompatibility of the Bible account with other sources of knowledge, but instead as a means for recovering the original intention of Scripture.

As will be seen, I have been very much influenced by the work done in recent years on the biblical "metanarrative," especially by Evangelical scholars. This enterprise has arisen from the rubble of the abandoned nineteenth-century consensus on hypothetical Old Testament sources, apparently reawakening OT scholars to the realization that the concentration on the history of texts can blind one to the existence of a history *in* the texts.

In my view, Genealogical Adam is an important tool in that historical and narrative kind of biblical theology. It helps us create a firm foundation in world history for all such attempts. So it is my main purpose in this book to show the relevance of Genealogical Adam to biblical theology. The divine appointment of a vice-regent back in Eden is necessary to account for the crucial fact that there is a man ruling all things in heaven now, and that he will also reign with us in the renewed earth in the age to come. I will attempt to establish that case in the real world using evidence both from within the pages of the Bible and from elsewhere.

Here, and throughout this book, I have referred to the paradigm as "Genealogical Adam." This was the "working title" of the idea as it was being developed, but Joshua Swamidass has opted in his book to be more inclusive and use "Genealogical Adam and Eve" consistently. This is appropriate to his primarily scientific treatment. After consideration, I have retained the earlier usage simply because my focus in this book is on biblical theology, and in that sphere it is the role of Adam that is the paramount consideration. This is, of course, by no means intended to denigrate the role of Eve, who is an archetype of womanhood in her own right.

The title, *The Generations of Heaven and Earth*, comes from Genesis 2:4, the first of the so-called "*toledot*" statements of Genesis. The scholarly consensus is that these act primarily as introductions to the sections of the book, pointing to the "outcomes" of the named individuals such as Adam (5:1), Noah (6:9), and so on. These "outcomes," or "generations" are mainly their offspring, but also the events they took part in. "The heavens and the earth" are, of course, the entire Genesis 1 creation, and it may seem strange to see the garden narrative as if it were a genealogy for a parental cosmos.

And yet, if I am correct in my thesis that Genesis 2 introduces the theme of new creation that occupies the whole of the rest of the Bible, then there is a theological, as well as a poetic, truth in the concept of the heaven and earth bringing forth a new creation that literally unites and replaces them.[4] The title, then, describes the whole theme of the book, and not simply the genealogical relationships of the human race.

4. Rev 21:1.

ACKNOWLEDGMENTS

RICHARD COEKIN TRIGGERED MY interest in biblical theology back in 1995, when I asked him to teach a Bible overview at our church for a Lent course, and instead he encouraged me to prepare my own, pointing me to Graeme Goldsworthy's landmark work. Their Moore College influence was later reinforced by my erstwhile pastor, Tim McMahon, who trained there, and who has also focused my mind on a number of the issues raised in this project during a brief, but valuable, visit in November 2018. The recent influences on my thinking on the subject, to whom I express my gratitude, are clear from the text, but I must particularly single out Richard Middleton, who has been willing to keep me personally abreast of his own developing work on "Biblical Worldview" despite the disparity in our academic status, whilst expressing appreciation for my own, somewhat different, approach.

Genealogical Adam, being a newcomer, has far fewer advocates than does biblical theology. But I must, of course, acknowledge my debt to David Opderbeck, who first wrote about it and awakened my interest in 2010, and to Joshua Swamidass, who has been encouraging me to collate and develop my thoughts since 2017, latterly urging the writing of this book.

In the early days, those thoughts were encouraged, and the spark of the Genealogical Adam idea kept alive in my mind, to be honest, by discussions at my blog The Hump of the Camel, including not only my co-writers there Merv Bitkofer, Sy Garte, James Penman, and Edward Robinson, but also astute critics and encouragers including George Domazetis, Preston Garrison, Kenneth Turner, and Noah White. The online community at Swamidass's Peaceful Science forum has also been supportive since it formed in 2018.

I must also acknowledge the encouragement and indulgence of the leadership team at the Baptist Church, Kilmington, especially my pastor Darrell Holmes. They have been generous in recognizing that time closeted away in my study is work for the kingdom, even when it is not work for the local fellowship. Anthony Chape's theological discussions, often across the top of a piano after Sunday services, have also been invaluable.

Most irreplaceable of all, as ever, has been the support of my wife, Cynthia.

INTRODUCTION

MOST NEW IDEAS TURN out to be old ideas whose time has come, or even ideas that have returned after a long and undeserved absence.[1]

Take, for example, a familiar concept like "air." In the ancient world, air was not considered a material substance. The Greeks had words for the bright *"aether"*[2] of the blue sky, and for murky fog, but not for the stuff that we assume surrounds us, and clothes our world like a blanket. Ancient gods of the air, therefore, were deities of a *space*, not a substance. The winds they governed were not merely "air in motion" but something more mysterious and dynamic—which explains, for example, why the "spirit/wind (*ruach*) of God" in Gen 1:2 lacks the ambiguity in Hebrew that it has in English, and why the same word, when used for "the breath of life" (e.g., Gen 6:17; 7:15, 22) has divine, rather than merely physical, connotations.

It was the Sicilian Greek philosopher Empodocles who, in c 450 BCE, was the first to name "air" as a material substance, finding that a bucket inverted in water retained a pocket of air. Such a phenomenon must have been seen by many, for millennia before, but not interpreted as significant.[3] *Genealogical Adam* did not have to wait quite so long to be seen as important, but its seeds have certainly been around for a long time.

There is a long-standing party conversation piece in Britain, to the effect that everyone in Europe is descended from Charlemagne, Holy

---

1. This chapter is adapted from a blog post I wrote for the Peaceful Science website in November 2018.

2. *Aether* derives from *aithein*, to burn or shine, which provides an interesting commentary on the old problem of how the writer of Genesis considered light to have been created before the sun.

3. Garvey, "Short History of Air."

Roman Emperor from 800 CE. Why he in particular is singled out I do not know—he had about twenty children, which is not unusually large for a polygamous king. Johann Sebastian Bach had the same number with a more usual number of wives.

But the party spiel reminds us that our ancestors double with each generation. We all have four biological grandparents, eight great-grandparents, sixteen great-great-grandparents, and so on. A little calculation shows that this gives each of us around a thousand ancestors in the tenth generation, and a *million* in the twentieth. With some fifty generations separating us from the Emperor Charlemagne, each of us has a *quadrillion* ancestors from that time, which is clearly absurd—until one remembers that most of those ancestors must be shared many times over. Many lines of descent must pass through the same individuals, causing our *real* genealogy to resemble far more a tangled meshwork than a family tree.

The population of Europe in Charlemagne's time is estimated at twenty-five to thirty million. Taking that figure of one quadrillion ancestors for each of us, on average each person from that generation would be our ancestor around forty million times over. Some of those ancestors— and perhaps, virtually *everyone* who has left any descendants at all—will, inevitably, be ancestors of everyone in Europe. Genealogy is more like a pudding being stirred than a tree growing and branching.

In 2002 a freelance writer, Steve Olson, published a trade book called *Mapping Human History*,[4] which I bought when browsing my local bookshop because it described some findings from the new studies of genetics across human populations. It was a good source to understand the popular "Y-chromosome Adam" and "Mitochondrial Eve." It also highlighted intriguing studies like those showing the prevalence of a particular Y-chromosome type among Jewish bearers of the surname Cohen, the descendants of priests. In a majority of cases, it was found, they are also descendants of one male ancestor in the late second millennium BCE, according to the genetic divergence.

But Olson's primary interest was in stiffening up the "Charlemagne scenario" to suggest that pervasive genetic mixing renders the whole idea of pure "races," and major ethnic differences, obsolete and purely cultural, not biological. In fact he claimed that it is likely that humanity's most recent ancestor lived just two or three thousand years ago. The brotherhood of man is far more real than people had realized.

4. Olson, *Mapping Human History*.

Olson had drawn on a paper by statistician Joseph Chang,[5] which had explored for the first time how a two-parent model of population genetics would deal with common ancestry. Surprisingly, up until then (as in the research leading to "Mitochondrial Eve") only single-sex inheritance had been used. Nevertheless despite his use of this unexceptionable paper many geneticists dismissed Olson's recent date for a common ancestor as an absurdly low figure, thinking more in terms of the six-figure numbers of Y-Adam and Mito-Eve.

But Olson then took the initiative of enlisting Chang and a software engineer, Douglas Rohde, to run detailed computer simulations. This resulted in two papers,[6,7] one of which appeared in *Nature* in 2004, demonstrating that Olson's intuition was correct. Using virtually any reasonable input for population movements and growth, the simulations showed consistently that our probable most recent *genealogical* ancestor lived two or three thousand years ago, and even more strikingly, that *anyone* living more than five or six millennia ago, who has left any descendants at all, is a common ancestor for the whole human race. If, like me, you have at least five grandchildren, it is "virtually guaranteed"[8] that you will be an ancestor to everyone living two to three thousand years from now.

This ancestry includes even "isolated" populations. The Andaman Islands are often cited against Genealogical Adam, as being cut off from the rest of the world since time immemorial. Yet their religion shows otherwise, for cultural exchange accounts for some complexities of their primitive monotheistic religion across the various tribes:

> [W]e now know for certain that this complication is in very
> large measure due to crossing with later, matrilineal cultures
> from Farther India.[9]

Whilst I nodded approvingly at Olson's demolition of any rational justification for racism, I thought nothing about any theological implications when I read his paperback, even though the catchy subtitle was *Unravelling the Mystery of Adam and Eve*. But somebody else was more perceptive.

5. Chang, "Recent Common Ancestors."

6. Rohde, Olson, and Chang, "Modelling the recent common ancestry."

7. Rohde, "On the common ancestors of all living humans."

8. "Steve Olson (writer)," *Wikipedia*, https://en.wikipedia.org/wiki/Steve_Olson_(writer)#Research_on_ancestry.

9. Schmidt, *Origin and Growth*, 258.

In April 2010 David Opderbeck, a lawyer by training (note the absence of geneticists in the story so far), published a piece at the Theistic Evolution website BioLogos,[10] citing one of the Rohde articles. He identified how, if Adam and Eve were a couple arising from within an existing human population, they could be ancestors, if not strictly speaking sole ancestors, of the whole race. This proposal would also account for the hints in Genesis of others outside the garden, such as the perennial matter of Cain's wife, as well as for the scientific evidence of worldwide populations from times close to the very beginning of our species. He stated, on the one hand:

> What I'm suggesting is scientifically plausible. There is no problem at all in suggesting that every person alive today physically can trace his or her lines of descent—his or her "family tree"—to encompass a single pair in the recent or distant past. The problem arises when we try to suggest that this pair were the *only* humans alive at the time and that all of our present genes derive *only* from a single pair.[11]

But on the other, theological, hand he continued:

> . . . it seems to me that it could preserve Paul's federal theology and provides a plausible, even Augustinian, mechanism for the propagation of original sin.[12]

This viewpoint seemed to me to tick many boxes in the origins debate, and that November I wrote my first study paper[13] on it (for my own use), and aired it in several discussions at BioLogos. But for the most part it engendered little interest there. In fact, a year or so after the Opderbeck piece, the then BioLogos President Darrel Falk was lambasted merely for giving a voice to those (in Falk's words in a blog comment) "very few theologians" holding "the view that Adam and Eve were real historical individuals, but not the sole genetic progenitors of humankind."[14] Falk, following his departure from BioLogos, has subsequently spoken[15] in support of Genealogical Adam.

---

10. Opderbeck, "'Historical' Adam?"
11. Ibid.
12. Ibid.
13. Garvey, *Adam and MRCA.*
14. Blog comment at BioLogos, 06/04/2011, since deleted.
15. Swamidass, "Genealogical Rapprochement."

BioLogos went on to make a firm commitment to the impossibility of a historical Adam and Eve, as ancestors of the whole present human race, on scientific grounds, though they drew back from that uncompromising position more recently.[16] Individual BioLogians, like their Resources Editor Kathryn Applegate,[17] have also expressed personal support for a historical Adam arising within an existing population.

A couple of scholars who did support Opderbeck's idea, or something similar, found themselves accused of racism, despite the fact that, as it was first presented by Steve Olson, the very *purpose* of uncovering "genealogical common ancestors" was to *refute* racism.[18] It is true that Genealogical Adam implies some kind of distinction between Adam and those outside the garden, and the gradual merging of those distinctions through interbreeding as Adam's genealogical descendants spread across the world. But since the same is true of the gospel of new birth, I began to sense that the Bible actually supports that interpretation.

In 2016 physician and computational biologist Joshua Swamidass burst upon the origins scene, engaging with both the Intelligent Design website Uncommon Descent and its rival, the theistic evolutionist BioLogos. He largely opposed the former, but propounded the kind of providentially orthodox understanding of theistic evolution I had been championing for several years. Within a short time he was seeking to bring the various origins factions into discussion, an effort that eventually culminated in the Peaceful Science web forum. But in April 2017 he started a BioLogos thread[19] about his own recent acquaintance with what came to be known as Genealogical Adam, and was surprised that one or two of us had already been thinking and writing about it for a while.

In his hands, it would appear, Genealogical Adam's "time had come," because of Swamidass's knowledge of population genetics and computer modelling, his enthusiasm for the idea, and his gift for networking. The great value of his work so far has been to put the theory on a rigorous scientific footing, with obvious benefit for scientists both theistic and otherwise, as well as encouraging those of us interested in it to develop

---

16. Hardin, "On Geniality."

17. Applegate, "Why I Think Adam was a Real Person."

18. "Genetics research is now about to end our long misadventure with the idea of race. We now know that groups overlap genetically to such a degree that humanity cannot be divided into clear categories." Olson, *Mapping Human History*, 6–7.

19. BioLogos Staff, "Genealogical is not Genetic."

its implications for theology. His book[20] has now taken the idea to a far wider audience.

At this point I should add a couple of other factors which make Genealogical Adam an "idea whose time has come." One is the increasing trickle of thinkers propounding a "*Homo divinus*" model, in which Adam is similarly selected from an existing population, and somehow specially endowed for relationship with God, perhaps with the divine image, or in some other way.[21]

Derek Kidner had proposed the germ of such a concept from within conservative Evangelicalism in his 1967 Genesis commentary.[22] Andrew Alexander had developed a similar idea,[23] which was restated by Catholic scholar Kenneth Kemp in 2011,[24] and supported by analytical Thomist philosopher Ed Feser.[25] However, without invoking genealogical science these schemes all tend to fall foul of problems like an extremely ancient (and so primitive and prehistorical) Adam, contradictions with genetic science, and so on.

Still, they have been rendered more plausible because of strong recent trends in recent OT theology, suggesting that the biblical authors identify the divine image more with vocation to a task[26] than with specific attributes like rationality or biological form, the emphases of traditional theology.

A further, related factor opening the way to Genealogical Adam is the renewed interest in biblical theology, particularly in Evangelicalism, arising from the collapse of the source-critical consensus in recent decades. To put it crudely, academics have become less obsessed with how the Bible evolved, and more interested in what it says, leading to the exploration of its overarching historical narrative by many scholars.[27] This makes finding the place of Genesis within history a necessary task.

20. Swamidass, *Genealogical Adam and Eve*.

21. One forthcoming book, Loke, *The Origin of Humanity*, takes Swamidass's work into account in such a scheme.

22. Kidner, *Genesis*.

23. Alexander, "Human Origins and Genetics."

24. Kemp, "Theology, and Monogenesis."

25. Feser, "Monkey in your soul?"

26. For example Brock, "Jesus Christ the Divine Animal?"

27. Currently these include Greg Beale, C. John Collins, Richard Middleton, John Sailhamer, John Walton, Christopher J. H. Wright, and N. T. Wright, amongst many others.

If Christians are to understand their significance as being participants in a real historical process governed by Christ,[28] then the beginning of that history is as crucial, in its own way, as its culmination in the incarnation.

Genealogical Adam is probably best viewed as a *paradigm*, rather than as a specific theory. Joshua Swamidass has his own theological viewpoint, which he expresses tentatively as a "narrative experiment,"[29] but also presents examples of how those with other theological understandings might approach it. As Opderbeck's original article suggested, it is compatible with an Augustinian understanding of original sin—but it does not entail it. Likewise, it is entirely compatible with the special creation of Adam and Eve. However, for those who wish to see a greater biological continuity between Adam's line and his predecessors that too is possible.

In the end, its strength is that it enables the traditional doctrines associated with Adam, both in Scripture and in historical theology, to remain intact, whilst leaving no quarrel with "secular" findings on history and archaeology, nor even with various evolutionary understandings of creation.

For my own part, having been persuaded that my "pet theory" was actually a worthwhile research project, my interest since 2017 has largely been in exploring to what extent Scripture itself might endorse it. This is not as absurd or anachronistic as it might seem.

Concordist schemes seeking to show that, for example, the writer of Genesis had knowledge of modern science are doomed to failure. But if Genealogical Adam is true, then Genesis may be about relatively recent history, preserving a real tradition arising from the events themselves. If so, the Bible writers might be expected to be well aware that other human lines than Adam's had existed, and I believe there is some evidence they did. In fact, Genealogical Adam may well be an example of the second kind of idea I mentioned to begin with—one which was once well known, but eclipsed for a time.

---

28. "For by him all things were created, in heaven and on earth, visible and invisible, whether thrones or dominions or rulers or authorities—all things were created through him and for him. And he is before all things, and in him all things hold together. And he is the head of the body, the church. He is the beginning, the firstborn from the dead, that in everything he might be preeminent. For in him all the fullness of God was pleased to dwell, and through him to reconcile to himself all things, whether on earth or in heaven, making peace by the blood of his cross." (Col 1:15–20.)

29. Swamidass, *Genealogical Adam and Eve*, 17–83.

In this case, the eclipse partly has to do with the way our modern thinking on ancestry has become conditioned by genetics. The rejection of a historical first couple by many Evolutionary Creationists is based on its alleged scientific impossibility (from which allegorical readings follow by necessity), and on seeing inherited sin as necessarily genetic, and therefore implausible (and so also in need of doctrinal revision).

But the discovery of genealogical science is, in reality, only a rediscovery of what ancient peoples knew from experiencing life in a relational, rather than a materialistic, way. We are only beginning to scratch the surface of such an understanding in our presentations of Genealogical Adam.

To sum up how Genealogical Adam bears directly on biblical theology, consider these two implications, assuming it to be correct (and assuming we have good reasons to reject a purely allegorical or mythical Adam). In the first place, it removes any reason to deny that the relatively recent Adam implied in Genesis comes from historical times, about which we also have many other sources of information.

Secondly, this Adam arose in a world that had been widely populated with "biologically modern humans," and previously by their evolutionary forebearers (including the hybrids between them), for hundreds of thousands of years, for which there is abundant evidence.

The first implication means that we would expect the story of Adam, whatever its peculiarities of genre, to have come to the author of Genesis *via* a human tradition, and not simply by divine dictation (as would necessarily be the case if Adam were, say, living in the ice age beyond the range of collective memory). This conclusion is endorsed by the literary links we already know to exist between the first chapters of Genesis and Mesopotamian narratives whose origins date back, as far as we can tell, to the very birth of written literature around 2,500 BCE.

As an illustration, many believe that the great flood described in Genesis corresponds to the Akkadian Atrahasis flood, which is probably in part a recollection of the river flood that affected the region of Shuruppak around 2,900 BCE, an inundation amply confirmed by archaeology. If the two are parallel traditions, rather than Genesis being simply the theft of folk-motifs by the biblical author, then those who originated them would have been well aware that the flood was regional, not universal, and the mere four centuries that passed before the stories were first written down would be insufficient to erase that knowledge. I will be examining the longevity of oral historical narratives in chapter 2.

The second implication of a fully populated world outside the Garden of Eden means that the original bearers of the Genesis narrative tradition (such as Adam himself) would have been fully aware of the state of their world, with its other inhabitants. That awareness would be likely to be discernible in the text we have. Someone constructing an origins myth for the distant past might well invent a single primordial couple. But a *real* historical founder couple, aware that their uniqueness was a special divine calling from within a populated world, would surely understand their significance in *that* setting, and would embed it in the tradition.

And so the capacity of Genealogical Adam to make a recent historical setting for Adam plausible also confirms the account itself to be potentially historiographic, in the sense of arising from events within a particular culture and being passed as a tradition on from generation to generation, as cultural memories customarily are. Whether it is *intended* as history (in the broad sense) or as myth must therefore be decided on literary and theological grounds, not by pleading scientific impossibility. We may even have to unlearn a two-century habit of over-allegorizing Scripture.

Whether it is *true* as a historical account must then be judged in the same way as are other biblical events, such as the lives of the patriarchs, which lie beyond the scope of strict historical corroboration. The considerations would include cultural verisimilitude, for example, and in the later chapters of Genesis 1—11, perhaps, possible mapping to known historical events.

One reason for considering the early chapters of Genesis to be essentially historical is that they are not simply an aetiological tale of origins, looking back to a lost past to explain why things in the present exist. Rather these chapters are forward looking, laying a foundation of hope for the divine resolution of the tragedy of sin, death, and estrangement from God they describe. Genesis does not, in the end, look only backwards to explain the beginning of things. The story-cycle that begins in the Garden of Eden has an ongoing trajectory leading up to the account of the tower of Babel, at which point Abraham's family begins to be introduced as the first sign of the fulfillment of that hope.

In this way, it explains the *raison d'être* of Israel, for whom the form of the narrative we have was first written, and of the church, which has inherited in Christ the vocation of both Adam and Israel.

Genealogical Adam appears to be a means for this generation to recover the full power of that biblical narrative.

§1: Generations of Heaven

(Time)

". . . let them be for signs and for seasons and for days and years . . ."
GEN 1:14.

1.

GENRE AND METAPHOR

Literal or Metaphorical?

THE EMPHASIS ON SCRIPTURE'S literal meaning was an important distinctive of the Protestant Reformation, although it should never be forgotten how William Tyndale explained that,

> the Scripture uses proverbs, similitudes, riddles, or allegories, as all other speeches do; but what the proverb, similitude, riddle, or allegory signifies, is always the literal sense, which you must seek out diligently.[1]

This concern for the literal meaning was in strong reaction to largely allegorical readings of Scripture that had begun early in the Catholic era, particularly under the influence of Neoplatonism. But even that most Platonist of the Church Fathers, Origen, who openly regarded as absurd some of the details of the account of Adam,[2] nevertheless seems to have taken the basic historicity of the story for granted,[3] even as he emphasized the more "spiritual" understanding.

1. Tyndale, *Obedience*, 72.

2. "And who is so foolish as to suppose that God, after the manner of a husbandman, planted a paradise in Eden, towards the east, and placed in it a tree of life, visible and palpable, so that one tasting of the fruit by the bodily teeth obtained life? And again that one was a partaker of good and evil by masticating what was taken from the tree?" Origen, *De Principiis* IV.1.16, 315–16.

3. "For every beginning of those families which have relation to God as to the

13

Despite the tradition of Protestant historical-grammatical interpretation, modern Evangelical scholars are insistent on avoiding a dichotomy between "an imagination shaping fairy tale or a newspaper account."[4] David Opderbeck was mentioned in the Introduction as the original proponent of *Genealogical Adam* at BioLogos. In a different context he sees Origen's approach, whilst overly influenced by Platonism and often used nowadays by those espousing "Eastern" theology to make excessively "broad generalizations,"[5] as being a useful stimulus "to a contemporary Christian theology of Adam and original sin."[6]

This is a salutary reminder that the ancient biblical writers put much less of a barrier between the literal and the metaphorical than we do. The difficulties of placing Eden in space and time are, as Brian Brock says, a warning to us to base our theology on the Bible, not on a history reconstructed from the Bible:

> A properly theological account does not attempt to explain nor insist on pinpointing human origins beyond what we are offered in the scriptural narrative. . . . The issue here "is not whether we have a historical account of the Fall, but whether we have the account of a historical Fall."[7]

We should heed such warnings not to seek to dismember what should be taken entire. Both the literalistic approach (insisting on the account as *réportage*) and the scientistic approach (insisting it must correspond with current secular knowledge) fall into the trap of "the myth of modernity," as Aaron Riches explores in an essay on the *Colossian Forum*. The inner truths of metaphor and meaning are indispensable, but paradoxically find their significance in the primary reality of lived experience:

> Adam is placed at the beginning of the Sacred Scripture so that love might bear a human face and a name, so that it might be "personal." Our Lord has a face and a name: he is the person of the Son. So likewise in this story of God's intimacy with the human creature at the origin of human history, this

Father of all, took its commencement lower down with Christ, who is next to the God and Father of all, being thus the Father of every soul, as Adam is the father of all men." Ibid., IV.1.22, 328.

4. Brock, "Jesus Christ the Divine Animal?," 65.

5. Opderbeck, "Origen on Adam."

6. Ibid.

7. Brock, "Jesus Christ the Divine Animal?," 67.

love-with-a-face-and-a-name truly had God as his father, and so was the first creaturely "son of God." (Lk 3:38)[8]

There is, then, a place for seeking to establish the historical basis for our theology, because it is that which grounds it in created reality. As historian Mark Noll writes:

> The Christian stake in history is immense. Every aspect of lived Christianity—worship, sacraments, daily godliness, private devotion, religiously inspired benevolence, preaching—every major theme of Christian theology—the nature of God in relation to the world, the meaning of Christ, the character of salvation, the fate of the universe—directly or indirectly involves questions about how the present relates to the past.[9]

This is the reason that the biblical theologians, especially those of a historical bent like N. T. Wright, stress the importance of the messiness and particularity of the events of the Bible narratives, rather than "eternal verities." To Wright:

> It is ironic that many people in the modern world have regarded Christianity as a private worldview, a set of private stories. Some Christians have actually played right into this trap. But in principle the whole point in Christianity is that it offers a story which is the story of the whole world. It is public truth. Otherwise it collapses into some version of Gnosticism.[10]

Similarly missiologist Lesslie Newbigin emphasizes the singular importance of Christian historicism in the words of a Hindu critic:

> "As I read the Bible I find it a quite unique interpretation of universal history and, therefore, a unique understanding of the human person as a responsible actor in history. You Christian missionaries have talked of the Bible as if it were simply another book of religion. We have plenty of those already in India and we do not need another to add to our supply."[11]

---

8. Riches, "Mystery of Adam 1."

9. Noll, Mark A., quoted in Cole, "Peril of a 'Historyless' Systematic Theology," 55.

10. Wright, *New Testament and the People of God,* 41–42.

11. Newbigin, *Gospel in a Pluralist Society*, 89.

Metaphorical Elements in the Eden Account

So I will keep the theological end in view as I try to perform the necessary task of placing Adam more firmly in history. The first part of that task is, perhaps, to make some attempt to sort the historical from the metaphorical by identifying the genre of the early chapters of Genesis. Inevitably this is a somewhat subjective exercise, because even when considered as historical events what is described is unique and supernatural. As Brian Brock further observes:

> Given the peculiarity of the real events being named, it is clear that Genesis should not be understood to offer a newspaper account of the first days of creation, since the conventions of modern positivist historiography assume the stability of the universal causal laws of our contemporary experience as the framing condition of what could conceivably be counted as a true story about the past. Genesis is a story about something that happened before we existed that radically departs from Darwin's positivist account of history.[12]

There is a comparison to be made here with apocalyptic accounts of the realized new creation, such as the final chapters of the book of Revelation. If an entirely new cosmos is to be described to those in the present one (and a new creation is what is irrupting into the world in Eden) what literal genre could possibly do it justice?

But another factor lies not in the *necessity* for a metaphorical account, but in its *appropriateness* to the subject in hand. In the ANE, apart from the fact that the very existence of literature was so new that historical writing, as we understand it, had yet to be invented, the weighty nature of the matters deemed worthy of committing to writing demanded, at the least, some rhetorical flourishes. This is especially so since texts often derived from oral public performances designed to excite wonder, loyalty, or worship. High poetry is the language of the bard and the religious assembly. And so a theogony like the Babylonian *Enuma Elish* could scarcely be expressed prosaically, nor yet the mythical exploits of a hero like Gilgamesh. *Listening* to (as opposed to reading) *The Epic of Gilgamesh* recited, in Sumerian (with subtitles, fortunately!) shows it to be not just "old myth," but powerful, wonderfully paced, drama.[13] Even accounts of wars, when serving as propaganda for kings rather than

12. Brock, "Jesus Christ the Divine Animal?," 65.

13. Pringle, "Epic Of Gilgamesh In Sumerian."

for their private annals, deserved epic poems rather than terse combat diaries.

Various terms have been coined to describe the genre of Genesis 1—11. Gordon Wenham cites the Assyriologist, Thorkild Jacobsen, who coined the term "mytho-historical" to describe both the early chapters of Genesis and the partly parallel *Eridu Genesis*. Jacobsen did this on the basis that they both clearly have mythical subjects, but are also interested, like histories, both in cause and effect and in chronology. However, because of the way that Genesis carefully connects events both to each other, and to the narrative of the rest of Genesis, Wenham sees "mytho-historical" as surrendering too much historical ground, and prefers the term "protohistorical."[14] The key to the difference, in his view, is genealogy. In chapter 11 we will explore how genealogy serves this historiographic function throughout the Bible.

If we restrict the discussion, for the moment, to the Eden account of Genesis 2—3, there are various features in the text that are often regarded as "mythic elements," when seeking to place Adam into a plausible history, which aim is of course the main reason for considering a hypothesis like Genealogical Adam at all. However, it is not as easy as it seems to draw firm distinctions between the historical and the metaphorical.

Creation of Adam and Eve

The creation of Adam from dust is frequently seen nowadays as indicating only his ultimately earthly origins, perhaps *via* evolution or selection from an existing earthly tribe. John H. Walton, for example, discusses parallels with Akkadian and Egyptian texts in which humans are made out of clay, suggesting that the Genesis use of "dust" "represents what people return to when they die."[15]

This is a long-standing, and almost certainly correct, line of figurative understanding. As Matthew Henry observed long before the age of critical scholarship:

> Man was made out of paradise; for, after God had formed him,
> he put him into the garden: he was made of common clay, not of
> paradise-dust. He could not plead a tenant-right to the garden,

---

14. Wenham, *Rethinking Genesis 1—11*, 32–33.

15. Walton, *Genesis*, 165.

for he was not born upon the premises, nor had anything but what he received.[16]

Likewise the creation of Eve from Adam's rib, clearly full of theological symbolism, is equally open to metaphorical interpretation. Walton makes the novel, and plausible, inference that Adam's deep sleep[17] is visionary in character, and hence the episode would be didactic rather than creative even within a historical account.[18]

However, there are many to whom the special creation of Adam is theologically crucial. For example, the Evangelical leader Tim Keller, who is supportive of evolution generally, created a small *furore* when, in a video discussion, he included the special creation of Adam amongst his non-negotiable origins doctrines.[19] This is one reason that Joshua Swamidass includes special creation in his "basic model" of Genealogical Adam.

There are grounds for maintaining that, even if his biological origins were in an existing people-group, there were ontological distinctives about Adam, apart from the mere fact of his calling, which required a radical transformation of his body, spirit, or both—an act, in other words, of special creation, even if not *ex nihilo* or from literal dust. Such changes, even if outwardly invisible, would be no less remarkable in themselves than what we have in the text, which is, as Swamidass points out, entirely compatible with the science.

The Nakedness and Clothing of the Man and the Woman

There is clearly much of figurative importance in the innocent nakedness of Adam and Eve, especially given the disapproval of nudity in the Hebrew culture compared to, say, the Greek. Greg Beale, thinking in terms of biblical theology, has an interesting discussion on their nakedness in which he envisages it, like their lack of wisdom, as a probationary state before their intended acquisition of "priestly" clothing of divine righteousness. The attempt to clothe themselves,[20] followed in due course by the removal of these inadequate scraps and their gracious replacement

---

16. Church, ed., *Matthew Henry*, 6.

17. Gen 2:21.

18. Walton, *Lost World of Adam and Eve*, 79–80.

19. Keller, "Non-Negotiable Beliefs."

20. Gen 3:7.

with divinely wrought skin garments[21] he compares to the clothing meta-
phors of new birth used by Paul in more than one passage.[22]

Such a metaphorical intention is more likely because, in any period
likely for Adam, clothing was already long-established amongst humanity. The evolution of body-lice suggests that clothing was being worn as
long as 170,000 years ago.[23] But if Adam and Eve were specially created,
and knew nothing of the outside world in their innocent state, that fact
might, perhaps, be irrelevant.

One Sumerian myth, *Ewe and Wheat*, presents the primitive state of
man as nakedness,[24] which may therefore be a cultural indicator of naïvety. However, there are other meanings for nudity in Sumerian sources.
Generally, in their art, it may indicate those of low social status: a line of
men bearing offerings is depicted naked on the Warka Vase from Uruk
(c 3,000 BCE).

However, some interpret these men as priests, and some priests, at
least, seem to have officiated unclothed in Sumerian religion according
to other evidence. So it might be tempting, given Adam and Eve's priestly
status in the garden sanctuary, to see echoes of this ancient practice in
Genesis. But in the Eden story their nakedness becomes, though it was
not initially, a source of shame. God does not remove their embarrassment, but clothes them. Here, then, we may indeed be dealing with a
meaning more spiritual than literal. But we certainly cannot rule out the
latter altogether.

The Trees of Life and Knowledge

You will recall from the beginning of this chapter that Origen denied that
actual trees could confer eternal life or knowledge. And there are good
reasons to treat them metaphorically. Elsewhere in Scripture the tree of
life motif is reused in connection with the eschatological kingdom, and
the source of eternal life in the New Testament is Christ himself.[25] Would
dwelling obediently in the presence of Yahweh in the garden not have
been sufficient to banish death?

21. Gen 3:21.
22. Beale, *New Testament*, 452–55.
23. Hogenboom, "Clothes are not a necessity."
24. Oxford University, "Sheep and Grain," 12–25.
25. John 4:13–14; 7:38.

Likewise, does not the command to avoid eating from the tree of knowledge symbolize graphically that the fear of the Lord is the beginning of wisdom?[26] The very desire for gaining wisdom apart from God's will would have been rebellion, tree or no tree.

Yet Origen should have seen that actual trees might serve a sacramental function, for in the Eucharist he believed he received the actual body of Christ.[27] So even literal trees, in the unique sacred space of the garden, could be a historical reality.

The Creatures Named by Adam

It would indeed be bizarre to think that in Genesis 2:19–20 God literally brought to Adam every single species of animal in existence, presumably including several million species of insect, to be named and classified after the manner of a Linnaeus. The commentators agree that naming the creatures, i.e. discerning their natures,[28] was an indicator of Adam's status as a wise ruler, echoing the naming by God of what he created in Genesis 1, and foreshadowing the wisdom of Solomon, which itself may well have been seen by the biblical author as an echo of Adam himself:

> 33 He spoke of trees, from the cedar that is in Lebanon even
> to the hyssop that grows on the wall; he spoke also of animals
> and birds and creeping things and fish. 34 Men came from all
> peoples to hear the wisdom of Solomon, from all the kings of
> the earth who had heard of his wisdom.[29]

Yet the text might imply only that God showed him the main species in that garden at that particular time, the naming being an entirely pragmatic demonstration of Adam's authority and wisdom there and then. Once again an intelligent reading renders a historical reference more plausible than it might seem.

---

26. Ps 110:10; Prov 9:10.

27. "We give thanks to the Creator of all, and, along with thanksgiving and prayer for the blessings we have received, we also eat the bread presented to us; and this bread becomes by prayer a sacred body, which sanctifies those who sincerely partake of it." Origen, *Contra Celsum*, VIII.33, 519.

28. Kidner, *Genesis*, 65.

29. 1 Kgs 4:33.

The Talking Serpent

The issue readers have with this, apart from the ability of the serpent to speak, is the ability of Eve not to be surprised that it does. The problem is not made easier by the fact that a couple of the ways in which the spiritual significance of the event is understood are not obviously compatible with each other.

It is, on the one hand, common and reasonable to interpret Eve's capitulation to the serpent's deception as the reversal of the authority structure God had set up. Yahweh was the source of the command not to eat, which he gave to Adam before the creation of Eve as his helper. We assume that Adam passed the command on to her, and she should, as co-ruler with Adam over the beasts, have put the serpent in its creaturely place. Instead we see Eve submitting to the serpent, and Adam heeding her rather than the divine command (and then starting the chain of blame for his disobedience back through Eve to the serpent when God confronts him). Greg Beale understands it in this way:

> Adam as the priest-king, who prevented unclean things from entering the temple, should have discerned Eve's misquotation of God's word and the serpent's capitalizing on it.[30]

On the other hand, the involvement of Satan in the temptation—who would be expected to have the power of speech—is affirmed directly in a number of other Scriptures, and implicitly in his character as primordial deceiver, or liar, much more widely.[31] Jesus' wilderness temptation, as well as being a recapitulation of Israel's wilderness experience, is in its context a clear repeat of the temptation in the garden, a test that Jesus passes, thus beginning the defeat of Satan, the tempter.[32] And both John the Baptist and Jesus refer to their adversaries as a "brood of vipers,"[33] an allusion to the "seed of the serpent" in Genesis 3:15 that is clearly of spiritual, not biological significance.

Perhaps, then, Satan "co-opted" an ordinary snake, which Eve should have controlled as a beast. Another possibility is that recently proposed by Michael Heiser, who suggests[34] that we should understand

30. Beale, New Testament, 34.

31. John 8: 44; Rom 16:20; Eph 5:6; 2 Thess 2:8–10; 2 John 7; Rev 12:9; 20:2, 8.

32. Beale, New Testament, 222–23, 417–22.

33. Matt 3:7; 12:34; 23:33; Luke 3:7.

34. Heiser, Nachash and His Seed.

the serpent, or *nachash*, of Genesis as a spiritual being with every right to be in the garden of God, as a member of Yahweh's divine council—but no right to countermand the word of God. Heiser's case from linguistic studies, ANE parallels, and a particular interest in the angelic creation of the Bible, which we often ignore, is intriguing.

It may also be significant in this regard that the Hebrew word *sara-phim*, or "burning ones," is used both of the spiritual beings of Isaiah's temple vision,[35] and of the serpents that bit the Israelites in Numbers 21. Since his is the only biblical use of the term in this angelic way, it may well be his alternative term for the cherubim covering the ark on the holy of holies.[36]

Given that Eden is, as it were, an outpost of God's heavenly dwelling on earth, and if Adam and Eve, as I shall explore in subsequent chapters, were being "trained up" to be vice-regents to God, then it would actually be rather strange if representatives of Yahweh's angelic host, attested throughout Scripture,[37] were *not* present in Eden. In the present context, though, this idea once again shows there is an alternative to a non-literal understanding of the text.

These few examples, then, show that it is possible to reduce significantly the features of the garden narrative often regarded as metaphorical, provided of course that one accepts the irreducibly supernatural nature of the account as a whole. They do not in any way reduce the theological *significance* of each element of the story. The meaning of Eve's stated origin from Adam's side is as true in a visionary revelation as in a creational one. Eternal life is as real when available sacramentally through a living tree as it would be by a metaphorical one, through dwelling with God. Illicit knowledge of good and evil is likewise gained through any form of disobedience, physically represented or not. And it makes a minor difference in the end whether Eve was deceived into disobeying God by Satan as a divine being in all his glory, or in disguise as a snake, or as a seducing voice in Eve's mind, come to that.

---

35. Isa 6:1–7.

36. See Ezekiel 28:14: here the "cherub" refers either to Satan, or perhaps to Adam himself, in his own guardian role in the garden, perhaps pictured as becoming, potentially or actually, a member of the divine council.

37. In Genesis itself, consider the theophany of Genesis 18, where it seems Yahweh is accompanied by two companions, for no other reason than to attend him.

At the same time, the form of the story, and hence its choice and treatment of details, has been written with a theological end in view. As C. John Collins says:

> The author is talking about what he thought were actual events, using rhetorical and literary techniques to shape the readers' attitudes towards those events.[38]

Anachronism

Collins, a scholar with whose approach I generally closely agree, includes amongst these literary techniques that of anachronism. He rightly points out that "historical verisimilitude," the practice of paying attention to authentic detail in telling a story of the past, is of fairly recent origin,[39] and one has only to look at classical European paintings of biblical characters in mediaeval garb to see that to be true.[40] Indeed, Collins goes on to say how the period detail of the narrative of Abraham and the other patriarchs is evidence of their ancient origin.

But he cautions against using the detail of Genesis to date the account, citing the agricultural pursuits of Cain and Abel as an example, because of his allowance for "a level of anachronism":

> When I use the term "anachronism," I mean that a text may well have described aspects of the older times in terms of what the writer and his audience are familiar with. This does not necessarily detract from the historicity of the text, since the text still refers to actual events.[41]

Whilst this is certainly a generally valid truth, I would question the need to invoke it in this instance. If the garden account is "history" in the sense that it has been handed down by a tradition rather than given to the author from nowhere by divine inspiration, then it is extremely likely that it occurred within the period when agriculture and farming livestock had already been developed. Otherwise, we are to accept the

---

38. Collins, *Did Adam and Eve Really Exist?*, 16.

39. Ibid., 60.

40. The custom of verisimilitude seems to be in decline, as in the film *Braveheart*, which paints William Wallace as a woad-painted Pict rather than a mediaeval noble, and as in recent films that depict Robin Hood or King Arthur as superheroes.

41. Collins, *Did Adam and Eve Really Exist?*, 113–14.

possibility of accurate oral transmission of historical events for well over five millennia—or even far more if Adam is placed back into deep pre-history. In that case Cain's city of Enoch, mentioned only in passing as a fact of interest,[42] would have to be taken as a gratuitous anachronism, proto-cities like Çatalhöyük having developed around the same time as farming, and certainly being absent before it. It seems to me that anachronism ought to be invoked only as a matter of last resort.

Literary emphasis

The considerations above show how limited, in fact, the "fabulous" features of the Eden story are, as opposed to the truly "mythic" (or better, "archetypal") character of the main events described. Events with deep meaning do not have to be fictional, though the literary form will emphasize the meaning.

One very clear example of this is in the overall form of the garden story. Different interpretations have been offered for its main purpose down the centuries. It has been seen as an etiological explanation of mortality (akin to the failure to gain immortality in the *Epic of Gilgamesh*). The Renaissance saw it in Promethean terms as the gaining of authentic human independence.[43] I have even heard it described as primarily intended to differentiate mankind from the animals.

But Gordon Wenham, citing analyses by Walsh and Auffret, shows how the whole episode is written in chiastic, or palistrophic, form:

> The whole narrative is therefore a masterpiece of palistrophic writing, the mirror-image style, whereby the first scene matches the last, the second the penultimate and so on: ABCDC'B'A.[44]

The central focus of the story, thus understood, turns out to be the temptation and taking of the forbidden fruit. But furthermore, Wenham writes, this central scene contains an *inner* palistrophic pattern, shining the spotlight of the whole narrative on Adam's act of disobedience: "and he ate."[45] And so, like any well-told story, the composition has been molded to the *purpose* for which it was written—in this case to show the

---

42. Gen 5:17.
43. See Garvey, *God's Good Earth*, 107–12.
44. Wenham, *Genesis*, 51.
45. Ibid., 75.

disobedient act of our first father. A *transgression* is the main point of the narrative, and a transgression is an actual event in time.

Patriarchal Longevity

Outside of the garden narrative itself events that seem overtly metaphorical are even less usual. One of the most obvious examples is the great ages of the line of Seth. These are hard to account for adequately in any manner. They appear to lack numerological significance, and they lack plausibility in literal terms if only because, in later generations, Seth's line has diffused throughout the ANE, and there is no external evidence that people of that time lived to great ages, or had a disproportionate number of children. Even the antediluvian patriarchs, from the Genesis genealogies or those of 1 Chronicles, had only the usual number of children despite living centuries (and starting families late—Adam waits until his 130th year to replace his murdered son Abel,[46] which scarcely seems consistent with "filling the earth" with any semblance of alacrity).

The great ages do not appear to be there in order to explain the rapid population of the earth, for Seth's descendants start producing children late in life until the time of Shem, Ham, and Japheth. The Table of Nations (of which more in chapter 6) covers a time when the ages begin to fall, after the flood.

It seems more likely that, like the Sumerian king lists, the particular genre of the protohistory demanded giving high ages to ancient heroes (though there is no great correspondence in the *magnitude* of the longevity between Genesis and the king lists).

Alternatively, or additionally, the longevity may be due to the fact that, for some reason, numbers are particularly prone to transmission error in these ancient texts. The Masoretic, Septuagint, and Samaritan versions of Genesis all give different numbers for the patriarchal ages. Various explanations have been given for them on the basis of scribal errors, of which the most convincing to me are those suggesting the exaggerated figures arose by their repeated transcription across the various ancient and less ancient Mesopotamian, and then the Hebrew, numbering systems. Discussing these in detail is beyond the scope of the present book.[47]

---

46. Gen 5:3.

47. See, for example, Hill, "Making Sense of the Numbers." Another attempt is

Another, less than convincing, explanation is that the figures given are accurate, but that they bridge gaps of several generations in the genealogies. If that were the case, though, it is likely that the ages of the individuals would be known to the author as well as the aggregates, and he might as well have simply lengthened his account to include them all. Neither does it deal well with the ages at which characters bear children. Nevertheless, the theory reminds us that it is quite likely that, like other genealogies in the Bible, at least some generations *have* been skipped, which discourages us from trying to be too precise about dating.

What is very much less credible, when Adam is placed thousands or tens of thousands of years earlier than a literal reading suggests, is that the genealogies contain gaps of tens or hundreds of generations. If, as I deem probable, the genealogies are the historical "pulse" of the text, then Adam's named descendants will have lived within the chronological range of a few centuries, or at very most a millennium or two, for the later generations begin to match known historical settings and even, possibly, events. Nobody would find much use in a genealogy that informed us that the Ealdorman Æthelfrith of Mercia begat Caspar W. Weinberger a millennium later.

In this book I assume that, at least after expulsion from the Garden of Eden, Adam and his line lived to the same ages as the peoples around him, from which he came. If nothing else, that humanizes the account dramatically: Adam and Eve, struggling to build a home and bring up children, were people just like us, as was Cain, an exile from Eden making good in a foreign land, or Enoch, being taken to the Lord at an unusually young age. They are like real people, not demigods.

Is the Whole Garden Metaphorical?

Having looked briefly at some of the less obviously historical details of the Genesis narrative, I will turn to the general "setting" of the story in space and time, which is again frequently said to be full of clues to the metaphorical nature of the story. At this point I will deal only in generalities, returning to look at some aspects in more detail in a later chapter.

The position of Eden is helpfully given by the writer in Genesis 2:10–14, except that, to us, the description is far from helpful. Gordon Wenham, for example, wrestling with the data, cites Speiser's suggestion

---

Best, *Analysis of the Numbers.*

of a lower Mesopotamian location, but since Speiser's four rivers converge, whereas the "four heads" of verse 10 suggest they *diverge* (which is an implausible thing for any large river), he has recourse to metaphor as an explanation and offers that,

> [m]aybe the reversed flow of the rivers suggests that paradise is beyond man's present experience. Their names affirm that there was a garden there, but maybe the insoluble geography is a way of saying that it is now inaccessible to, even unlocatable by, later man.[48]

But we have, in such a scenario, to imagine the *figurative* River Tigris flowing backwards past the *actual* city of Asshur, a rather outlandish, and unparalleled, concept for the author of Genesis to include in the text. The names of the rivers themselves have invited symbolic interpretation, especially the unidentified Gihon "winding around the whole land of Cush."[49] Since "Gihon" is the name of the small stream supplying Jerusalem with its water, a spiritual link to the temple has been made by some. However, to others, it seems better to take the identification of "Cush" as Ethiopia or, by association, Egypt, which would make the Gihon the Nile, even though "winding" is scarcely what the Nile does. This identification puts Eden mystically between great world rivers to the north and south, enabling the Pishon to become some other identified world river such as the Ganges.[50] The rivers would then be a convoluted way of suggesting that Eden was at the center of the world.

Greg Beale even speculates on the thematic link between the riches of Solomon's temple and the "'gold . . . bdellium and onyx,' in Eden,"[51] even though in the text these riches actually occur in the land of Havilah, around which the Pishon winds long after it leaves (or before it enters) Eden.

All these spiritualizing interpretations of the geographical information in Genesis 2:10–14 seem to me to confuse what appears a genuine attempt on the part of the author to place Eden in the real world, even though he makes clear that, guarded by the cherubim and the flaming

---

48. Wenham, *Genesis*, 66–67.

49. Gen 2:13.

50. Josephus, *Antiquities* 1:3.

51. Beale, *New Testament*, 68.

sword[52] it is, like the fictional Scottish town of Brigadoon, no longer accessible to human sight.

Although the geography is problematic to us, if we knew the intended identity of all the locations involved the account itself would read quite prosaically, as if to say, "This actually happened, and you can find it on the map if you take the trouble." The rivers are described in the present tense, and some are matched to local features, not as if they were ahistorical myth.

This has long been a conclusion of scholars. In an 1884 study Francis Brown quotes Friedrich Delitzsch:

> The writer conceived of the territory where the garden was as in existence in his own time, supposed himself to know its locality, and desired to communicate to his readers such knowledge as he had. Par. pp. 2, 3, 44.[53]

And then he adds his own assessment:

> The first statement and the last are undoubtedly true, witness the various details of the description—mostly unimportant for his narrative, and of use only as means of identification.[54]

There is a clear implication that the two currently known rivers, the Tigris and the Euphrates, are considered as radiating out of (or into) Eden. But in relation to Israel as a political entity, only the Euphrates is of significance, being "the River" of its ideal northern border.[55] It would seem likely that it is for this reason that while the Euphrates is simply named, the Tigris has to be explained in terms of its flowing east of Asshur.

This mention of Asshur has been regarded as a possible dateline for the antiquity of the account, as it appears to indicate the city, not the region, and that was at its most prominent before 1,400 BCE.[56] Whatever the case, Asshur was a geographical, not a metaphorical, city.

Similarly, the land of Havilah, through which flows the Pishon, is described in terms of its commercially valuable (not simply precious)

---

52. Gen 3:24.

53. Brown, "Recent Theory of the Garden of Eden," 3. Here he is citing Delitzsch, *Wo Lag das Paradies*.

54. Ibid.

55. Gen 15:18; 1 Chr 18:3.

56. Wenham, *Genesis*, 66.

products. If indeed there are hints of richness coming from, or flowing into, Eden, the fact remains that the writer is describing a particular source of natural resources that is *not* Eden.

Likewise, the only reason Cush appears to be named is to identify the Gihon River by a somewhat more familiar (to the original readers) regional location. If we exclude Ethiopia or Egypt as lacking any such river as a winding Gihon, or any geographical connection to the Tigris and Euphrates, we have an alternative "Cush" in Asia that is probably even referenced in Genesis,[57] the land of the Elamites which, even now, gives its name to Khuzistan.

Conclusion relative to Genealogical Adam

There is actually relatively little in the account of the Garden of Eden— and indeed, in the first 11 chapters of Genesis—that unequivocally suggests a metaphorical or mythical, rather than a historical, account. That fact at least gives us a justification for more detailed study.

But it also forces us to deal with the fact that the human population of the world is known to have been widespread across the world for hundreds of thousands of years. If the text is asking us to accept a historical Adam, then our historical setting has to make room for him. Historical events within a completely untraceable history might as well be mythical. Of what value would the gospel be if Jesus was crucified in the land of Shangri-La?

57. Gen 10:7.

2

BIBLICAL SIGNS OF PEOPLE
BEYOND EDEN

Where Are All the People in Genesis?

IT IS A REMARKABLE fact that Genesis scarcely talks about any foreign gods *at all* in its fifty chapters. That seems remarkable, and is seldom, if ever, remarked upon, though it must undoubtedly have been noticed by *someone* over the last three thousand years. I have no explanation, but perhaps one exists in the literature.

Yet considering the book spans a time from "the beginning" to, perhaps, 1,600 BCE, and involves characters who are active in Mesopotamia, Canaan, and Egypt, but not in a theocratic Israelite state, and that it mentions tribal origins over much of the then-known world, one might expect the gods of the nations at least to receive a mention or two, and some criticism, perhaps. But they do not.[1]

I have absolutely no explanation for this paucity of these references, for the false gods of Egypt and the nations are prominent in Exodus and the rest of the OT. But my reason for mentioning it is that the absence of the gods makes the apparent absence of *people,* other than Adam and his offspring, in Genesis 2—11, less unique and surprising than it might

---

1. There are a very few possible exceptions: "Foreigners" in Genesis 35:1–4, Laban's *teraphim*, Genesis 31:19, 24–37, which may not be gods at all (van der Toorn, "Nature of the 'Teraphim,'" 222), and Joseph's wife, daughter of a "priest of On."

otherwise seem. As some scholars have suggested,[2] the narrative is exclusively focused on the line of Adam for one good reason—that he is regarded as the forebear (and forerunner) of Israel, for whom Genesis was written.

We know that many deities were worshipped in the Mesopotamia of Abraham and his ancestors, in the various regions of the Levant in which his family wandered, and of course in Egypt where they ended up for four hundred years. Likewise in the period of history after the flood, and probably before it, if it is the same flood as that of the cuneiform texts, we know there were whole nations of people worshipping them, rather than Yahweh (who is unknown, it seems, from non-biblical sources of that period). Indeed, religion is attested all over the world at any plausible date when Adam might have lived. Yet Genesis 2—11 deals only with those who worship Yahweh.

The most likely reason for the absence of people outside Adam's line, then, is not that only the biblical characters existed in the world, but that the writer was as uninterested in the others, for his literary and theological purposes, as he was uninterested in their pantheons.

In particular, the passage in which the absence of other people is most marked is in the narrative of the fall. But this is to be expected simply from the nature of the account. Adam, formed outside the garden, a sacred sanctuary of Yahweh, is placed in it both for sacred service and, we find, to test his faithfulness. It is a setting for a new kind of personal encounter with God.

Even apart from that, biblical parallelism makes the absence of other human beings an expectation, not a mystery. When Moses is commissioned by Yahweh, he encounters him alone in the wilderness of Mount Sinai.[3] When, later, he takes the Israelites to meet God on the same mountain, his Midianite father-in-law Jethro, who has hitherto been a useful adviser, is sent away first. The assembly of Israel is brought into the presence of God in order to forge the new nation as one—and no outsiders are witnesses to it. It is as if Yahweh and his nation are the only people in the world at this point. This isolation is implied, also, for all the time of testing in the wilderness.

2. See especially Postell, *Adam as Israel.*

3. Exod 3:1–6.

The temptation of Christ is a recapitulation both of the testing of Adam in the garden, and the testing of Israel in the wilderness. Once again, this serious business with God is done in isolation from others.

There are, however, a number of hints in Genesis 1—11 which, if they do not indicate an incompetent author actually trying to write about a sole human progenitor, suggest the presence of others outside Eden.

Geographical Names

Attempts have been made to derive "Eden" from the Akkadian term for "steppe,"[4] but etymologically it is more likely to derive from "pleasure" or "delight."[5] Eden is therefore the proper name of a land or region, and so is Nod, the land to which Cain later flees. "Land of X" (*eretz* + name) in Scripture always refers to an inhabited territory. The word implies some kind of geopolitical entity. So, of course, do names like "Havilah," "Asshur," and "Cush" in Genesis 2. It could be argued that these denote lands that had come to exist only at the time of writing, not the time of the events. But how would the author know their locations, if they had had no populations to name them, and therefore no names, at the time of the events? Such named regions indicate namers for them, that is to say human populations beyond Adam's clan in Eden.

Cain and Abel's Occupations

If we accept Cain and Abel's occupations of agriculture and herding, respectively, *pace* C. John Collins's previously mentioned suggestion that they might be anachronisms (they are, after all, the circumstantial explanation for the murder of the latter), then we must explain why they followed these occupations. Even if Adam and Eve had been unusually fertile—and the fact that Seth is the first-named in the genealogy of Genesis 5, and named as a replacement for Abel by Eve[6] is against that—then both agriculture and keeping flocks[7] seem excessively intensive pursuits for the purpose of maintaining just one nuclear family.

---

4. Delitzsch, *Wo Lag das Paradies*, 4, 6, 79ff.

5. Wenham, *Genesis*, 61.

6. Gen 4:25.

7. Gen 4:3.

Agriculture appears, from a wealth of evidence, to have been developed in the ANE because of the pressure of increasing population. It was a more efficient way of feeding large numbers of people than hunter-gathering had been. Even if we grant the effectiveness of the curse on the ground, it would still seem to have been sufficient to tend a small plot of land and hunt the occasional wild sheep, rather than to practice farming.

This leaves to one side the recent evidence that the hunter-gatherers who built Göbekli Tepe in Anatolia in the tenth millennium BCE comprised a population of thousands, which only later moved to an agricultural and pastoral economy. Only wild animal bones have been found in association with their settlements, themselves quite large and populous.

It appears consistent with the text, then, that on their expulsion from the garden, Adam and Eve's continued life in Eden was actually amidst a population that would benefit from, and so compensate economically, the effort of Cain and Abel in their farming. A farming and trade economy is implicit in Genesis 4.

Cain's Exile

The marking of Cain, to prevent his finders killing him, follows on from the sentence of exile that Yahweh pronounced on Cain for the murder of his brother. And that, of course, raises the question of who would wish to kill him, and why. Cain's fear is the *result* of his being sent away—he shows no fear of vengeance by Adam, or by future kin at home. Blood vengeance scarcely seems a likely outcome within such a family household anyway, let alone their pursuing a manhunt across a large and unoccupied land of exile.

No, Cain's fear must be, and naturally reads as, that of being a stranger encroaching on another group's territory without good reason. It is strangers who are likely to be killed if they stray into foreign territory. That group, we suppose, consisted of whoever occupied the land of Nod, though since "Nod" is translated as "wandering," it probably had another name amongst its own people (this is by no means unprecedented: the name "Wales" derives from "foreign," whereas the Welsh name for their land, "Cymru," means "fellow-countrymen").

Cain's Wife

The identity of Cain's wife has been debated for centuries, and of course the traditional interpretation, amongst both Jews and Christians, was that he married his sister, or perhaps his niece, Eve having been busily producing the population of the world without its being mentioned in the text, which only tells us that "[Adam] had other sons and daughters."[8]

One problem with this interpretation is why God would have exiled Âwân (the name given to Eve's daughter, Cain's wife, in the second temple *Book of Jubilees*) for a murder her husband and brother, Cain, had committed. But the bigger problem is that Cain is said, in a matter of fact manner, to have built a city and named it after his son Enoch.

Now we know a lot about the building of cities in the ANE, and archaeologists have excavated many examples. The oldest true city, according to both archaeology and Mesopotamian tradition, was Eridu, founded around 5,400 BCE. Like other Mesopotamian cities, it was the product of population growth, the centralization of resources, the stratification of society, and strong leadership. Cities were, from the first, built to maintain large populations (and to manage regional economic resources). A city for one family is called a "house."

But even a so-called "proto-city" like Çatalhöyük, established from around 7,500 BCE, had an average population of 5,000. It was never a family farmstead, and even if Cain and Âwân lived for centuries, that kind of population growth is frankly incredible.

However, what *would* be realistic is for the immigrant Cain, bearing the inheritance of Adam's royal election and the ruthlessness of sin, to have married a local woman, and gained power and influence in a local population, to the extent of building a city—and probably not the first ever constructed, or at least Scripture does not tell us it was.

Calling on the Name of Yahweh

After naming Cain's descendants, the writer of Genesis returns to Adam's third son Seth, and to *his* son Enosh. But then he adds the strange comment that "at that time men began to call on the name of Yahweh."[9]

8. Gen 5:4.
9. Gen 4:26.

Which men would those be? In Genesis, the phrase "calling on the name of the Lord" usually implies sacrificing to him as Abraham did. But Adam had known Yahweh face to face, as had Eve, and we have already been told that both Cain and Abel "brought an offering to Yahweh."[10] It is hard to believe that Seth or his family didn't also share in the family worship. Even if they only began to do so late in life, they would not be the *first* to do so. The verse, then, appears to suggest that some *outsiders* began to worship Yahweh either under his covenant name, or at least in substance.

Now the introduction of outsiders to Yahweh, like the growth of population recorded in these chapters, would actually be a limited fulfilment of the commission that God had always intended for Adam, and so it has a logical place in the unfolding story. This mission was impaired, but not cancelled, by the fall, just as the parallel commission of Israel, marred from the start by the rebellion at Mount Sinai, nevertheless moved forward under the hand of God.

Greg Beale deals with this at length in *A New Testament Biblical Theology*, tracing the commission down through its various bearers from Noah onwards, and writes:

> After Adam's sin, the commission would be expanded to include renewed humanity's reign over unregenerate human forces arrayed against it. Hence, the language of "possessing the gate of their enemies" is included, which elsewhere is stated as "subduing the land . . ."[11]

Such an understanding takes what otherwise is both a curious, and (in the absence of an outside population) incomprehensible snippet of information, and ties it into the whole missiological purpose of Genesis, the *Torah*, and indeed the whole Bible. Adam's people are damaged goods, but God's word was not spoken in vain. But in order for this to be the case, we need to see and acknowledge the "invisible" population surrounding the new-creation population which Yahweh has seeded into the world. Somehow people began to perceive the Lord through this family—perhaps through intermarriage, even—and to call on the name of the Lord.

10. Gen 4:3–4.

11. Beale, *New Testament*, 53.

Paul tells us that "Everyone who calls on the name of the Lord will be saved."[12] Perhaps this verse includes some of the very first followers of Christ in history.

Marriage, Sons of God, and Daughters of Men

The Law of Moses detests incest,[13] and it is not mentioned at all in Genesis 1—11, despite the later custom of the patriarchs of close endogamy, which is fully described in the relevant passages. The circumstances in the beginning may have been exceptional, but that is purely an assumption, based on the further assumption of the sole existence of Adam and Eve. Marriage outside the Adamic line makes perfect sense as an alternative interpretation of their custom, and would render the Genealogical Adam something implicit within the text, rather than being simply a modern accommodationist rationalization. Cain's wife, casually mentioned, is in favor of that.

The "sons of God, daughters of men" passage of Genesis 6 is certainly a reference to marriage outside the Adamic line, but its meaning is too contested throughout history to be more than suggestive evidence in a discussion like this. Nahum Sarna is certainly correct to see the story as a mere fragment of what was once a well-known story, and therefore beyond the reach of reliable interpretation.[14] Trying to settle the matter finally is certainly beyond the reach of this book.

Some Second Temple literature from *1 Enoch*[15] (second century BCE) onwards takes the "sons of God" to be angelic beings intermarrying with Adam's line, to produce giants (the *nephilim*). This view *appears*, at least, to be reflected in the New Testament,[16] though those passages do not actually mention intermarriage, so it is scarcely a full endorsement of the interpretation. It is true that the Old Testament (but not Genesis) uses the phrase "sons of God" of angels.[17] It is also true that there are probable references to the divine council in the plurals of Genesis 1:26,

---

12. Rom 10:13.

13. Lev 18:1–30.

14. Sarna, *Genesis*, 45.

15. "Book of the Watchers," *1 Enoch* 6–26, in Charles, trans., "Book of Enoch."

16. 2 Pet 2:4–5; Jude 6.

17. Job 1:6, 38:7; Ps 82:6; and in the singular, Dan 3:25.

3:22, and 11:7, and possibly in the presence of the serpent in the garden if that creature be interpreted (as later Scripture does) as an angelic being.

But modern Judaism rejects this supernatural view of Genesis 6 entirely, and the view that the phrase means "Sons of Seth" (as opposed to "daughters of Cain") is attested from the second century CE in both Jewish and Christian sources. So both human and angelic interpretations have a good pedigree, and neither is close enough to the origin of the events to carry much authority.

In a historical account the "angelic beings" interpretation is problematic, not because angels do not exist but because it is hard to see immaterial, spiritual beings being created with unneeded biological reproductive functions. In any case, more than impregnation after the pattern of Zeus's lust is described, for they "took wives" for themselves.[18] We have to envisage new neighbors moving in, with their growing family of predatory demons, and the wife, when asked what her husband does, replying that he is an angel. If that is unrealistic, then what would the "realistic" situation be like?

Whether or not Genealogical Adam theology is true, the science is strong, and would predict that the "mighty men of old" born to such unions would become universal common ancestors just as surely as the Emperor Charlemagne. I don't know any theologian who would argue the case that the whole human race is a hybrid of mankind and angels.

For that reason let us consider non-angelic interpretations. If the reference were to Seth's and Cain's lines mixing, that would be problematic too, because we have already had to explain Cain's line, in the absence of non-Adamic humans, by his marriage to a daughter of Adam. The lines were *always* mixed. All other explanations imply, in some way, that Adam's line married outside their own, thus confirming my basic thesis, that there were already humans outside the Garden of Eden.

"Sons of God" is applied to God's chosen people in both Testaments, used of Israel in the Old, and of the church in the New. In the genealogy of Luke Adam is also said to be the son of God,[19] and for the same elective reason. Greg Beale argues in detail for the sonship of Adam and his line[20] (including a reference to Genesis 6, whose alternative interpretations he does not discuss except in a brief footnote) and concludes:

18. Gen 6:2.
19. Luke 3:38: see chapter 11.
20. Beale, *New Testament*, 401–6.

> I have discussed in some detail how the first Adam was to rule,
> multiply and fill the earth. . . . As such, he was to be a faithful son
> of God, fully reflecting the image of his divine Father.[21]

Although Adam failed, Beale argues that the sonship motif is renewed in the birth of Seth in Adam's own image.[22] It would therefore
be quite natural, if the writer of Genesis assumes there are families other
than Adam's line, to speak of the sons of God marrying the daughters of
men, even if the reverse also occurred, that is the sons of men marrying
the children of God. "Sonship," in Genesis as in the New Testament, has
an ungendered theological reference.

It is unnecessary to read disapproval into this event simply because
it introduces the flood narrative, for it also follows naturally *after* the genealogy of Adam. The offspring described are "mighty men of old, men
of renown" rather than men of infamy. "Son of God" is also a designation
for the Davidic king in Scripture,[23] probably for the same reason, that he
is royally elected by God to rule Israel, just as Adam was to rule earth.
This royal allusion would fit in with the passage at hand, and also with the
heroic status of the offspring of these unions. Adam's special status brings
some new element of power and glory to mankind, whether for good
(furthering the rule of the earth) or ill (introducing sinful tyranny) or
both. This reading is also consistent with the modern Jewish view, shared
by a few Christian commentators, that "sons of God (*elohim*)" actually
means here "sons of rulers."

And so if angelic unions appear implausible, and Cain's line was already that of the sons of God ontologically, Genesis 6 quite naturally supports the assumed existence of people other than the children of Adam,
and provides an account of their beginning to intermingle.

The Nephilim

I am dealing with the giants, *nephilim*, of Genesis 6 separately because it
is not clear to me that they are intended to be the same as the mighty children of the mixed marriages just described. In fact, they are mentioned as
being on the earth "in those days, *and also afterwards*," "afterwards" being
when these mixed marriages occur. Perhaps the "mighty men" were the

21. Ibid., 913–14.
22. Gen 5:3.
23. Ps 2:1–12.

nephilim, or perhaps they were the children of the marriages—the wording is ambiguous—but they cannot have been the children if they also existed beforehand. The referent for "in those days" is probably "when men began to multiply on the face of the land."[24]

That being so, these abnormally large people either arose by genetic mutation within just a few generations of creation, within Adam's line, or they came from outside it. No mutation is, in fact, described—just the existence of a giant race, which is also described as existing after the flood,[25] thus incidentally showing that the author of Numbers, at least, did not consider the flood to have been universal. There they are said to descend from Anak, whose clan is said to be part of the *nephilim*. Anak was a Hittite. All this suggests some particularly strong or tall group independent of Adam's line, but probably subsequently related by genealogical diffusion via the Hittites.[26]

The Repopulation of the World

The flood narrative appears to tell us that the entire line of Adam, other than Noah's sons and wives, was destroyed, however large or small the actual scale of the deluge. In the young earth chronology, the entire earth was repopulated from these few. In Genealogical Adam, the same level of destruction to the Adamic line, by a regional flood, would leave most of the world's existing non-Adamic population intact. There would therefore be no scientific trace of a recent human population bottleneck of six people—and indeed there is not.

This section, though, tests the first alternative, based on the stated ages for Noah's descendants, and/or the number of generations, if we assume that the whole population of the world arose from Noah's three sons.

There are only ten generations from Noah to Abraham, and Genesis 11:10–32 gives us precise figures, making up a total of just 390 years between the two. Meanwhile, after the flood the patriarchal ages are said to decrease from around 500 years to around 120. Yet much of this undoubtedly represents a period within recorded history. Abraham is datable in several ways to somewhere between 2,000–1,600 BCE. The flood

24. Gen 6:1.
25. Num 13:33.
26. Gen 10:15. Heth was the father of the Hittites.

may be that of Shuruppak around 2,900 BCE, according to archaeology and the Mesopotamian literature. Since this gives us a figure between the flood and Abraham more than twice that of even the elevated biblical ages, we must suppose some generations have been omitted, though not enough to completely falsify the genealogy.

If, however, some previous flood were intended by the text, such as the Black Sea flood suggested controversially to have occurred around 5,600 BCE, those ten generations would have to cover around 4,000 years, making it utterly meaningless as a genealogy.

The period from 2,900–1,600 BCE is one in which large populations are known not only in Mesopotamia, Egypt and the rest of the Near East, but across the globe. Yet we also know from numerous data that disease, famine, natural catastrophes, and warfare were common, so achieving such a population would be a slow business.

Even if Shem, Ham, and Japheth fathered a child every year, it is more than hard to imagine how a population of seven could grow to a world population estimated to be between 27 and 72 million in that period, within anything like the time indicated by the text. But the Table of Nations, in fact, gives a far less extensive spread, mainly within the ANE. Given existing populations in the areas covered by the Table of Nations, the pattern recorded could be easily understood by the same kind of diffusion model which is now understood to underlie population changes such as the transition from "Celtic" to Anglo-Saxon England (immigrants influencing, but not replacing, the aboriginal genetic make-up of the land) and, indeed, the formation of Israel itself as it absorbed the Canaanite peoples into the nation after the occupation.

The Longevity of Tradition

When I was leading a home Bible study on the Genesis creation narrative last year, one man asked me, "Who was there to write it down?" I had not yet explained how to approach the text, so it was a good introduction to that topic, as well as being a good question. You will guess that my answer was not "God saw the whole thing," although he certainly did. But dictation is not the usual way that biblical inspiration works, and that is one reason for regarding Genesis 1 as something other than history (for which see chapter 15).

But, as discussed in chapter 1, there are good reasons for regarding the rest of Genesis 1–11 as being "essentially historical," for which I used Gordon Wenham's term "protohistorical."

I suggested in that chapter that if these texts are "protohistorical" in the sense of transmitting oral traditions, then there are limits to the chronological range in which they could possibly have arisen and still be remembered accurately, or at all. I have also mentioned that the genealogies, in particular, constrain the time-scales, for a genealogy that skips more than a limited number of generations is worthless as a genealogy.

The same consideration holds for the later chapters of Genesis, which if they are genuine traditions from the patriarchs, must have been remembered for, at the very least, the several centuries that Israel was captive in Egypt. The difference, though, is that Abraham came from a literate culture, so the family narratives might well have been written down from the start, whereas we know from the ANE parallels such as *Atrahasis* that the origins of the protohistory are from the very dawn of literature, or before.

This is not, however, to deny that a lengthy period of oral tradition is possible, for example from events in the fourth millennium to the time of Abraham in the early second millennium. A high view of Scripture suggests that these are, whatever else, reliable human testimony, rather than divine dictation. They are history because men remembered well what they had seen, or what was passed down to them. This view of inspiration is commonplace in Gospel studies, where minor differences in detail are readily assigned to the fact that reliable human testimony always differs on detail.[27] Word-for-word consistency between the accounts would suggest a conspiracy (it actually invalidated testimony in rabbinic law). Total agreement might be compatible with divine dictation as well as conspiracy, but only the naïve expect that.

And so, although it would be quite possible for the Holy Spirit to say to the author of Genesis 1, "Recite this description of what I saw as I hovered over the deep," it would be quite out of step with the pattern of the rest of the Bible. And so, I venture to suggest, something like the "temple inauguration" view of Genesis 1 fits the usual prophetic pattern better (see chapter 16). The writer is given insight that the creation is a temple built by God, somehow in conformity to the "pattern shown to Moses on the mountain" of the earthly tabernacle. Grasping the meaning

27. A good recent essay on the reliability of memory and eyewitness testimony is Bauckham, "Gospel Narratives."

and the imagery, the actual "factual" input into the account is simply what he knows by experience of the world around him. And so, in my view, he writes a phenomenological account in terms of temple building imagery. For those who reject the temple inauguration theory, then other models like the framework hypothesis make equal sense of inspiration. Spiritual insight, rather than new historical or scientific facts, is the content of inspiration.

Turning now to the Adam story, I mentioned in the last chapter that it is implausible to believe in the transmission of an oral tradition from many millennia earlier than its apparent Neolithic or Chalcolithic setting. This poses a problem for those who place Adam at the "Great leap forward" of 40,000 BCE, or at the arrival of "anatomically modern humans," or at some bottleneck more than 500,000 years ago according to some others.

On the grounds stated above, it is unlikely that God would simply dictate to the inspired writer an extraordinary series of events before recorded time, whilst also including a spurious "modern but ancient" setting. I consider it is no more likely, as an alternative, that the author would "instinctively" have known, as a human being, that there "must" have been an original innocent couple who sinned and introduced human death, and that all the rest of the tale followed by gentle inspired suggestion. In any case, given that the Adam narrative is part of a literary unit, he would also have to know "instinctively" of Adam's son killing his brother, of a polygamous and violent Lamech, of intermarriage between sons of God and daughters of men, of a catastrophic flood, and so on. These are all contingent and surprising events, remembered, selected, and interpreted. And so, therefore, must be the story of Adam and Eve.

The pattern of Scripture is that historical events are remembered historically, and that must apply even to a "historical core" in Genesis 2—3. Our "Moses" must have received some tradition of the momentous events of the "primeval history" of Genesis 1—11. And it is pretty certain that he did, because there are undoubted literary connections with the Mesopotamian accounts like *Atrahasis* and the *Eridu Genesis*. It is vanishingly unlikely that these derive from a dictated Israelite prophecy, and of course if "Moses" simply borrowed a manufactured Mesopotamian myth, we are simply not considering a "historical core" at all.

But Genesis 1—11, from its parallels with Mesopotamian sources, does appear to go back to the very beginning of Near Eastern literature, in the mid-third millennium, to take the chronology from its literary parallels. How long could a folk memory of primordial events have persisted in shifting oral cultures, or even in a determinedly self-contained Yahwist clan?

Tribal memories can certainly persist for centuries. The American who traced my wife's family tree (which was also his) found that on three separate continents there was a tradition that the family was originally Huguenot, even though the family surname appears on none of the Huguenot lists. Parish records later showed the earliest generation in England to be living near East Anglian ports, with French given names, at a time when Protestants were fleeing here from France and Belgium, 400 years ago. The family tradition, in this case, seems credible. In a more celebrated case Homer seems to have recorded an accurate tradition of at least the bare bones of the siege of Troy from five or six hundred years before.

There are credible theories that certain Welsh folk tales may recall land lost to the sea around 2,000 years ago, their persistence being due to the resistance of Welsh speakers to forgetting their ancestral oral heritage under threat from the English. Also in Britain, Neolithic long barrows seem sometimes to have been formed from buried domestic houses, and stayed in use as memorials for a thousand years or more before being deliberately decommissioned. It seems possible that they continued to commemorate tribal founders for that long.

In Iran there is a tradition of travelling storytellers, working from memory, not texts. Some of these stories recount the exploits of "Iskander," or Alexander the Great. However fabulous the tales may be, the historical figure at their root has been remembered orally for 2,300 years.

Most extreme of all are Australian aboriginal tales about the Great Barrier Reef being connected to the land, and if that is an accurate interpretation of a genuine situation, scientific study suggests that their origin would be as old as 10,500 years ago. That is an extremely long period of oral transmission. But the circumstances are also very special: the Australian aboriginal culture was a relatively isolated, highly traditional and stable one, in which the accurate transmission of "dream time" stories is the very spiritual basis of their hunter-gatherer culture.

The Ancient Near East, in contrast, was always a highly volatile and mobile region: the protohistory itself records large movements of people and changes in culture. So it is very optimistic to imagine the narrative tradition persisting for that absolute maximum of around 10,000 years.

That kind of folk-memory would situate Adam a millennium earlier than even Göbekli Tepe (earliest levels c 9,130 BCE.)

This does allow a fairly wide leeway, taken in isolation. But on the common definition of Young Earth Creationism as "Adam within the last 10,000 years" it is pushing the limits, and pushing them no further back than the very late Mesolithic.

I would suggest, therefore, that it is utterly inconceivable that any tradition of Eden could have been preserved from earlier times, such as the "Great Leap Forward," or even before that. If it were that powerful a recollection, from so far back, it would surely be a human universal, like how to make fire. "Ancient Adam," surely, cannot be a figure remembered by folk tradition. Such a very ancient Adam, therefore, seems to me to lie outside history, and could only be the true interpretation of Adam in Genesis (seen as a real individual) on an understanding of inspiration unique to that passage, one that is virtually the equivalent of God dictating the creation account as a history lesson.

We must also remember that Genesis does *not* give us an isolated tale of the origin of humankind: it gives us a chronological account *linking* Adam, by genealogy, to the pivotal character Abram, whose general historical and geographical setting is not in doubt. If Adam is historical, then, he must probably, then, be relatively recent, in the sense of being within spitting distance of "4004 BCE."

Conclusion Relative to Genealogical Adam

To these considerations from the biblical text, hinting that the writer was well aware of long-established human populations outside that of Adam, we must add the extra-biblical testimony of both history and archaeology about a world already well-populated in the historical times fairly clearly indicated in Genesis.

It may be plausible to argue that Genesis represents some mythic version of the whole of mankind's origin, but it is not credible to take the geographical and historical clues in Genesis and then say that the Cro-Magnon or Aurignacian cultures post-date a flood in the last few millennia, a countable number of generations after Adam, and before Abraham. That is to ride roughshod over the text.

Such problems all disappear entirely if we take it that Genesis specifically mentions only Adam's line because only Adam's line tells the story of Yahweh's dealings with the ancestors of Israel. Israel was being taught that it was already part of the story of the true God's dealings with mankind through creation,[28] but in an even more special way through Adam, as well as being warned that just as Adam had failed and brought much grief on the world, so might they fail to be faithful and secure God's blessing.

Not for nothing does so much in the account of the fall parallel the story of the exodus, Israel's idolatry and immorality, and the final exile. This does not mean that the former was simply invented to illustrate the latter, but it is does make the story powerfully archetypal.

28. Gen 1:26–29.

3.

THE LORD IS NOT SLOW

The Problem of Time

IN A RECENT BOOK chapter N. T. Wright suggests that if we view creation, as we should, from a christological perspective, we ought not simply to substitute "Jesus" for "God" in some philosophical argument for God, without changing our thinking. Instead we should take lessons from how Jesus, as the bringer of the new creation through his incarnation, would probably have carried through the old.

> To begin with, if creation comes through the kingdom-bringing Jesus, we ought to expect that it would often be like a seed growing secretly; that it would involve seed being sown which went to waste and other seed being sown which produced a great crop. We ought to *expect* that it would be a strange, slow process which might suddenly reach some kind of harvest. And we ought to expect that it would involve some kind of overcoming of chaos. Above all, we ought to expect that it would be a work of utter self-giving love; that the power which made the world, like the power which ultimately rescued the world, would be the power, not of brute force, or of some vast robotic machinery controlled by a distant bureaucrat, but of radical outpoured generosity.[1]

1. Wright, "Christ and the Cosmos," 102–3.

Wright goes on to speak positively about evolutionary processes, but decidedly *not* about "Epicurean" chance, nor about the "semideism" so common in evolutionary accounts. In fact, what he does *not* say is intriguing, for whilst his model includes the mustard-seed growth of the kingdom, and the drama of the resurrection, he doesn't say how the latter might apply in biology. But he is a theologian and historian, not a biologist, of course.

In fact even the resurrection, that most climactic event auguring the entire new creation, and healing the woes of the old, was treated by Christ as an opportunity to teach his disciples a lesson in humility and quietness. He appeared first to Mary Magdalene, looking like the gardener, which tells us, at least, that he was alone and on foot too early for anyone to be visiting the place for pleasure. His resurrection appearances were equally modest—he turned up in the upper room, or by the lake of Galilee, or once, according to the earliest record we have, that of Paul in 1 Corinthians in 55 CE,[2] to 500 of the brethren.

But even there, it seems, he "made an appearance," rather than celebrating a triumph with a delegation of a few million of the angelic host who must have been celebrating infinitely more rapturously in heaven than they customarily do over one sinner who repents.

Now this situation was temporary, it is true. After forty days Jesus was taken up to heaven, where he was declared in power to be ruler of the kings of the earth, and where he reigns at the right hand of the Father in glory. But those forty days tell us a great deal about the character of God within creation, if we have ears to hear.

As I said, Wright does not really indicate how such high drama, or even *restrained* high drama, would apply in evolution. Fortunately, my subject here is not evolution, as such. But it is about the kind of time scales that evolutionary theory, together with a whole range of other sciences, has made manifest. I will aim to show in this chapter that the Genealogical Adam hypothesis makes more sense of God's timing in history than do many other schemes.

> 9 The Lord is not slow about His promise, as some count slowness, but is patient toward you, not wishing for any to perish but for all to come to repentance.[3]

---

2. 1 Cor 15: 3–8.

3. 2 Pet 3:9.

This text is one to be accepted by faith—the Lord knows the best timing for all things, and the reassurance that the delay in full salvation is owing to his patience, not his idleness, is important in times of trial.

Nevertheless, one of the challenging things about the Christian narrative is why, if sin is so deadly and Christ's work so necessary, the history of salvation seems to unfold so slowly. If, to begin with, we take the case of a "4004 BCE Adam," and place it within a Young Earth chronology, then the disaster of the fall occurs right at the beginning of history. God's world is "good," and his Sabbath reign lasts, for only as long as Adam remains sinless, which in the understanding of Church Fathers like Irenaeus, was only until the evening of the day he was created. That would appear to be a very unsuccessful creation.

Salvation begins in earnest, with Abraham, somewhere in the early second millennium BCE. So men are without a remedy for sin for some 2,300 years before Abraham's call. But God's "kingdom of priests"[4] for the world, Israel, was not called out of Egypt until 400 years later than his grandson's time. Even then Israel's failure to grasp the opportunity fully, ending in the exile, developed over another, perhaps, six centuries, and the promised Christ arrived, as we know from Daniel as well as secular history, three world empires after that. Furthermore, since then the gradual spread of the gospel prior to Jesus' return, which prompted Peter's remark on slowness, has run on for another two millennia. The kingdom is a mustard seed, indeed, but two thirds of world history and more, on this chronology, gave most people no access to the means of salvation.

We must not forget, of course, that from the start there has been a continuous line of faithful people "who call on the name of Yahweh," with whom we have a spiritual solidarity and who, we may be confident, will like the "witnesses" of Hebrews 11 be included in the salvation of the Christ for whom they hoped, however dimly they perceived him. Still, even on this most literal, short time scale, there have been 6,000 years from the time of the fall, and many have still not heard news of salvation.

In an old earth scenario, as many have pointed out, things seem at first to be worse. If we postulate an Adam in some earlier time frame, perhaps to match one of the common anthropological definitions of humanity (such as the "Great Leap Forward" in culture c 30–50,000 BCE), or a possible genetic bottleneck of two which, on the recent, highly technical, calculations by Joshua Swamidass, Richard Buggs, and others could not

---

4. Exod 19:6.

be less than 500,000 years ago[5]), we end up with a truly vast number of generations "without God and without hope in the world."[6] And that is no less true if, like many Evolutionary Creationists, one rejects a literal Adam altogether, but accepts the crucial importance of Christ's gospel to save people from sin that was theirs because of their evolutionary heritage. That is "slow" as nearly *anybody* would understand slowness.

Yet if we consider creation as a whole—all 3.8 billion years of life, 4.5 billion years of planet earth, or all 13.8 billion years of the known universe, then even the highest estimates for the existence of man make our existence seem futile. Creationists may ask why God would make all those millions of species for no good reason except to die, when the ruler of creation, Adam, formed on "Day 6" of this day-age scenario, and whose first job is to name the beasts, has no knowledge of the vast majority of them, since they are long extinct.

Secular skeptics will, in contrast, regard *humans* as futile, a mere flash in the pan, and of no significance to history. Since the world managed without anyone to rule and subdue it for countless aeons, what is the point of mankind?

When evidence for an ancient earth began to accumulate, around the beginning of the nineteenth century, one of the earliest Christian responses was the "Gap Theory," which suggested that between Genesis 1:1 and 1:2 there was a chronological gap of any interval that science might discover. In this gap another creation, or even a whole series of creations, responsible for geological formations and fossils, had occurred, each being successively obliterated by catastrophic events.

Although catastrophism went out of fashion, in favor of gradualism and the principle of uniformity, through Charles Lyell (and his supporter Charles Darwin), we now know that major changes in the world's flora and fauna have indeed occurred through recurrent cataclysms. These have involved volcanism, asteroid strikes, and ice ages. But theologically, the problem the Gap Theory raised remains with us: that the Bible appears to tells us about only a tiny instant within creation, with the rest of the long ages being entirely irrelevant to us. It is not surprising that this marginalizes concern for the Bible's message, since if climate change doesn't send us the way of the dinosaurs, geology suggests something else will.

5. Swamidass, Buggs, et al., "Adam, Eve and Population Genetics."
6. Eph 2:12.

How Genealogical Adam Helps

In my view, one good answer to this conundrum is Genealogical Adam, which whilst detracting neither from N. T. Wright's vision of a creation that operates at a leisurely pace, like the mustard-seed growth of the kingdom of God, nor from the patience that Peter attributes to the Lord as Savior, does make the time scales we discover seem more rational.

It is my contention that the whole subject matter of the Bible, beginning with Genesis 2:4, is about the drama arising from God's desire to build a new creation through humankind, from within the old. Genesis 1, the creation story, serves the literary function of setting the scene for the drama of the new creation, and therefore takes the old creation almost for granted.

As I will develop in more detail further on in this book, Genesis 1 is a phenomenological account of the world in which the story of Adam then begins, described in terms of creation as a cosmic temple, as is now a commonplace mainstream understanding.[7]

The old creation was physical and perishable, but also "very good." Since it is not the principal subject of the Bible, that being instead the new creation, its age and its history is not discussed there. But scientific evidence now indicates that, at times slowly and at times dramatically, but always under the intimate care of Christ the *Logos*, it produced wonders that pleased and served their Creator, that enjoyed their existence according to their various capacities, and that resulted in conscious praise to God from the angelic realm, and in latter days from those of us humans who have found delight in their study, as well as those who simply enjoy the world they inhabit now. Transience is no evil if one's nature is transient.

The God of heaven governed and loved this creation for what, in human terms, is a very significant period of time indeed. During this, the fall of every sparrow (or pterosaur, or dragonfly, or asteroid) was important to him. In due time, this perishable world was reaching the end of its particular role, but its last crowning glory was the gift of its own "rational animal," humankind, created in the image and likeness of God, able to join the angels in rational worship whilst enjoying his Lordship, and themselves subduing nature in a way no other creature ever had before.

---

7. See, for example, Beale, *Temple*; Middleton, *New Heaven and a New Earth*; Walton, *Genesis 1 as Ancient Cosmology*.

Archaeology, as we have discussed in the last few chapters, cannot tell us exactly how long humankind in the image of God lived in natural obedience, but *Homo sapiens* has been around for at least 300,000 years, which is a significant portion of the average lifespan of a species, of about one million years. It is futile to talk about things like cultural "progress" or "stasis" in this context. As Don Richardson points out,

> Each society or group of societies had its own starting line, its own starting time, its own course, and its own finish line. . . . A culture pursuing harmony with nature, for example, should not be judged by the norms of a culture pursuing technological mastery over nature![8]

God's plan to make a new creation out of the old, by transforming it through the same mankind he had formed to rule it in its old form, was intended—and is still intended—to change creation from something extremely long-lived to something eternal. This, of course, is the Christian cosmic hope of the eternal temple spanning heaven and earth, which is explored by some of the same writers who are seeking to understand the cosmic temple theology of the Old Creation.[9] In between the thirteen-billion-year-old creation and the eternal new creation is the time spanned by the subject matter of the Bible, covering, to date, around 6,000 years on Archbishop James Ussher's dates.

I find it somewhat ironic that, for all we have learned about both the antiquity of the earth and the chronological and genealogical habits of the ancients, the time frame of the Bible narrative still matches quite reasonably the frequently mocked chronology of Ussher from 1650, which graced the margins of King James Version Bibles for centuries. It is often forgotten that Ussher's work was regarded at the time as a masterpiece of applied science, the culmination of a research program that also included Isaac Newton, and it relied on the best historical corroboration available to him. The physicist Robert Boyle was both a family friend and an admirer of his.[10] Consequently I may occasionally find it convenient in this book to use "4004 BCE," Ussher's date for the Creation, as symbolic shorthand for a relatively recent Adam's introduction to the garden.[11]

8. Richardson, *Eternity in Their Hearts,* 143–44.

9. Notably Beale, *Temple*; Middleton, *New Heaven and a New Earth*; but also Wright, *Surprised by Hope.*

10. Davis, "Heart of a Great Scientist."

11. I also have a soft spot for Ussher because his next-but-one predecessor as

This relatively short time period of a few thousand years, then, forms the pivot, or perhaps the bridge, between the two creations. This interval, plus however much remains until the return of Christ, is the time that God has employed in readying the world for the remedy he has provided for Adam's sin and Satan's deception, in Christ. In terms of either creation, he is not slow—it is the mere blink of an eye.

As for that time, let us assume that, in accordance with traditional theology, it was necessary for all men to be "in Adam" before they could be "in Christ."[12] Perhaps this necessity is along the lines that "God has shut all up in disobedience so that he may show mercy to all."[13]

Granted that necessity, though, genealogical science tells us that within two thousand years, Adam might have become a common ancestor of all mankind. He had certainly become the common ancestor of all in Eurasia and Africa who might come under the influence of Israel and her priestly role. Christ's coming for all humanity was, on that time scale, almost immediately after the time when all humanity became children of Adam.

Conclusion relative to Genealogical Adam

Genealogical Adam, which works with the usual scientific dating of the earth, and posits "natural humans" living alongside, and long before, Adam and Even in the Garden of Eden, makes sense not only of the age of the earth, but of the long period, humanly speaking, of salvation history. In the first place, both old and new creations grow slowly, as Scripture teaches of the work of Christ's kingdom. In the second place, God's patient dealings with humanity gain a clearer perspective.

Scripture tells us that in the course of time, Christ died for the ungodly "at the right time."[14] There might be many reasons why 30 CE *was* the right time: the completion of OT prophecy and the culmination of Daniel's succession of empires, or the widespread Jewish diaspora that provided a foothold for a Jewish gospel, or the *Pax Romana* making travel easier. But one reason might well be that this was just the time

---

Protestant Archbishop of Armagh, my probable ancestor John Garvey, was a relative of his by marriage. Genealogical blood is thicker than water!

12. 1 Cor 15:22.

13. Rom 11:32.

14. Rom 5:6.

when Adam's genealogical lineage became that of every human being on earth. The science tells us that it was, at any rate, not too much longer than would guarantee this, even without considering special divine knowledge.

Genealogical Adam does not second guess God's timing. But it does cast some light, I think, on some of the divine wisdom behind God's apparent slowness.

§2: Generations of Earth

(Place)

Let the waters below the heavens be gathered into one place,
and let the dry land appear . . .

GEN 1:9.

4.

CLUES FROM THE ANCIENT
NEAR EAST

Adam and Adapa, Priest-Sages

GENESIS IS A UNIQUE piece of literature. But Genesis 1—11, showing signs both of great antiquity and a literary relationship to other ANE literature, is also a product of that ancient culture. We may be able to find clues in other literature that help address my suggestion that, despite traditional appearances, Genesis was written in the full knowledge that other people existed outside the garden.

Assyriologist Leo Oppenheim makes an interesting (and usually unnoticed) distinction between the two so-called "creation stories" of Genesis.

> The relationship between man and nature in the ancient Near East is nowhere as pointedly formulated as in Genesis 1:26, where it is said that God gave man "dominion over the fish of the sea, and over the fowl of the air, and over the cattle, and over all the earth, and over every creeping thing that creepeth upon the earth." The parallel version of the Creation story (Genesis 2:19) formulates the same relationship differently, and in a way that is more relevant to the characteristic attitude of those civilizations that relied on writing for the preservation of their intellectual traditions. It says, "God formed every beast of the field, and every fowl of the air; and brought them unto Adam to see what he would call them: and whatsoever Adam called

every living creature, that was the name thereof." While it was thus man's privilege as the lord of creation to give names to the animals, the knowledge of all their names and their individual features and behavior was considered the privilege of the sage. This is illustrated by the passage (1 Kings 4:33) that extols the wisdom of Solomon: "And he spake of trees, from the cedar tree that is in Lebanon even unto the hyssop that springeth out of the wall: he spake also of beasts, and of fowl, and of creeping things, and of fishes."[1]

I mentioned the similarity between Adam and Solomon, in naming the animals, in chapter 1. But notice in Oppenheim's description of Adam the designation of "sage."

Oppenheim is suggesting that, whereas man and woman in Genesis 1 are being presented as the creature set over earthly creation by virtue of bearing God's image, in the light of the ANE parallels, Adam in Genesis 2 is presented as a male sage-priest. This is particularly significant given the now widely recognized temple imagery of Eden itself.[2] Adam is not presented as the first man in the world, but as a designated priest in a sacred space *within* the world, and it is there that the drama of his innocence, rebellion, and subjection to exile and death is played out.

Genesis 2, in its protohistoric genre, never actually claims Adam specifically as the first man. It just fails to mention any other people and majors on the history of his genealogical descendants. It is true that it also names Eve as "the mother of all living." But the same is true nowadays, genetically speaking, of Mitochondrial Eve, and she certainly wasn't the first woman.[3] Although the natural tendency has been, like Oppenheim, to see the two Genesis accounts as parallel (or in critical circles, conflicting) views of the same creation event, some have seen them as dealing with different circumstances, with texts like Genesis 5:1–3 intended to bring the two accounts into harmony rather than congruence.

John H. Walton, for example, sees Genesis 1 as recounting the creation of the whole human race (as a functional account, of course, with

---

1. Oppenheim, "*Man and Nature.*"

2. See chapter 16.

3. There is also rich theology behind the designation, in that Eve, "dead in sins and trespasses" has been promised, by Yahweh, the seed that will trample down Satan. "Mother of all living" therefore has a spiritual, even christological, connotation. This may account for the strong emphasis on the choice of wives and their difficulty with childbearing in the patriarchal narratives of Genesis 12—50.

the whole cosmos serving as God's temple),[4] whereas the Eden account is that of an archetypal human from that race, set in a temple precinct on earth for a specific role.[5] In his particular interpretation, Eve already existed naturally (like Cain's wife later on), and he presents a case that her creation from Adam's side is a didactic vision about the divine nature of marriage, akin to the visionary experience of Abraham in Genesis 15.[6]

As moderns we will miss the allusions to Adam as a sage-priest, though they may have been self-evident to the original readers from the naming of the animals, that is to say, the classification of the world, the specific activity of wise men and priests in the ANE. But further support for the idea, and greater insights, might come from what has sometimes been considered a Mesopotamian parallel to the Adam story, the tale of Adapa, dweller in the world's first city, Eridu. At times Genesis 2—3 has been said to be derived from *Adapa*, at times the reverse, and at others that there is no connection. But there are sufficient parallels to make it likely that they share some kind of literary heritage, though put to very different uses. It is quite possible that "Adam" and "Adapa" even share an etymology, those usually proposed for both being quite conjectural.

Adapa is the first of seven sages who serve the kings of different cities before the flood (which was probably the major inundation centred on Shuruppak around 2,900 BCE). He is certainly not the first man; in the myths the gods have made humankind to serve the gods in the cities, once the kingship descends from heaven. Here is what is said on the tablets[7] about Adapa's origin:

> He possessed intelligence . . . ,
>
> His command like the command of Anu . . .
>
> He (Ea) granted him a wide ear to reveal the destiny of the land,
>
> He granted him wisdom, but he did not grant him eternal life.
>
> In those days, in those years the wise man of Eridu,
>
> Ea had created him as chief among men [= "model of men" or archetype (Andreasen)],[8]
>
> A wise man whose command none should oppose,

4. Walton, *Genesis 1 as Ancient Cosmology*, 175.

5. Walton, *Lost World of Adam and Eve*, 74–77.

6. Ibid., 77–81.

7. Rogers, "Adapa," Tablet No. 1.

8. Andreasen, "Adam and Adapa," 188.

> The prudent, the most wise among the Anunnaki [= offspring of the sky-god Anu] was he,
> Blameless, of clean hands, anointed, observer of the divine statutes,
> With the bakers he made bread
> With the bakers of Eridu, he made bread,
> The food and the water for Eridu he made daily,
> With his clean hands he prepared the table,
> And without him the table was not cleared.

Niels-Erik Andreasen notes:

> Although Adapa, unlike Adam, is not the first man on earth, he does represent mankind in a special sense. According to fragment A, line 6, he is a "model of men," a human archetype; and as B. R. Foster suggests, this particular aspect of Adapa's character identifies him as a wise man whose abilities extend in several directions.[9]

Though not the first of men, then, note that Adapa, like Adam, is created apparently supernaturally, without mention of human parentage. As a sage he is engaged in the service of the Eridu temple (that being the significance of his interest in bakery). The story continues to speak about his similar role in catching fish for the temple, and that leads to his adventures, which need not detain us except to say there is a quasi-parallel with Adam in his failing to obtain eternal life.

Note also that, though he is not even the king of Eridu (that was Alulim, first of the Sumerian antediluvian rulers), Adapa's wisdom and blamelessness are intended to make him an archetype for men. It appears that the role of the sages was to teach the wisdom of the gods to men, presumably so that the formerly uncivilized race would be fit for their new divine calling.

Though the details, and the *denouement*, are very different in the two tales, summarizing *Adapa* in this general way actually casts light on what the story of Eden is already suggesting to some modern scholars, as they pick up on the various allusions to the garden as a sacred space in which man and Yahweh commune but from which Adam and Eve are exiled for disobedience, to the tragic loss of all of their descendants.

If we approach Adam as a priest-sage, we see him within the Pentateuchal literary context of the foundation story of Israel, in which they

9. Ibid.

too are called to be a nation of priests amongst the gentiles. There is even a parallel to Israel's potential or actual failure in that role. We are less likely, with that background knowledge, to jump to the conclusion that Adam is the original, generic inhabitant of earth, and less likely to have big issues with the thought of his having dealings with "non-Adams" outside the garden, as Adapa did with "ordinary" people. Zombies or apes are not in view in either story.

Genesis already gives hints of mediation between Yahweh and the wider race by suggesting Adam's priesthood. And in *Adapa*, too, we have the cultural memory of a supernaturally wise man bringing knowledge of the divine to an existing human race hitherto in ignorance. They might even be the same man.

It may be harder to explain how the failed priest of Genesis becomes the father of universally sinful humanity in the New Testament, but it's by no means completely implausible. On the one hand, if Adam, by his unique appointment to become intimate with and obedient to God, was intended to achieve wisdom and eternal life (the tree of life) for all men, then his failure deprives us all. On the other, if like Adapa he is God's appointed archetype ("model of men"), then the example he set was disastrous, whether it was transmitted to mankind through generation as in the Irenaean and Augustinian theories, or in some other way.

Some such understanding retains the biblical uniqueness of Adam as the human origin both of knowledge of Yahweh, and of the rebellion against his word which constitutes sin. And it also makes evolutionary denials of the Adam story irrelevant, because not only does Adam become an historical (and not a biological) figure, albeit couched in some "mythic" imagery, but he becomes a plausible character in a specific historical setting—that of the earliest civilization in Mesopotamia, which even, perhaps, passes on some kind of distorted memory of him in the *Adapa* story. Genesis is then consonant with the culture, with the historical fixed point of a known flood, and with a specific cultural (and in the stories divinely created and appointed) role as a priest-sage for all men.

The main incongruence is that Mesopotamia did not worship Yahweh, but "images made to look like mortal man and birds and animals and reptiles."[10] But we already knew that Adam failed in his role, and passed his imperfect knowledge of the true God only down his

10. Rom 1:23.

genealogical line until God called his descendant, Abram, from that very land to the land of promise.

Adam, the Ewe, and the Wheat

There is another Sumerian text that might cast some oblique light on the apparent solitude of Adam and Eve. That text is not the *Atrahasis Epic*, but I want to refer to that first since it is commonly compared and contrasted with Genesis, and with good reason because the two have many literary parallels.

One key point taught in *Atrahasis*, and in a number of other Mesopotamian texts, is that humankind was created to ease the labor of the inferior gods. These deities had been assigned the work of irrigation (this was the Euphrates flood plain, remember), which was necessary for cultivation in order to produce both grain and pasture for livestock. The minor gods protesting at their workload (in some accounts taking strike action), humankind is created, *en masse*, from clay and slain god's blood, specifically for this role of agriculture and pastoral activity, in order to feed the gods, which is done *via* the whole cultic apparatus. This functional reason for humankind's creation is central, because it is the gods' hunger that later on ends the flood and has them all clustering around Atrahasis's sacrifice "like flies."

The parallel with Genesis is that both in Genesis 1 and Genesis 2, *ādām* and Adam (respectively) are also created for cultivating work. The hugely important theological difference is that in both passages in Genesis there is a strong sense of mankind's being created not as slaves to save God work, but as co-regents to administer his world. But the point to remember for now is that, both in Genesis and *Atrahasis*, humankind is created for cultivation and stewardship of the land, appearing to suggest that before agriculture there was no humankind:[11] in both traditions we were created *de novo* for a specific purpose.

Richard Middleton's book on the *imago dei*, *The Liberating Image*,[12] quotes another Sumerian text, *Ewe and Wheat* (formerly known as "Sheep and Grain"), whose text may be found online. Middleton's purpose in citing it is to critique the Mesopotamian concept of man as slave to the

---

11. Gen 2:5.

12. Middleton, *Liberating Image*, 156–58.

gods (and its social consequences), but I want to pick up on something entirely different.

The story is basically a "disputation text" in which two gods, responsible for sheep and grain, argue about their respective importance. But the story begins with a "cosmological introduction" in which the gods have trouble getting enough food and clothing, eventually resulting in the solution of forming deities who will be responsible for inventing pastoral and agricultural activities.

If we were to seek to integrate this into the mythological structure of the *Atrahasis* story, we would place it chronologically *before* the gods started doing those jobs, *before* they got fed up with them and therefore long *before* the creation of man to do them instead. But in fact, part of the *Ewe and Wheat* introduction says this:

> The people of those days did not know about eating bread. They did not know about wearing clothes; they went about with naked limbs in the Land. Like sheep they ate grass with their mouths and drank water from the ditches.[13]

Now whether these primitive people were simply invented to add relish to the story, or came from some residual folk memory of hunter-gatherer life before agriculture (bearing in mind that, like *Atrahasis*, it comes from the very dawn of literature in the mid to late third millennium), the fact is that it states clearly that people existed long before agriculture, whereas *Atrahasis* says people were created expressly for an existing agriculture.

Now, I wouldn't want to press the matter too far. We simply don't know how far either *Ewe and Lamb* or *Atrahasis* were taken literally, or believed to be factual at all, in their original contexts. There may have been rival traditions on origins, or the culture may not have been that concerned with consistency between different stories.

Nevertheless both these ancient stories come from the same culture, and were preserved by the same scribes for centuries, and they were able in some way to hold together the fact that *Atrahasis*, like Genesis 2, has humanity created for its role *de novo*; and that *Ewe and Wheat* presupposes people existing from time immemorial. These "former" people led an existence somehow removed from "people today," whose customary labor of irrigation, farming, and cultic duties is explained by the first account, but not the second, whilst the "discovery" of that farming way of

13. Oxford University, "Sheep and Grain," 12–25.

life appears in the second, but not the first. Absence of evidence of wide-spread humanity in an ANE creation text is demonstrably *not* evidence of absence, but only of literary purpose.

We can only conjecture how a Sumerian scribe confronted with this contradiction would reply, or whether his response would even make sense to our modern sense of logic. One obvious explanation, with possible relevance to Genesis, is that the scribe might say that *Atrahasis* didn't mention other people simply because it wasn't about them, but about *real* people, civilized people.

It is by no means impossible that, for a Sumerian priest-scribe with a highly functional and theologically orientated view of things, bringing people together in cities so that the real gods were fed and worshipped correctly (thus holding creation together, in Mesopotamian belief) was what constituted the creation of humankind in the first place, the divine blood and clay being figurative, and barbarians living long before, or far away, being simply irrelevant to his conception of "human" or "creation."

Israel was not dependant on Mesopotamia for its beliefs, but it undoubtedly shared some of its thought-life. So if, as I contend, Genesis was written to the nation that God called to transform the world, because Adam had failed to do so, then the history of Adam's line is the main story being told, and nobody else requires to be mentioned. Yet even so, people outside Adam's line might be as implicitly present in the idea of the world that was to be transformed, as the non-Sumerians are when they peep out shyly from one small passage in Ewe and Wheat.

Curses for All

In my book *God's Good Earth*[14] I pointed out the parallels between God's specific punishments for Adam and Eve (the curse on the ground of Genesis 3:17–19, and the curse on childbearing of Genesis 3:16) and a passage in *Atrahasis*. In this, as the gods are increasingly troubled by mankind's "noise," but before the flood, they first cut off nature's gifts, producing starvation:

> When the second year arrived
> They had depleted the storehouse.
> When the third year arrived

14. Garvey, *God's Good Earth*, 29–30.

The people's looks were changed by starvation.

When the fourth year arrived

Their upstanding bearing bowed,

Their well-set shoulders slouched,

The people went out in public hunched over.

When the fifth year arrived,

A daughter would eye her mother coming in;

A mother would not even open her door to her daughter. . . .

When the sixth year arrived

They served up a daughter for a meal,

Served up a son for food.[15]

Furthermore, at this time Enlil also curses childbirth:

Let the womb be too tight to let the baby out.[16]

If there is indeed a literary connection here, then Genesis might have borrowed, rather obliquely, from *Atrahasis* or, less likely, *Atrahasis* borrowed from Genesis and projected the curses forward in time. But a third explanation is that God's curse on the ground affected the whole region, by famine or by drought, for the entire period up to the flood, and the curse on childbearing affected Eve's line over the same period—a line which had, by the time of the flood, grown extensive not least through the intermarriage of Genesis 6.

If, in these ways, the curses were experienced, and passed into literature, by the Sumerians, then it would constitute yet another pointer to the existence of others apart from Adam and his immediate descendants. Their actions affected an entire culture.

Conclusion Relative to Genealogical Adam

Here are three non-Hebrew sources that might cast light on the world into which Adam and Eve came after their expulsion from the Garden of Eden, a world in which there had existed others from much earlier times, and a world which they themselves affected both for good and ill.

Not only do these literary parallels suggest the world in which Adam may have existed—a world in which we know that large populations had

15. Dalley, trans., *Myths,* 25–26.

16. Ibid., 25.

existed for millennia—but there is a direct parallel, in Adapa, of a single man specially created, and yet living within a human population.

Furthermore, the creation of humankind itself in Atrahasis, comparable both to Adam's formation and the Genesis 1 creation, exists alongside stories of earlier humans existing from an indefinite period beforehand. There seems no reason to exclude a similar "non-Adamic" population being assumed by the author of Genesis, and some good reasons for thinking it likely.

5.

CULTURE AND GEOGRAPHY

Cultural Pointers

IN CHAPTER 1 OF this book I pointed out that some features of the early chapters of Genesis strongly suggest a setting in or after the Neolithic—flock-keeping and agriculture in Genesis 2—4, and city building in chapter 4. I might add to that the division of animals, from the very start in Genesis 1, into beasts of the field (wild animals), "creeping things" (Heb. *remeś*, which John Walton understands to mean wild prey animals such as deer, wild cattle, or antelope), and domestic livestock—the animals which only became "livestock" through Neolithic domestication.[1] In fact, the primordial metal-working of Tubal-cain in chapter 5, only five generations after Cain, pushes the account even further forward to the Chalcolithic, which began in Anatolia, where it spanned c 5,500–3,000 BCE.[2]

I also pointed out that, however abbreviated the genealogies in Genesis 1—5 may be, for them to make any sense at all *as* genealogies there is a limit as to how many generations can have been omitted. Lastly, I gave

---

1. Walton, *Genesis*, 341.

2. It is not necessary to assert that Tubal-cain was the first metalworker: only that his skill made him the archetype of metalworkers. Thus we not need believe he personally worked with iron—though it is not impossible that he did, for meteoric iron was first worked in around 4,000 BCE in Egypt, and the Anatolian Hittites are the first known true iron-smelters, around 2,000 BCE.

a general introduction to the indicators that a genuine location, rather than a purely mythical symbolism, is described for the garden in Genesis 2:10–14.

As discussed in chapter 1, the whole Genesis protohistory is abbreviated, theologically oriented, and has metaphorical elements to a greater or lesser extent. In other words, it is greatly underdetermined for my purpose here of grounding it in space and time. I pointed out in that chapter that this is probably part of its author's intention. He wants us to know *that* it is history, but to focus our attention on its relevance to the reader's situation, archetypally.

Nevertheless, once the text itself points us to a particular window in history and geography, as I have shown above that it does, we are in our times forced to grapple with the knowledge that the world was widely populated long before that time. We have to ask whether there are any real settings for it that might be plausible: and there certainly are, though none is without difficulties. That very possibility, given the nature of the text and our distance from both the events and the culture, is itself significant. One would expect that a purely mythical account ought to be impossible to map to any real situation.

Eden in Israel

I offer first the example of Israel, or the land that would become Israel, as an instance of an *implausible* mapping to a literal Eden. The area of Mount Moriah, now in Jerusalem, is the region suggested by John Sailhamer and Seth Postell for the garden,[3] and theologically it certainly makes good sense, tying the holy place of Abraham's offering of Isaac, the Temple, and even the Passion of Christ into a unified geographical continuity with Eden.

The general eastward trend of the Genesis narrative, ending at Babel and theologically denoting progressive estrangement from God, would also fit the location. Abraham's journey west from Ur would then be a kind of return to Eden, and the exile a recapitulation of the movement east in Genesis. However, the same neat pattern is not true of the flood narrative, in which the symbolic re-creation of the world after its destruction would take us back not to the place where it started, but to Ararat, somewhere far to the northeast of Jerusalem and so seemingly irrelevant,

3. Postell, *Adam as Israel*, 89–90.

in typological terms. The fact that Ararat, as a location, is so arbitrary to the whole biblical narrative points to real, somewhat messy, events rather than myth.

Sailhamer's (in two cases) vague identification of the four rivers of Genesis 2 at least places Israel somewhere between them. He takes "Cush" as Egypt (rather than the usual meaning of Ethiopia), and so identifies the Gihon as the Nile, and then reasons his way to Havilah as somewhere to the southeast of Israel, the River Pishon, and the territory itself, being deduced rather than identified on the ground.

But in Genesis 2, a river flows through Eden to water the garden, and the only river of any size that has ever been described to flow from Jerusalem, which is built on permeable limestone, is the eschatological river of life of prophecy.[4] This river certainly involves Edenic imagery, as well as temple imagery, but it is impossible to link it with any actual river, divided into four "heads," in historical or even geological time. The one major river that does exist in Israel, the Jordan, is entirely absent from the account. Yet in Eden, its own river gave rise to (or possibly flowed from) the others, which are clearly intended to be real.

All this, for an Eden set in Canaan, renders the geographical pointers in the text, to the city of Asshur for example, gratuitous. Once one rejects un-evidenced changes in world geography to account for these impossibilities (sometimes still invoked and attributed to a global flood, in the teeth of the scientific evidence), one has to regard the text as deeply metaphorical throughout, and assign some theological meaning to the city of Asshur, as has sometimes been done for the products of Havilah, matched to the riches of the Temple furniture or of Solomon's reign, and stripped of all geographical significance.[5] Nobody seems to have attempted this.

Israel as an actual geographical location for an Eden within the time frame which, I suggest, the Bible itself has set out is therefore untenable, although if one prefers an entirely metaphorical or allegorical understanding of the garden story it will do fine—but then, where does one place one's *historical* Adam and Eve in that, and with what justification?

However, the author of Genesis, conscious of the spiritual parallelism of Eden and Jerusalem, might have introduced some literary allusions to the Holy Land. That would confuse us as paleo-geographers, but

4. Ezek 47; Ps 36:8; 46:4; Zech 14:8; Rev 22.
5. Beale, *New Testament*, 68–69.

ought not to prevent us entirely from identifying the true location, if the author's geographical pointers are intended to help us, rather than throw us off on a mythical goose chase.

Northern Eden

Some candidate locations for Eden are based on ancient traditions. For example, Sumerian mythology seems to attribute some Edenic qualities to Dilmun (Bahrain) in the Persian Gulf:

> In Dilmun the raven was not yet cawing, the partridge not cack-ling. The lion did not slay, the wolf was not carrying off lambs, the dog had not been taught to make kids curl up, the pig had not learned that grain was to be eaten.
>
> When a widow has spread malt on the roof, the birds did not yet eat that malt up there. The pigeon then did not tuck the head under its wing.
>
> No eye-diseases said there: "I am the eye disease." No headache said there: "I am the headache." No old woman belonging to it said there: "I am an old woman." No old man belonging to it said there: "I am an old man." No maiden in her unwashed state . . . in the city. No man dredging a river said there: "It is getting dark." No herald made the rounds in his border district.[6]

But the differences outweigh any similarities. In the light of the information in Genesis, there are only two main contenders for the site of Eden: at the headwaters of the Tigris and Euphrates, where their sources are relatively close together, or at their mouths, where at various times in history (including now) the two rivers have been confluent.

Both areas have changed considerably in climate and topography over the millennia, making the drawing of conclusions from the present state of things risky. But this also opens up intriguing possibilities, sometimes arising from new discoveries about the situation in the past.

There is a case to be made for setting most of the events of the early chapters of Genesis in the region of the upper Tigris and Euphrates. Typologically this area fits the bill, having territories to the east suitable for the subsequent events of Genesis, and being both well-watered, and mountainous enough to resonate with the Hebrew cosmos in which a

---

6. Oxford University, "Enki and Ninhursaja," 11–26.

mountain is the usual place to meet God. Ezekiel even attributes a divine mountain to Eden.[7] Historically speaking, this region is the cradle of many aspects of civilization, including agriculture.

There are potential candidates in Eastern Anatolia (ancient Armenia) for the four rivers of Eden that match the description of the river being divided into four "heads," if they are understood as distributaries rather than tributaries, as the alternative southern theory (see below) demands. The Armenians lay claim to Eden in their traditions, but of course the mention of Ararat in the flood account would be sufficient to generate such national pride. This location seems preferable to other alternatives topologically, though as I mentioned in chapter 1 many commentators seem willing to entertain the possibility that "heads" can mean "headwaters," and that the river of Eden was fed by these, rather than them by it.

The Tigris and Euphrates rise less than fifty miles from each other, and another nearby river, the Çoruh, winds north to the Black Sea through a land of historically good gold deposits, Colchis, which might therefore be the biblical Havilah. The Aras (or Araxes) might fulfill the role of the Gihon, flowing into the Caspian, if Cush, like Havilah, is rebranded from the usual understandings of its location.

But there is no river connection between these four, unless one invokes their mythical Mesopotamian origin in the subterranean waters of the *Apsu*.[8] The underworld scarcely fits the description of Eden, however. Furthermore rivers seldom split into major branches watering disparate lands. The Tigris and Euphrates even have competing watersheds.

A glance at the literature shows that although the upper courses of the Tigris and Euphrates have altered considerably within historic times, particularly as the climate changed after the ice age, there is no current evidence suggesting a common source of these rivers at any time. Ice-age Armenia was cold and dry, rather than glaciated, and subsequent warmer and wetter periods offer no mechanisms to change the river drainage so radically as to fit the account literally.

But more positively this early period, in which changed river drainage may at least be imagined, overlaps the dawn of agriculture in the Mesolithic, and therefore the earliest possible cultural setting for Adam. However, in the much later Chalcolithic, or late Neolithic, setting that is

7. Ezek 28:14.

8. Walton, *Genesis*, 168.

indicated by both the narrative and the genealogies, the rivers behaved much as they do now in their upper courses.

There are other clues in support of the northwestern situation, though. The first, as I have mentioned, is that the general movement of the story is from Eden to increasing ruin, involving progress towards the East. The cherubim guard the garden on that side, Cain is banished to the east, and migration east leads to the founding of Babel and its tower, where the protohistory culminates. That directionality parallels the later exile of both Israel and Judah to the east, the latter ending in Babylon.

I discuss the eastward spread of "Semitic" culture into Mesopotamia in the next chapter. At the very least, the migration of Akkadian-speaking Semitic peoples from the mountains to Sumer is a close match to the men of Genesis finding a plain in Shinar as they moved east. In considering the northern location, it is significant that most of this movement takes place after the flood.

Then again, it is not impossible for the high plateaus of eastern Anatolia to be the situation for this flood. The plateau of Şanlıurfa province, in Southern Turkey, is prone at least to short-lived, though catastrophic, floods from torrential rainfall in the mountains. It is the location of Abraham's town of Haran (his move west from Ur towards Canaan being a parallel with the Jewish return from exile), and also of the earliest temple sites in the world, notably Göbekli Tepe, as well as the (possibly) earliest proto-city Çatalhöyük. It is therefore a very suitable place for a human origins account.

A 2015 study[9] on flooding in the city of Batman, situated on this plateau, reviewed the geological and archaeological evidence of paleofloods at settlements on the Tigris in the region. Many of these sites are now permanently flooded, owing to the damming of the Tigris. But former excavations showed periods of accumulation of alluvium (because of large historic floods) alternating with periods of incision (reflecting drier times). The accumulation periods of interest to us were the Early Neolithic prior to 6,000 BCE, the Early Chalcolithic 5,500–4,000 BCE, and the Early Bronze Age 2,650–1,200 BCE.

One point of interest is that the paper also compared this data with paleofloods in the upper Euphrates, and with those famously recorded in lower Mesopotamia, such as Woolley's flood level at Ur (3,500 BCE), and the Shuruppak flood (2,900 BCE). The latter two, it turns out, correspond

9. Sunkar and Tonbull, "Paleoflood Analyses."

to periods *not* associated with flooding on the upper Tigris. What is true of the Tigris is not, therefore, necessarily true of the Euphrates, as their weather systems may differ. And flooding in their upper reaches may not closely reflect downstream effects.

This shows that any attempt to pin down a regional flood as being that of Genesis must be locality dependent. Therefore a chronology reconstructed from the choice of Upper or Lower Mesopotamia as the biblical Eden, or the site of the biblical flood, will possibly differ by several centuries, at least. That may mean we can only ever identify a broad period in which to situate the flood.

The plateau of the Upper Tigris is bounded on the north by the mountains of ancient Urartu, where the ark grounded in Genesis 8. A course from this location is more plausible than an ark which ended up there, against the current of a river in flood, having started in the environs of lower Mesopotamia near Shuruppak in the southern theory. Historians have also pointed out that, at the likely time of the flood, the olive leaves that the dove brought back did not grow in lower Mesopotamia, nor the vines that Noah planted, and also figs (for Adam and Eve's improvised clothing) are rare there. However all of these did grow in Anatolia, where not only viticulture, but agriculture and herding, and the metalwork attributed to Tubal-cain, have left their earliest evidence.

So although there are many difficulties, the region of Eastern Anatolia, especially the upper reaches of the Tigris, can present a case for being the site both of Eden, and of the Flood.

Southern Eden

The German Assyriologist Friedrich Delitzsch in 1881 proposed a theory placing the historical Eden in the region of northern Mesopotamia, north of Babylon and south of modern Baghdad.[10] This involved proposing the (probably mistaken) etymology of "Eden" as the Sumerian *edin*, "plain" or "steppe," and identifying the minor rivers with artificial irrigation channels. For these and other reasons, this theory has few adherents now.

But an earlier theory, of a southern Mesopotamian situation close to the Persian Gulf near ancient Ur, which was supported amongst others by John Calvin, has regained favor in recent decades.

---

10. Delitzsch, *Wo Lag das Paradies.*

Archaeologist Kenneth Kitchen points out that all the variant forms of ANE Flood and Creation stories, with their more or less loose literary links to Genesis 1—11, date in their present forms to around the early second millennium BCE. These include the Sumerian king lists, The *Eridu Genesis* and *Atrahasis*, as well as (possibly) the *Adapa myth* and the famous *Epic of Gilgamesh*, which undoubtedly used a source like *Atrahasis* as material for the relevant flood episode, in what is a composite epic poem about the antediluvian king Gilgamesh.[11] We can add to that list Irving Finkel's recently published tablet with yet another variant of the Atrahasis story, this time with a circular "ark."[12]

Kitchen suggests that the dates of all these varied but parallel sources would be more or less contemporaneous with the patriarch Abraham. Only at this early period could the first chapters of Genesis take the overall shape they have. They would have been very differently composed in the much altered literary conditions of, say, the Babylonian exile in the sixth century. If so, we must conclude that Genesis is of equal weight with the cuneiform texts, if we are seeking to discover the original basis of the narratives, being roughly of the same antiquity and geographical provenance.

However, the varied character of all these sources, compared with their shared memory of an epochal flood long before, suggests that they have their roots in divergent much earlier traditions, written or oral, from the third millennium. This raises the possibility that Abraham's family preserved an otherwise lost variant (without our making any faith-based judgement at this point on its relative historical value).

Taking all these traditions together, there seems little reason to doubt nowadays that lower Mesopotamia, at least, always prone to periodic river floods, once suffered something far beyond the usual inundations, which seems to have marked, archaeologically speaking, the transition between the "Uruk" period and the next phase of civilization. This event is routinely regarded, in the Mesopotamian tablets, as the dividing point of their history. The seventh-century Assyrian king, the scholarly Ashurbanipal, wrote that he studied pre-flood documents in his extensive library. Kitchen writes:

> As to definition, myth or "protohistory," it should be noted that the Sumerians and Babylonians had no doubts on that score.

11. Kitchen, *Reliability*, 423–27.
12. Finkel, *Ark Before Noah*.

They included it squarely in the middle of their earliest historical
tradition, with kings before it and kings after it, the flood acting
as the dividing point in that tradition, from long before 1900.[13]

Various hints in the documents and scattered evidences from archaeology place this flood around 2,900 BCE, though conclusive evidence for its exact date and extent is ambiguous and scattered. I'll return
to some new evidence later, but first let us consider Eden.

The Mesopotamian literature helps to demonstrate the genre of
Genesis 2—3, both in showing the general literary conventions in use at
the time, and in suggesting that Gen 1—11 shares the *Atrahasis* pattern of
"protohistory with divine elements." So the flood narratives, overall, em-
ploy various symbolic elements, different theological points and varied
details about who and what was rescued, but can at least be referred to a
significant historical event. It seems to follow that Genesis 2—3 have the
same historical basis, being part of the same account.

Assuming Genesis 2:10–14 to be a true geographical description,
then, it is not very plausible to interpret the passage as meaning that
Eden's river split into four downstream of the garden: rivers just don't
break into major distributaries serving different lands. But upstream
tributaries do *combine* to make single rivers, as the Tigris and Euphrates
do now.

It was long suspected that the second-mentioned river, the Gihon,
represents the present Karun river, flowing from the north, from the
"Cush" possibly identified with Elam in Genesis 10, into the combined
Tigris-Euphrates. But only relatively recently was it shown that, to the
southwest, an ancient river system once flowed to the head of the Gulf,
across what is now Kuwait, from the hinterland of Northern Arabia, the
biblical setting of Havilah, where gold was mined until the 1950s, and
where aromatic resin ("bdellium") was a major export throughout antiquity. So this now-dry river is a perfect candidate for the River Pishon.

The bad news, however, is that, owing to a drying climate, this Pishon stopped flowing c 2,500 BCE, half a millennium before our earliest
cuneiform Genesis parallels. All that is left in Iraq is the Wadi al-Batin,
which only flows occasionally. If Genesis contains a reliable tradition, it
would have to have originated *before* 2,500 BCE and been passed down to
Abraham and the Genesis writer either orally or in writing for 700 years
or more.

13. Ibid., 426.

An additional problem is that in the early second millennium, and for over a thousand years before that, the shoreline of the Persian Gulf was far inland from its present position. The earliest cities like Ur, in their heyday, hugged the ancient shoreline. The Pishon and Gihon would then have opened into the Persian Gulf, not the flood plain as they do now, and in fact even the Tigris and Euphrates apparently had separate mouths then. It was knowledge of this last fact that led earlier writers like Delitzsch to reject the southern theory.

Only much later did alluvial deposits push the shoreline back far enough to conceive of all four rivers converging in a land of Eden, and by then all memory of the Pishon as a true river must have long faded.

The precise history of the Gulf shoreline is difficult to determine exactly because of a complex interplay between rising sea levels after the ice age, climatic change (the late prehistoric period was wet, becoming drier as southern Mesopotamia was settled), and alluvial deposition. All agree the whole Gulf was dry, if swampy, in 17,000 BCE, being flooded rapidly as sea levels rose soon after the ice age, far too early to be likely as the setting for Eden. It seems generally agreed that the "highest" (i.e. most westerly) shoreline existed around five thousand years ago—the approximate time of the epochal Flood of Mesopotamian tradition.

A 2015 article by Nils-Axel Mörner,[14] though, provides some interesting new detail relevant to my purpose here. By studying the "fossilized" shorelines of the Gulf, this researcher found that the levels changed through intermittent relatively rapid incursions and retreats, rather than gradually. He found, as well as the present shore, two (and only two) old shores. The earliest was at approximately the same level as the present one. The second marked the highest extent of the sea-level rise, carbon dated from deposits to around 3,000 BCE.

Mörner's historical interest is the archaeologically confirmed flooding of Ur, rather than the biblical account, and he considers that the rapid rise of sea level he discovered would have had significant hydrological effects very far upstream which, with unknown contributions from unusually heavy rainfall, could have been sufficient to account for a cataclysmic flood of the land. The shoreline appears, from archaeological remains, to have returned to more or less its present level by about 2,000–1,500 BCE.

At present there is insufficient information to date accurately the earliest shoreline mentioned in the study by archaeological methods, for

14. Mörner, "Flooding of Ur."

ephemeral remains would have been first flooded by the sea's rise, and then stranded (and buried under many meters of alluvium). But it would seem probable that the transition must have been relatively rapid and incremental, or other shorelines would have been preserved. So the sea was probably close to its current levels even just a few centuries before the flood, if that occurred around 3,000 BCE.

Nowadays the Tigris and Euphrates join at al-Qurna to form the Shatt-al-Arab to the sea, but though the nature of the land has caused many variations in the two rivers' courses, historical records suggest that, having had separate outlets from the early third millennium or before, it was only around 100 BCE that they rejoined each other. That is far later than any possible date for the Genesis events, or for its writing.

If we accept the theory of a southern Eden there was a time, according to the text of Genesis, when the four rivers named did indeed flow into one, watering a fertile alluvial plain between their junctions and the sea. The *earliest* time for this is limited both by human memory and the post-ice-age filling of the Gulf. But the very *last* time that it can have occurred in southern Mesopotamia would have been in the fourth millennium BCE, and well before the flood that is remembered in Babylonian history as well as Genesis, and whose deposits have been found in the ancient cities by the Assyriologists in their excavations.

It was around 3,800 BCE that a formerly wet climate began to dry, leading to prolonged drought and low rainfall in the ANE. This was the time when the Ubaid culture began to irrigate the plain of Shinar in earnest.[15] So at that time a southern Eden would have been watered primarily by annual river inundations, like the Nile. Two pieces of biblical data correspond to this.

Firstly, Gordon Wenham[16] suggests that the word *ed* often translated "mist" in Genesis 2:6 is a cognate of Sumerian/Akkadian *id*, the freshwater cosmic river, and informs us that the old versions translated it as "spring." This may, then, be a geographical prompt describing a land watered by inundation, though without crops until cultivated by man. This makes more sense than the cloud-forest suggested by translating *ed* as "mist."

15. Roux, *Ancient Iraq*, 66. Roux points out that some irrigation agriculture had been carried out in southern Mesopotamia for up to two millennia before this. The drier climate increased the need, and the population.

16. Wenham, *Genesis*, 58.

Secondly, Genesis 13:11 describes the area of the cities of the plain, according to recent excavations[17] probably to be situated across the alluvial fan of the Jordan from Jericho, as "like the garden of the Lord, and like the land of Egypt as you go to Zoar." Both the identifiable sites here are on alluvial sites watered by inundation rather than rainfall. It therefore appears likely that the author is making some specific comparisons with his geographical understanding of Genesis 2, rather than a general observation about fertile country.

How such an incredibly ancient tradition as a fourth millennium Eden might have lasted through to the writing of Genesis is impossible to say, though I covered the capabilities and limitations of oral transmission in chapter 2. But it remains true that nobody familiar with the geography of lower Babylon in historical times, and wishing to situate Eden there, could possibly have invented such an anachronistic narrative and written it down without being universally ridiculed. There was no written script in the fourth millennium with which to record the changing topology, even if there had been hydrologists around to do so. And it seems highly unlikely that someone ignorant of the geography, such as some scribe in first-millennium Israel, could have accidentally hit on a geographical description that so closely matches the long-lost time and place it purports to describe.

An illuminating survey[18] of the interplay of the various physical processes in the development of the lower-Mesopotamian geography, by English archaeologist Andrew Sherratt, also shows clearly that there was a time, before the fullest extent of the sea-level rise c 3,000 BCE (coinciding with the most likely historical date for the flood), when the two great rivers did flow together for the last part of their course, as Genesis describes. This period would have been back in the fourth millennium—in other words, remarkably consistent with the Ussher dates for the Eden narrative. If the detailed Genesis topography is not sheer fiction (and why, and how, invent an imaginary confluence of rivers which, at times, have had a real confluence?), then it must be recalling the land as it was way back in fourth millennium, centuries before the earliest written records we have from the region, but consistent with a "4004 BCE" Adam.

The only real geographical loose end I see in Sherratt's work is that the advancing northern arm of the Persian Gulf, separating Sumer from

17. Collins and Scott, *Discovering Sodom.*
18. Sherratt, "Evolution of Mesopotamia."

Susa (Khush) seems to give the Karun River (*aka* Gihon) a separate sea outlet. But as the author admits, precise reconstruction of such a complex system is extremely difficult. It may well be that there was, indeed, a time when all four rivers flowed into a single confluence in the center of the developing flood plain, but if so it must have been for a historically brief period.

More problematic to the southern theory are matters of ethnicity. On the positive side, the people dwelling across that northern arm of the Persian Gulf, which was certainly crossed for trading purposes in the third millennium, were probably of a different ethnic origin to those in Sumer. This would make a very plausible situation for Cain's exile amongst a potentially hostile people.

On the negative side, though, the ethnicity of the southern Mesopotamians at this time was that of the Sumerian "black-headed people," who appear to have been for all intents and purposes indigenous to the region. This divorces Adam from the apparently Semitic ethnicity indicated so strongly in the ensuing chapters of Genesis—unless, of course, Genesis 2:7–8 be taken to imply that Adam was a sojourner in an unfamiliar promised land, like Abraham after him.

The other major difficulty of the southern location is the loss of the eastern movement that is so prominent in the text of Genesis 1—11. We have to suppose either that the flood took Noah's ark all the way upstream from the Persian Gulf homeland to the region of Ararat, whence the eastern drift began again, or else that Adam's line had gradually migrated west, though that is unmentioned in the text.

In summary, there are intriguing evidences that make a southern Eden at least conceivable, as we found there were with respect to a northern Eden in Armenia. At the same time there are difficulties in both cases that will only be resolved by further discoveries, or by accepting a degree of agnosticism about the exact location. There are, at least, indications that there *was* an actual location, rather than a purely mythical and otherworldly Eden being intended in Genesis.

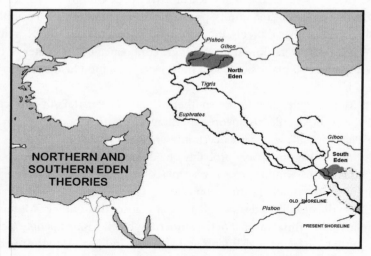

Conclusion Relative to Genealogical Adam

If we reach the conclusion that Eden was in an actual location, within an actual time frame constrained by the limitations described so far, then we need to account for the archaeological presence of considerable populations of people, with advanced cultures including the building of both towns and megalithic cultic monuments. The sizes of these populations are not in doubt, and neither is their antiquity, right back to the end of the ice age.

But once we no longer insist on finding a lone, original couple, then the spiritual business God did with a couple drawn from such a population, and the subsequent history, are not at all implausible.

It would be quite conceivable for the Garden of Eden to be a private place, either by natural or supernatural means, amidst or beyond the margins of such a population. It is inconceivable, however, for Adam and Eve to have existed alone in those times and places. Something like Genealogical Adam is necessary if we are to give any weight to the geographical references that Genesis makes, apparently in order to assist us in identifying its location.

6.

THE TABLE OF NATIONS

Language

ONE FEATURE OF GREAT theological significance in the protohistory of Genesis 1—11 is the apparently obsessive desire of Noah's sons to spread over the earth. The writer is clearly concerned to show how, despite the failure and exile of Adam from Eden, God's creation ordinance of Genesis 1:28, repeated after the judgement of the flood in the Noachic covenant in Genesis 9:1, is being progressively fulfilled—but not necessarily righteously.

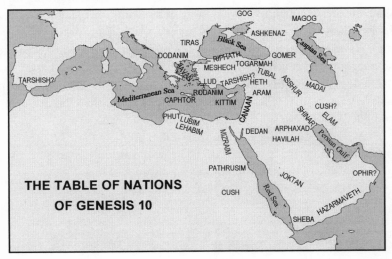

THE TABLE OF NATIONS
OF GENESIS 10

This migration is documented in the "Table of Nations" of Genesis 10, which is unique in ancient literature. Fig. 2 shows a typical mapping of the table to what is known, or may be reasonably inferred, from various sources. In my university days, in the early 1970s, a linguistics lecturer made a deliberate mockery of it when he facetiously began the course by saying that all modern languages stem from Babel. This, of course, is not true.

Yet since then genetics has shown beyond reasonable doubt that for Europe, at least, the Neolithic Revolution spread across the continent not just by diffusion of ideas, but by a mass migration of people from Anatolia. That seems an intriguing match, geographical if not chronological, to the biblical narrative, especially if Ararat, where the ark landed, is taken to be the mountain range in northern Mesopotamia, that is to say, bordering Anatolia. I explored the arguments for possible geographical sites for early Genesis in chapter 5.

But I want to draw attention to something particular about that map of the Noachic nations. Though it is necessarily somewhat approximate, there is a decided bias towards occupation of the territory west and south of the Caspian Sea, and little to the east of that. The spread of the Noachic peoples largely ceases at the mouth of the Euphrates and the Arabian Peninsula.

This, to a large extent, overlaps the area in which the language group traditionally known as "Semitic" (a term popularized by Johann Gottfried Eichhorn as long ago as 1795) was spoken. Linguistically, the more outlying northern groups in the Table are absent from the Semitic-speaking area (though we have no way of knowing what languages were spoken there so long ago, since these outliers lacked any preserved writing). However, the overlap does include northern Africa, where Semitic languages were spoken in what are now Tunisia, Algeria, and Libya. The Table does not mention the Horn of Africa, where Semitic was spoken only after 800 BCE. The list gives some indication, therefore, of being compiled before that time, at least in its original form.

A recent study suggests from Bayesian analysis that the origin of the Semitic language group was in the Levant in around 3,800 BCE.[1] The paper is aware of the anthropological significance of this:

1. Kitchen, Ehret, et al., *Bayesian phylogenetic analysis.*

Semitic populations are associated with the oldest written languages and urban civilizations in the region, which gave rise to some of the world's first major religious and literary traditions.[2]

To remind us of the significance of this language in relation to Genesis, it was the Semitic tongue Akkadian which gradually replaced the earlier, non-Semitic, Sumerian tongue in Mesopotamia in the mid-third millennium BCE. If we accept the possibility that Noah's descendants were the Semitic (speaking linguistically rather than biblically) survivors of Adam's line, rather than of all mankind, this corresponds very well with the statement:

> 2 It came about as they journeyed east, that they found a plain in the land of Shinar and settled there.[3]

This is a highly compressed account of a very long and complex period of history. But however this move eastwards is interpreted, the settlers would not have found a virgin land, but one already occupied by the Sumerians, who are generally regarded as indigenous to the area well back into the Paleolithic.[4] It is significant that this observation in the text is made together with an observation about the linguistic unity in the land (*eretz*), and then describes the confusion of Babel.

Richard Middleton suggests that the Babel episode might actually allude not to the miraculous division of an original language into many, but the *imposition* of the Akkadian language across the Assyrian Empire by Sargon of Akkad (2,334–2,279 BCE),[5] since it occurs in Genesis *after* the Table of Nations, in which mention is made of various languages being spoken.[6]

The chapter would then be intended as an "ideology critique" of the violent political power exercised by the sinful Adamic line, in the form of Sargon's regime, usually considered the first empire in the world. The confusion of languages and the abandonment of building would then be about Yahweh's governmental breakup of the first empire, in which revolt against the suppression of "inferior" native language and culture

2. Ibid.

3. Gen 11:2.

4. Roux, *Ancient Iraq,* 48.

5. Middleton, *Liberating Image,* 221–28.

6. Gen 10:20.

was undoubtedly a factor historically. Such an empire, if it involved the offspring of Adam, would certainly warrant inclusion in the Genesis narrative.

This is a more lucid explanation than the usual rather arbitrary one that it accounts for the languages of the earth (the traditional explanation seized upon and dismembered by my linguistics lecturer) and it ties the theme of a progressive growth of sin more closely to the ensuing narrative of Abraham, God's first definitive answer to sin. It would also be the first of a long pattern of assertions of God's controlling discipline over empires through both Old and New Testaments. Noah's descendants are seeking to make a name for themselves[7] by imposing their own language and culture forcibly (echoing Cain's violent example), whereas it is Yahweh who will make a name for Abraham[8] as he lives at peace in a foreign land, trusting in God's promise.

But this interpretation depends on the assumption that the writer of Genesis *knew* of the non-Adamic peoples, and saw them as originally intended for blessing through Adam, but in fact being harmed by the effects of his sin. Through Abraham, in contrast, God will bless all the families of the earth. Does the table give us any more evidence of such knowledge of non-Noachic, and therefore non-Adamic, people?

Culture

Figure 3 comes from an article on the origins of the Neolithic revolution in Asia.[9] It shows the known Neolithic sites in Western and Central Asia as black spots.

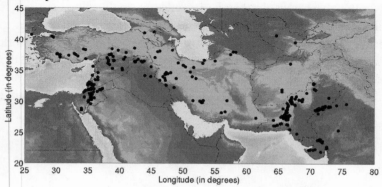

7. Gen 11:4.

8. Gen 12:2.

9. Gangai, Sarson, and Shukurov, *Near-Eastern Roots of the Neolithic.*

There seem two distinct foci, as if agriculture arose independently both in the ANE, and much farther east, around the Indus valley. But this is actually not the case. The article shows that the dates of settlements, based on carbon dating or the archaeological levels, are more recent in proportion to their distance from Gesher in Israel, believed to be close to the origin of the Neolithic. So the sites in the west range from about 10,000 to 6,000 BCE, and those in the east maybe from 6,500 to 4,000 BCE, with a chronological gradient between them. It suggests a pattern of diffusion of the culture eastwards.

This pattern is broadly comparable to the more familiar diffusion of Neolithic culture from the Near East across Western Eurasia, though it was rather slower in the east because of the inhospitable intervening terrain. In the west the Neolithic reached the distant outpost of Britain around 4,000 BCE. In fact, the western spread of the culture seems to follow the same routes taken by the Semitic language from Anatolia, but it occurred several millennia earlier, being completed well before that language is thought to have developed. So the route is similar (presumably because it depends on the geographical communications), but the chronology is incompatible.

Fig. 3 illustrates the other notable difference between the spread of the Neolithic, and that of the Semitic language, in that the language, unlike Neolithic culture, did not spread east beyond the Persian Gulf. It is absent, in fact, from the same areas that are left unmentioned in the Table of Nations. But this is not because mankind had not spread further east, as the Neolithic settlements show. Neither does it mean that the occupied lands to the east were unknown to the author of Genesis.

It is often assumed that the Table of Nations is intended to attribute Noachic origins to all nations known at the time:

> Some maintain that this Table names the peoples of the whole world, others that it mentions only those peoples of the Near East with whom the Israelites were likely to come into contact.[10]

But the Indus Valley civilization is now known to have had extensive trading links with the civilizations of Mesopotamia as early as 2,600 BCE. Materials unique to that area and numerous artifacts have been found in Iraq, some of which bear the as yet untranslated symbols of the Indus Valley Script.

10. Mitchell, "Nations, Table of," 869.

There are clear signs that the Indus Valley script was used for language, but it lacks a "Rosetta Stone" to enable it to be easily decoded. Recent research on some examples from Mesopotamia,[11] however, shows unusual combinations of characters that almost certainly mean that a resident trading community was using the Indus script to transliterate the local language. In other words, a sophisticated culture to the East of Shinar was well known, and in a regular trade relationship, at all periods in which the Table of Nations might have been composed, from the Persian period right back to the mid third millennium.[12] The educated author of Genesis must have known about that civilization. Yet it is not mentioned in the Table of Nations.

The most obvious explanation for this, if we free ourselves of the assumption that Genesis is about the beginning of all humanity, is that the Table of Nations was written to record the spread not of mankind after a universal flood, but of the Adamic line after a regional one. The Indus Valley civilization was excluded for the simple reason that it was not, at that stage, a recipient of Noachic culture.

People

Another article, in *Science*,[13] deals with the genetic makeup of the western and eastern centers of Neolithic culture discussed above. Its net conclusion is that there was a clear genetic distinction in Neolithic times between the western population of Europe and the ANE, and that of the area spreading east from Zagros. And this clear distinction is found to date from a separation tens of thousands of years *before* the Neolithic:

> These results suggest that Neolithic populations from NW-Anatolia and the Zagros descended from distinct ancestral populations.[14]

So not only was the spread of the Semitic language a movement into already occupied regions, but we cannot even say that the much earlier west-to-east spread of Neolithic culture, from the ANE to the Indus Valley and surroundings, was the result of the first human population

11. Rao, "Computing a Rosetta Stone."
12. Kenoyer, *Meluhha*.
13. Broushaki,Thomas, et al., "Early Neolithic genomes."
14. Ibid.

migrating east. Mainly, it seems, it was the result of local people, already present for many millennia, adopting the Neolithic lifestyle.

This is not to say that there would not have been intermarriage—there always is, as the Genealogical Adam hypothesis describes and much genetic evidence confirms. But there was less migration involved in the cultural movement towards India than is apparent in the spread of the Neolithic into Europe, where significant genetic changes did occur.

How does this relate to the Table of Nations? Negatively, it is more evidence that other people and cultures existed (and as I have shown, were known to the author of Genesis to exist) both when Noah's descendants migrated, and when Genesis was written.

But it also casts some light on *how* Noah's culture may have spread, together with their Semitic language. We do not have to suppose that Shem, Ham, and Japheth moved into virgin country and settled there. We do not even have to imagine the bloody replacement of existing peoples, once we accept that they existed. The picture that we get from Genesis, and the picture that comes from the distribution of the language and, perhaps, the scraps of information from Mesopotamian history, is of a small but culturally dominant group forming a ruling class within the territories designated in the Table of Nations.

We should not expect to find much evidence of this from genetics. England is historically an Anglo-Saxon culture. Our nation's name, our laws and customs, our language and many of our personal names come from the tribes of Angles, Saxons, and Jutes who invaded us way back in the fifth century, after the Romans withdrew. Yet research shows that the vast majority of our genetic makeup comes from the founder population that has been in Britain since the end of the ice age.

The so-called Cheddar Man, a skeleton found in a cave in the Cheddar Gorge and dating from Mesolithic times, c 7,100 BCE, has been shown to have had dark skin and blue eyes. Even at that early date, he was the result of many waves of migration around Europe, Asia, and Africa. And there have been many and complex migrations since, one bringing white skin and farming from Anatolia, one bringing the Indo-European tongue from Iran, one bringing the Romans and their cosmopolitan legionaries, another the Anglo-Saxons, then the Vikings, then the Normans, and so on.

Those successive waves are why, in treating the Genesis Table of Nations as a historical document, it is not easy to identify just which radiation of ANE people might be represented in the genes, history, and archaeology. But the attempt is worth making, and the results, whilst making the sole-Adam interpretation very hard to fit into the world, do fit the general pattern of the regular mixing of humanity that makes the Genealogical Adam hypothesis so realistic.

In the same way, even Jews share the same genetic palette as other nationalities originating in the Near East. And this corresponds to the increasing signs from archaeology (and from closer study of the Bible) that, although there was indeed an armed population movement into Canaan in the late second millennium, there was as much, or even far more, cultural infiltration and intermarriage than there was destruction or expulsion of the Canaanites.[15]

This is interesting in itself, because it suggests that biblical genealogy has a place for such cultural accommodation, as well as for biological descent from the twelve tribal patriarchs. Adam's intended role may have involved influencing the existing culture with the knowledge of Yahweh, as well as the procreation of godly offspring. Over time, the two aspects coalesced as Adam became a common ancestor of all. The English genetic makeup, based on disparate racial origins, does not alter the fact of our being truly Anglo-Saxon Englishmen (and Englishwomen), nor that of Jews with a strong Canaanite heritage being true Jews. The concept of pure races, arising *de novo*, turns out to be as alien to the Bible as it does to science. But we are also all biological children of Adam.

In the same way it is sufficient for the writer's purpose that the Table of Nations describes where, amongst the nations, Noah's offspring took root and brought their Adamic heritage into the population, for good and for ill. The good would have included some knowledge of Yahweh, and of man's high calling. The evil would have included the sin that had marked even righteous Noah, of whom God said after the flood, "Every inclination of the human heart is evil from childhood."[16]

Conclusion Relative to Genealogical Adam

Contrary to tradition the Table of Nations does not correspond to all the nations that were known to Israel at the time Genesis was written. But it does appear to correspond to the spread of Semitic language and culture at the relevant time, realistically matching the patterns by which

15. Kitchen, *Reliability*, 159–239.
16. Gen 8:21.

populations and cultures migrated from the ice age onwards. The Table of Nations is a snapshot, from a very specific time, which endorses the basic historicity of Genesis—but only if we accept that the Genesis events are set in a wider human culture, that is, that there were people not of Adam's lineage in the region.

According to genealogical science, by the time of Christ Noah's descendants would have included everybody on earth. And God's word of command, and promise, to Noah would have come true:

> And God blessed Noah and his sons and said to them, "Be fruitful and multiply, and fill the earth."[17]

---

17. Gen 9:1.

§3: Generations of Adam

(Humanity)

"Let us make man in our image, according our likeness; and let them rule . . ."

GEN 1:26.

7.

WHAT IS MAN: WHAT'S IN A NAME?

Three Meanings of Adam

ONE OF THE DIFFICULT, and contentious, issues in deciding between a broadly historical and an entirely metaphorical understanding of Genesis is the complexity of the way the word *man* is used throughout. This is even more important, and complicated, if we consider Genesis in the context of Genealogical Adam, in which it is postulated that there were already other human beings throughout the world at the time the events took place.

Genesis does not define what it means by humanity, except in terms of its creation "in the image and likeness of God" in Genesis 1:26–27. This description is itself subject to many interpretations. Joshua Swamidass points out that there is no consistent *scientific* definition of "human" either.[1] The lack of either a clear biblical or a clear scientific definition of humanity makes for many potential problems, and some interesting solutions, some of which I will try to clarify in the next two chapters. These problems involve both anthropological questions, and linguistic ones, the latter of which will be my concern in this chapter.

John H. Walton offers a good survey of the three distinct ways in which Genesis uses the Hebrew *'ādām*.[2] The first point is that "Adam" and "Eve" cannot just be the names two individuals happened to have

1. Swamidass, *Genealogical Adam and Eve*, 99.
2. Walton, *Lost World of Adam and Eve*, 58–62.

(like "Sid" and "Mabel") because they are Hebrew names, and on any understanding the couple pre-dated the Hebrew language by at least a millennium or two. The names must therefore have been assigned, or translated, because their meanings ("man" and "life" respectively) matter in the account.

What is less immediately obvious is the complexity of the usage of the word '*ādām*. Walton does a detailed study on the thirty-four instances of the word in early Genesis, based on both linguistic and contextual considerations. He concludes that in some cases the meaning is *generic*, describing "man" as a species (in Walton's usage, that is, though we ought to remember that to take that word "species" biologically is anachronistic). This usage implies only that Adam was a human, and that we readers too are "humans," but it makes no attempt to draw boundaries that would relate to paleontological or even philosophical, let alone theological, concepts of humanity. The generic usage of '*ādām*, Walton notes, is also sometimes employed in the text to distinguish male from female (just as happens in the English use of "man" for both the race and the male, at least before "gender neutral" language became the custom), although the normal Hebrew gendered noun for "man" is *ish*.

Far more often, on Walton's analysis, '*ādām* is used, with the definite article, to indicate "the man" either as a *representational agent* or as an *archetype*. These categories overlap to some extent.

What is surprising is that the unequivocal third use of '*ādām*, as a personal *name*, is limited to the genealogical section (5:1, 3–5), even once it is clear in the narrative that "the man" is actually a particular individual. Adam the individual, then, is deeply and deliberately endowed with some kind of representational character that is closely related to—though textually distinguishable from—humankind as a race or species. This is the most interesting and important aspect of this topic. Walton puts it thus:

> When the generic is used, the text is talking about human beings as a species. When the definite article is being used, the referent is an individual serving as a human representative. Such representation could be either as an archetype (all are embodied in the one and counted as having participated in the acts of that one) or as a federal representative (in which one is serving as an elect delegate on behalf of the rest).[3]

3. Ibid., 61.

Walton goes on to suggest that in all the representational cases, the *significance* of the events is intended to extend to those Adam represents. *Only* where the personal name, or a contextually generic use of *'ādām* without the definite article, is used is the significance restricted to him as an individual.

I should say at this point that Walton is not implying that Adam is representational in an *allegorical* sense, and that what happens in life to every person is simply pinned on a generically named fictional character. Such literary concepts do not appear to have existed in the ANE, and in any case the complex juxtaposition of undoubtedly generic with undoubtedly representational uses of *'ādām* shows something more sophisticated is going on. Walton again, in his glossary, writes:

> In a literary sense, an archetype refers to a recurrent symbol or motif, even a type of character. Fictional characters often serve as archetypes of good and evil, heroism or treachery, etc. In this book I am using the term in a narrower sense. An archetype here refers to a representative of a group in whom all others in the group are embodied. As a result, all members of the group are included and participate with their representative.[4]

Walton's word "participation" is reminiscent of what Owen Barfield suggested about ancient patterns of thinking.[5] He argued that primitive thinkers considered themselves part of the phenomena they observed or described, and furthermore that we do as well, but only unconsciously, because of the way that modern thought has objectified reality, making such participatory concepts hard to comprehend intellectually. Such participation is implied, as Walton notes, in Paul's use of the aorist tense (indicating a one-off, completed event) in Romans 5:12, when he says that "all sinned in Adam."

Because of this archetypal character of *'ādām* as "The Man" who represents both all men and all women, and its overlap with generic uses and its personal use for one man, it will be less confusing for the rest of this chapter if I avoid attempting to use gender-neutral terms, and translate *'ādām* consistently as "man."

Walton's use of the term "federal representative" is interesting. He writes how this concept arose in Reformed covenant theology, for example in John Calvin's thought, though traceable as far back as Augustine

---

4. Ibid., 240.
5. Barfield, *Saving the Appearances*, ch. 4, 28–35.

and Irenaeus. The historical setting for it, one should note, was after Barfield's ancient sense of "participation" had largely dropped out of sight. Federal headship is, therefore, a more forensic concept, in which Adam is designated by God as the head of the race so that the rest of humanity is implicated legally, as it were, in his actions. In particular, the guilt of his sin of disobedience is imputed to the rest of humanity.

This is a more restricted concept than participation, but does not contradict it. Walton seems to see both as complementary ideas that have validity in understanding the theology of Genesis. In other words, the rather difficult notion (to our modern mind-set) of real participation in an ancient archetype, and the forensic idea of Adam's being the race's appointed representative, are not mutually exclusive.

In fact the same concepts come together in comparing traditional Protestant understandings of the atonement, in which the righteousness of Christ is "imputed" to sinners in a forensic manner, with the controversial "New Perspective on Paul," in which our union with Christ is, in the best presentations, emphasized—which is to say, our actual participation in him in some sense.[6] Both approaches find their source particularly in Romans 5, in which, of course, Paul also deals with Adam as the contrast to Christ. Michael Bird has argued that whilst the union/participation language is exegetically more correct, federal representation truthfully conveys important understandings for theology.[7]

Walton enlists federal headship in his later argument that the genealogies of Genesis are related more to archetypal relationships than to merely genetic ones:

> [Adam's] federal headship would easily serve as an appropriate
> basis for the genealogy to go back to him.[8]

Where this whole discussion of the word *'ādām* in Genesis leads is that, by whichever alternative one views the representative nature of Adam, it is problematic to see him as a purely fictional, or merely symbolic, figure. Whether one is "counted as having participated in the acts of that [archetype]," or as legally accountable with "an elect delegate on behalf of the rest,"[9] one has only a case to answer before God only if the actions, and hence the original accountability, actually occurred. It is no

6. Wright, *Paul and the Faithfulness of God*, 530.
7. Bird, *Saving Righteousness of God*, 85–87.
8. Walton, *Lost World of Adam and Eve*, 188.
9. Ibid., 61.

more possible to participate in a fictional Adam than it is to participate in Mickey Mouse. Likewise to be held legally accountable for the acts of Adam as a federal representative would be entirely unjust if he, and his acts, were as mythical as those of Geoffrey of Monmouth's imaginary King Brutus of Britain after the fall of Troy. The Wright Brothers are archetypes of all aviators. Phileas Fogg is not.

One can, of course, reformulate Pauline theology to accommodate "Allegorical Adam," but that not only raises big questions about apostolic authority and the validity of the gospel, but requires one to explain how such an anachronistic allegorical Everyman character got into an Ancient Near Eastern text to begin with.[10]

Generic Adam: Who Is in the Genus?

One question for the Genealogical Adam hypothesis, in which Adam is a historical figure and universal common ancestor, but not the first man, is how he gets to adopt the word for all humanity as his personal name. Would this not be evidence that he is an allegorical figure, rather than a real person?

As I pointed out above, there is no definition of "man" in Scripture, which precludes us from simply assuming, without consideration, some biological definition like *Homo sapiens* or *hominins* in our theology. This, however, is frequently done unthinkingly, and the problems become obvious whenever we ask whether some group—such as Neanderthals, for example—is human or not. It is not at all clear what we even mean by the question. It may seem elementary simply to say that "man" means what we think of informally as "the brotherhood of man," if we are neither slave owners believing our chattels are subhuman, nor Bolsheviks classifying our opponents as "non-persons." People, we suppose, are simply people—unless you happen to be one of those postmodernists who are legally declaring rivers or orangutans to be "people."

Aristotle defined the species "man" as "rational animal."[11] But he did not have to consider the possibility that intelligent extraterrestrial aliens exist somewhere in the cosmos, ontologically unrelated to ourselves. Nor was he aware of the certainty that other species of hominins existed

10. ". . . allegory is not a genre familiar to the ancient world." John H. Walton, personal communication, 5/14/2012.

11. Aristotle, *Ethics* I.13; *De anima* III.11.

before, and even alongside, *Homo sapiens*. "Human" nowadays stands in need of more precise definition.

But even the ancient history of words for "people" is a lot more convoluted than our common intuition that all humankind is the same thing; and the Bible in its entirety *is* ancient history, and the early chapters of Genesis are *very* ancient history. I even question to what extent the very ancient world had a universal concept of "people" or "mankind" available to them, just as equally "obvious" ideas like "world," "universe," "nature,"[12] and even "air" (which I discussed in the Introduction) developed much later.

Steve Olson's *Mapping Human History*[13] describes how the Bantu-speakers of West Africa, acquiring several technological advantages around 2,500 years ago, migrated across Africa and displaced the forest dwellers (pygmies) and bushmen from most of their range to become the dominant group on the continent, as they are to this day. Olson points out that "Bantu" simply means "People"—with the implication that non-Bantu were not considered people. Even today, it seems,

> Pygmies are not considered citizens by most African states and are refused identity cards, deeds to land, health care and proper schooling.[14]

Various tribes still reputedly enslave the Batwa forest people—*Batwa* being a word derived from the Bantu for "outsider, foreigner," even though they are the aboriginal inhabitants.[15] Yet even *within* the majority Bantu population of Africa, that same self-identification of groups as the "real people" occurs:

> Meek writes that the Bachama tribe, Northern Nigeria ". . . call themselves the Gboare or Men, a term which is doubtless the same as Gbari (the name of a large tribe in the Niger and Zaria provinces), Bari (in Eastern Sudan) and Ka-Bwari (Tanganyika). The root gba = man is also found in the Upper Ituri regions of Central Africa under the form mu-gba or ba-gba."[16]

---

12. See the discussion of the history of these words in the relevant chapters in Lewis, *Studies in Words*.

13. Olson, *Mapping Human History*, 51–53.

14. "Pygmy Peoples," *Wikipedia*. https://en.wikipedia.org/wiki/Pygmy_peoples.

15. Ibid.

16. Jeffreys, "The Batwa."

The same situation occurs elsewhere. We read for example that "Most of the names that [Native American] tribes have for themselves mean 'the people' in their own language."[17] Thus:

> The Abenaki people also call themselves Alnôbak, meaning "Real People" (c.f., Lenape language: Lenapek) and by the autonym Alnanbal, meaning "men."[18]

Or:

> Elder John B Bigeye stated that his people call themselves "Denesuline," the people, or the real people.[19]

Similarly it seems the term "Inuit," used by themselves, translates as "people"—whereas "Eskimo," applied by outsiders, derives from a description of their using snowshoes. This self-identification simply as "the people" appears, in short, to be very widespread amongst tribal societies, as Arthur Custance writes:

> Among most primitive people the habit is to refer to themselves (in their own language, of course) as "true men," referring to all others by some term which clearly denies to them the right to manhood at all. Thus the Naskapi call themselves "Neneot," which means "real people." The Chukchee say that their name means "real men." The Hottentots refer to themselves as "Khoi-Khoi" which means "men of men." The Yahgan of Tierra del Fuego (of all places) say that their name means "men par excellence." The Andamanese, a people who appear to lack even the rudiments of law, refer to themselves as "Ong," meaning "Men." All these people reserve these terms only for themselves.[20]

Memories of this habit are preserved even in civilized England, together with a living example of how such a restricted idea of humanity eventually develops universality as culture becomes more cosmopolitan. Our two most easterly counties are Norfolk and Suffolk, being the territories of the "North Folk" and the "South Folk," known as the Angles to their neighbors, the Saxons and Jutes, whom the Angles evidently did not regard as "folk." History saw "folk" gradually acquire the meaning of "all people" (until the less folksy and Latin word "people" largely replaced it).

17. Stockton, "What do Native Americans call themselves?"
18. "Abenaki," *Wikipedia*. https://en.wikipedia.org/wiki/Abenaki.
19. Cardinal and Hildebrandt, *Treaty Elders of Saskatchewan*, 40.
20. Custance, *Noah's Three Sons*, II.1.23.

Even our word *man*, derived from another Proto-Indoeuropean root *manus*, in its Sanskrit form *manu*, is far from being just a generic term for humankind:

> Manu is a term found with various meanings in Hinduism. In early texts, it refers to the archetypal man, or to the first man (progenitor of humanity). The Sanskrit term for 'human' (*mānava*) means "of Manu" or "children of Manu." In later texts, Manu is the title or name of mystical sage-rulers of earth, or alternatively as the head of mythical dynasties that begin with each cyclic kalpa (aeon) when the universe is born anew.[21]

There are echoes of Adam as archetype there, in concept if not in folk memory. In the oldest texts of Hinduism, it is the archetype who names the race of man, not a generic descriptive term for man that is applied to an allegorical figure, as many conclude today about Genesis.

What, then, might be the case in the ANE in which Genesis arose? To the Babylonians, "the world" was conceived as being principally their own land, though they were fully aware of countries beyond.[22] Their kings called themselves "king of the world," or even "king of heaven and earth." And when the gods in the Mesopotamian myths created mankind to serve them, it was in order that mankind would serve the temples in Eridu or Shuruppak, and was not at all about distant people in Orkney building megaliths, or the Chinese worshipping their ancestors.

The Sumerians referred to themselves as "the black-headed people," and to their territory as "the place of the noble Lords." Interestingly as the Akkadian tongue replaced Sumerian (reflecting a more ethnically mixed society) people tended to be referred to by their ethnic origins: the culture had been compelled to begin to see people in a wider sense than just "me and mine."

Oddly enough one of the earliest names for Egypt also derives from "black," and the Egyptians called themselves "the black people." This may seem like an ethnic description, but their neighbors to the south were no less black, and in fact recent genetic studies suggest that the main gene pool of Egypt at that time was Semitic, not African. It seems possible that the term refers to their belief that they were descended from the supreme god Amun, usually depicted as black; in other words, once more

---

21. "Manu (Hinduism)," *Wikipedia*. https://en.wikipedia.org/wiki/Manu_(Hinduism).

22. Garvey, "Flood Geography."

ethnocentricity prevailed in their self-reference. How this relates to the concept of "humankind" appears in their attitude to foreigners:

> Another important continuity during this period is the Egyptian attitude toward foreigners—those they considered not fortunate enough to be part of the community of *rmṯ* or "the people" (i.e., Egyptians). . . .

> The Egyptian sense of superiority was given religious validation, as foreigners in the land of *Ta-Meri* (Egypt) were anathema to the maintenance of Maat—a view most clearly expressed by the admonitions of *Ipuwer* in reaction to the chaotic events of the Second Intermediate Period. Foreigners in Egyptian texts were described in derogatory terms, e.g., "wretched Asiatics" (Semites), "vile Kushites" (Nubians), and "Ionian dogs" (Greeks). Egyptian beliefs remained unchallenged when Egypt fell to the Hyksos, Assyrians, Libyans, Persians and Greeks—their rulers assumed the role of the Egyptian Pharaoh and were often depicted praying to Egyptian gods.[23]

So, in the light of this wealth of examples of ancient concepts of "man," could it be that in the very coining of the word 'ādām to mean "man," the Hebrews were following the common practice of referring, primarily, to their *own* people's origins, rather than to "worldwide humanity"?

Quite apart from these deliberate variations in the use of the word 'ādām in Genesis, the noun itself is generally believed to have a possible etymological link in Hebrew with 'adamah, meaning "red" and hence "red (= fertile and tilled) soil." This would not be strange, since our own English word "human" appears to derive from a Proto-Indoeuropean (PIE) root meaning "earth" (from the same root as "humus," thus distinguishing humans from the gods of heaven). This would be a very specific etymology.

If the PIE example means anything, the etymology of the word could derive from the belief that their first founder was either created from the soil (as described in Genesis), or was known as the cultivator of it, perhaps in a particular locality with a particular red soil.

The traditions of Genesis 1—11 were probably foundational to Israel even before the Exodus. They were in all likelihood "the Old Testament of the Old Testament."[24] Since Hebrew was scarcely, if at all, a language at

23. "Egyptians," *Wikipedia*. https://en.wikipedia.org/wiki/Egyptians.

24. Moberly, *Old Testament of the Old Testament*, 159–66.

the time of Moses,[25] it is at least possible that their generic word for "man" actually *derives from* their foundation story and its archetypal hero/anti-hero, Adam, the man formed from soil, rather than simply being applied to him.

Such an inference would appear at first sight to make Genesis an uncomfortably ethnocentric text. But whereas most tribal self-designations cover over the fact that they are no different from everybody else, Adam actually *was* different: he dwelt with the living God and, until he disobeyed, had access to eternal life. Even granted that special circumstance, just as "folk" became generalized in English to mean the "just plain" variety rather than only the tribe of Angles, Israel would later have generalized the word 'ādām to include "all men," so that to Paul, the Greek *anthropos* was a suitable Greek translation of universal scope for Hebrew 'ādām.

According to the Genealogical Adam hypothesis, Adam's progeny would by the time of Paul probably have encompassed the entire human race as we now understand it. For reasons to be discussed in chapter 15, I consider the creation text of Genesis 1:1—2:3 to be a preface added by the final author of Genesis to the traditional protohistory he received. If, as I argue, this author was aware of people outside the Garden of Eden, not descended from the man Adam, how was he to refer to them in Hebrew, when describing their creation in Genesis 1:26–28? By that time, the only generic word available to him was 'ādām.

We do not therefore, simply because of the noun used, have to assume that Genesis 1 refers to the Adamic line. That interpretation is by no means excluded by Genealogical Adam, though it seems to me that the author intends us to understand that even those not descended from Adam were created in the image of God, and so were truly "human," though not elected to Adam's new status. So for reasons of the history of the Hebrew tongue, there may be some ambiguity in the text, and likewise in Genesis 6 if the writer intends us to understand "sons of God" as the Adamic line, and "daughters of men" as the non-Adamic. The word 'ādām may, by the time of writing, have become the only Hebrew term covering both.

Analogously, we may assume that ancient *Homo sapiens* had a distinct term for Neanderthals, where they coexisted with them. But we

---

25. The evolution of the various languages of the region is contested.

have long forgotten any such word, and so have to designate Neanderthals as "early humans," or some similar term derived from our word for
ourselves.

In support of this, I think, is the evidence within Genesis itself of
a universalism that is unusual for those far-off times—at least, it is hard
to think of a parallel in ancient literature. That evidence is principally to
be found in the Table of Nations.[26] In this, the spread of Adamic humankind ('ādām) in a universal sense is expressed by the founding of many
nations by Adam's descendants, *via* Noah and his sons. To us, the table
may seem an aetiological requirement to explain how mankind spread
around the world. But as we have seen, other cultures never seem to have
realized such a necessity, making Genesis unique amongst early texts in
this respect.

There is no sense here of Israel's exclusive right to be known as the
"real people," even though their unique calling is always, and increasingly, within sight in the book. Remember, too, how the call of Abraham
in Genesis 12 is accompanied by God's promise that he will become a
blessing to all nations. Arthur Custance, whom I quoted earlier, goes on
from discussing the widespread tribal restrictions on personhood across
the world:

> It is a sign of a low cultural state when this attitude is taken,
> but then, when a people hold the opposite attitude, it is likely
> a sign of a high cultural state. Thus when any people achieve a
> stage of intellectual development at which they clearly conceive
> that all men are related in a way which assures them equality
> as human beings, they are then highly cultured, even though
> the mechanics of their civilization may appear at a low stage of
> development. From this we ought logically to gather that the
> writer of Genesis was a highly cultured individual. Indeed, it
> seems to me that only with a high conception of God would
> such a conception of man be possible, and therefore Genesis 10
> would seem to bear testimony to a very high order of religious
> faith. In the final analysis, one might ask whether it is possible
> at all to sustain a true conception of the equality of man without
> also a true conception of the nature of God. The former stems
> directly from the latter. The only ground for attaching to all men
> an equal level of worth is the tremendous fact that all souls have
> equal value to God.[27]

26. See chapter 6.
27. Custance, *Noah's Three Sons*, II.1.23.

Perhaps, then, the very concept we have of a universal "humankind,"
which we now take entirely for granted, came to us first through Adam
and the Hebrew Bible.

More on Adam as a Generalized Tribal Designation

The closest ANE literary parallel to Genesis 1—11 is the so-called *Eridu
Genesis*, taken from a broken Sumerian tablet of c 1,600 BCE, but thought
probably to have been composed c 2,300 BCE, making it the earliest
known narrative text in the world. It speaks of the creation of mankind
(but see below), and after a gap in the text, of the great flood that probably
dates to around 2,900 BCE.

I am not concerned here with any literary, or even historical, connections between this narrative and Genesis, but only with the facts that,
firstly, it is close in time and place to the origin of Genesis 1—11, and
secondly, like Genesis, it describes the creation of man by divine beings.
After an introduction it begins like this:

> When An, Enlil, Enki, and Ninhursaga
> fashioned the dark-headed people,
> they had made the small animals that came up from out of the earth
> come from the earth in abundance and had let there be, as befits it,
> gazelles, wild donkeys, and four-footed beasts in the desert.[28]

Now the text, as I have said, is Sumerian, and the Sumerians were
the first known inhabitants of Mesopotamia, who called themselves "the
black-headed people." But already by 2,300 BCE, the earliest likely date
for the written story, there was another people group in the land, the
Semitic-speaking Akkadians from Anatolia. In fact, that date marks the
height of the power of the Akkadian Empire under Sargon the Great, and
the start of the eclipse of Sumerian as a living language. But Akkadian as
a language had been spoken, and known in Mesopotamia, for centuries
beforehand.

Even before the Semitic people began to live alongside the Sumerians, they would have been near neighbors. There has never *been* a con-
tinental people-group that wasn't aware of their neighbors close at hand,
probably waving spears at their borders, and at least aware of rumors
of strangers farther afield, through trade. The Sumerians were certainly

28. Arnold and Beyer, *Readings from the Ancient Near East*, 13.

aware of their own neighbors. And yet the *Eridu Genesis* speaks of the creation of the "black-headed people," along with the animals, as if they alone inhabited the earth.

If absence of evidence is not evidence of absence in the case of the *Eridu Genesis*, then one needs to supply a solid set of reasons why that should not also be the case for the description of the creation of generic *'ādām* in Genesis 1, or of "Adam" the individual in Genesis 2. Genesis describes how *'ādām* was created, just as *Eridu Genesis* describes how *saggigga* (the black-headed people) were created. It does not follow, any more than it does in *Eridu Genesis*, that the writer was unaware of any others existing. The silence is a matter of genre, or if it is not, then an explanation that applies to Genesis but *not* to Eridu Genesis needs to be found.

I have mentioned the possible etymological link between *'ādām*, man, and *'adamah*, "red soil." Genesis puns on the two,[29] speaking of *'ādām* as *from* the soil, *for* the soil, and *returning to* the soil. And, of course, the rest of Scripture maintains the connection.[30]

This much is undisputed. What seems less remarked is that, as far as I know, the words for *man* or *mankind* in other languages, are *not* generally derived from the word for *soil*, the exception being that which I have already mentioned, the Proto-Indoeuropean root for "human" and "humus." This etymology appears to be a particular feature of Hebrew and of closely related languages like Aramaic, just as "black-headed people" (*saggigga*) was peculiar to the Sumerians.

It therefore seems plausible that the story came before the language, which evolved only *after* Israel's settlement in Canaan. If the ancient narratives were handed down through Abraham and the other patriarchs, it was in a language that preceded Hebrew, and no doubt helped to form it.

So *'ādām* may well have arisen as a specific name for the culture from which Adam came, or of which he was considered the progenitor,

---

29. "From the 'earth' (*eretz*) the water rises to water the 'land' (*'adamah*; 2:6). More precisely 'land' appears to be agricultural land which consists of dust (2:7) and which it is man's duty to till (2:5; 3:17; 4:2). Man's especially close relationship to the land is seen in his creation from its dust (2:7)." Wenham, *Genesis*, 58. Despite this, whilst granting that *'adamah* is the feminine form of *'ādām*, Wenham doubts their etymological connection. Ibid., 59. It is hard to understand on what grounds, in the light of the discussion above.

30. E.g., Job 10:9, 34:15; Ps 90:3, 103:14; Eccl 3:20; 1 Cor 15:47.

which later became generalized to the whole of mankind as the Hebrew language developed.

If, in this way, '*ādām* was originally as specific and local a term as *saggigga*, it does not imply, any more than in the latter case, that no other men existed, nor indicate that the writer was unaware of them. The example of the *Eridu Genesis* is clear evidence that other peoples could, and did, describe the creation of their own races, even with their own fauna, whilst being fully aware that other humans and animals existed in the world.

Conclusion Relative to Genealogical Adam

If human universalism is to be found in Genesis (as I believe it is), then the author's awareness of a widespread humanity is likely also to be an implicit part of the text. It follows that the inspired Hebrew writer probably had some idea of how the problem of Adam's sin, and the solution of the calling of Israel, came to apply to a worldwide and relatively ancient human race.

Once again, something like the Genealogical Adam hypothesis appears to be implied by Genesis itself.

8.

WHAT IS MAN: WHAT'S
IN AN IMAGE?

Image, Creation, and Election

THE CREATION OF HUMANITY, as envisaged by the Bible, isn't as obviously physical as is often assumed, which is important if one wants to take a "science and faith" approach that doesn't lapse into mere scientism. Take, as an analogy, the Christian who, according to the New Testament, is a "new creation." Every man or woman who has ever been a Christian was born by generation in the usual biological way, and if one accepts evolution, had ancestors that were apes—none of which has any bearing on the process of their *new* creation whatsoever, which is of the Spirit.

They are, in the eyes of John the Baptist, children raised up for Abraham "from these stones,"[1] for it is not a biological matter. There is no guarantee that they have Abraham as an ancestor (though it is not improbable that they have, for on the genealogical science understanding of humanity, anyone born four millennia ago will have the greater portion of humankind as their physical descendants). But the creation of children for Abraham from stones is a spiritual matter, not a genetic or even a genealogical one. Arguably, it is when such people become fully human.

---

1. Matt 3:9.

The biblical understanding of humanity therefore cannot be divorced from his relationship with God, because humankind is introduced there in that context. In Genesis 1, male and female are created "in God's image and likeness," and they are given various creation mandates to fulfill on God's behalf, or from another perspective given the earth as a gift from God to use for him according to their created nature. Either way humanity is described from the start with respect to its purposeful creation by God, for God.

In Genesis 2, Adam is formed by Israel's God Yahweh to serve in his garden sanctuary, and it is the failure of his relationship with God that defines humankind as "sinners" for the rest of the Bible. Adam's creation, therefore, is also at least as much the creation of his relationship with God as that of his body or mind.

This means that the making of "humanity" in the full biblical sense has elements both of *making*, and of *appointment* or *election*, for the comparison I have made with new birth in Christ shows there is some similarity and even overlap between them. That is especially important in considering what might constitute the difference between Adam's line, of which we are a part, and those who had not yet become a part of that family before, during, and for some period after Adam's life.

In Genesis 1, humankind appears primarily in the context of *creation*. He is not *chosen* from an existing species, but brought into being *de novo* (or into function from futility, in John Walton's functional understanding of the text[2]). Humanity was *created* in the image and likeness of God: the image is therefore what makes him a human being at all. If one regards the image as an *addition* to man, by God's election of the species, or of some members of it, one destroys the unity that in Hebrew thinking constitutes a human being. Our bodies become, as in "pie in the sky when you die" quasi-platonic popularizations of Christianity, the dispensable and even inimical encumbrances from which our spiritual souls need to be released. One is left with a dualistic, Gnostic concept of a human that is incompatible with biblical religion.

How one integrates the biological origins of humankind with what Genesis 1 means by its creation is a matter for another discussion. But whatever insights evolution may provide, it cannot give an adequately *complete* account of our true humanity. It cannot even *define* it because

2. "[T]he nuanced meaning of *bārā* that best suits the data is that it means 'to bring something into (functional) existence.'" Walton, *Genesis 1 as Ancient Cosmology*, 133.

of the problems evolution has with any kind of universal categories like "humanity."[3]

But this creation, biblically, cannot be an entirely biological matter. If, as I said before, Christians are a new creation, which is orthodox New Testament doctrine, their genetics, their evolutionary history, and even, of itself, their position in the tree of life were largely irrelevant to that. And so the creation of a human being—and notably the creation of a first human beings in the biblical sense—encompasses much more than biology, in the same way as does the new birth in Christ.

It is now well established, even within science, that you are not simply your genes. You did not enter your profession because it was "in your DNA," despite the colloquial cliché, or choose your favorite music or the football team you support on that basis. Genes did not determine who your spouse would be (if they did, the genetic diversity that sexual reproduction allows would be destroyed in a generation or two). Nor was your faith the product of a religion gene, but of the supernatural grace of God working in you.

Neither are you only your body. Our faith affirms that we will be raised in the body, but also that between our death and that time, "we" shall be with Christ, apart from the body. So if "I" am neither just my body, nor just the product of my genes, then neither were the first humans, described as being created in the image of God in Genesis 1.

In Genesis 2, by contrast, the emphasis is on calling more than creation. The garden narrative is not a creation account as such, but a dramatic episode *within* creation. That is probably why the Hebrew word *bārā*, "create," does not occur in it at all, appearing only in the summary linking it to the next section and so integrating it with Genesis 1.[4] Yes, it speaks of God's forming Adam from the dust of the ground and breathing his breath into him so that he *becomes* (note!) a living soul, but this idiom is widely used in Scripture and elsewhere in the ANE to show simply that our origin is from the earth and from God's hand: we are *all* but dust[5] and God formed *each* of us.[6]

What actually *happens* to Adam has more of the flavor of election, in that he is he is taken from the world into the garden and assigned his

3. Almost all versions of evolutionary theory are necessarily "nominalist," lacking a concept of "natures."

4. Gen 5:1.

5. Ps 103:14.

6. Ps 139:13–16.

work, he is personally privileged to name (that is, assign functions) to the animals, he is given an elect wife, he is given access to the eternal life of God and to communion with God himself, and furthermore it is hinted, by the prohibition against eating the tree of the knowledge of good and evil, or wisdom, that by obedience to God's command his wisdom will also, in God's time, become perfect. Now all these blessings are akin to what is promised to God's elect throughout the Bible, from Abraham onwards: they are what we, too, are promised in Christ. They constitute election to a relationship of faith.

Adam becomes, by this election, the archetype of the whole race. This is quite compatible with the idea that he might have been called, in the cultural time and place laid out in the text, from amongst a race of humans already created in and as God's image. Adam would then be a proto-Abraham, a proto-Israel, or a proto-Christ, chosen by grace from amongst men and becoming, in a similar—not to say archetypal—way, a representative on behalf of all men, though one noted primarily for his failure.

However, this is not to exclude the idea of creation from Genesis 2 altogether. As I have said humankind is only *fully* human, in the biblical sense, in personal relationship to God. We were made for God, and Adam was the first to know God and experience his glory. And so it is not surprising that Paul, in 1 Corinthians 11, bases his argument for church order on Genesis 2—3, saying that man was "created" first, and woman for man rather than *vice versa*. I do not think such language implies that the Adam story is just a rerun of the creation account, but it does suggest that his election to service in the garden involved God as Creator, as well as Covenant-maker.

Isaiah uses the word create (*bārā*) of the nation of Israel.[7] There he describes the passage through the Red Sea as an act of creation, so does that make the exodus a story of election, or creation? Surely, like Genesis 2, it is both, but predominantly one of gracious calling.

Thus, if Adam were indeed taken from the mass of mankind and placed in a sacred precinct, perhaps now covered by waters of the Persian Gulf or by meters of alluvium, he would still be something entirely new within creation; the fountainhead and archetype of a new humanity and the type of Christ.

---

7. Isa 43:1–17.

Imago Dei and Non-Adamic Man

It was a guest post by Reformed pastor and scholar James Penman at my blog, *The Hump of the Camel*, that first alerted me to the possibility that the image of God need not be restricted to an elect Adamic line, but could realistically have been the endowment of the whole race from which Adam was chosen. He wrote:

> First, I envisage God bestowing His image collectively on the whole of the existing race of anatomically modern humans. How far advanced linguistically, technologically, artistically, musically, etc., humans can be *without* possessing the divine image, I do not fully know. Nor am I sure what immediate and evident effects the bestowal of the image would have brought, in terms of observable differences in the historical record (what should we be looking for?).
>
> However, I postulate this collective bestowal of the divine image on the existing race of anatomically modern humans, which would perhaps have been experienced by them as a collective quantum leap into God-consciousness. It seems to me that Genesis 1 is best read as describing the creation of a race—humanity—rather than exclusively of Adam and Eve, who I think first appear in Genesis 2. In my model, then, Adam is not the biological father of all *Homo divinus* humans. But I see nothing in the text that requires him to be. He is the ancestor of his own line, the Adamic line, through which descends the Promise of the Messianic Seed.[8]

Penman makes two assumptions that differ from my own. The first is in seeing the *imago dei* as something *added* to "anatomically modern humans," whereas I have described it as an aspect of their very creation, which the text seems to demand. The second is in the application of the *Homo divinus* label to the whole race thus constituted, rather than to the descendants of Adam. But this only demonstrates the difficulty of nomenclature in anything to do with "humanity," which difficulty I have already labored to prove.

But his main point is well-made and valuable. He sees Adam and Eve as chosen members of a race already endowed with the *imago dei*. He sees that image as a kind of species-wide spiritual awareness, and I agree that such awareness must be part of the created nature of humanity.

8. Penman, "Place of Adam."

John Walton thinks along similar lines. To him Genesis 1 deals with the creation of mankind in God's image, and Genesis 2—3 deals with the priestly representative of the race who failed. But, he writes:

> Nevertheless, in the view that I have proposed, Genesis 1 and 2 are a continuum, and what applies to all people in Genesis 1 applies to Adam and Eve in Genesis 2.[9]

The image of Christ, in other words, would exist in humankind created as the apex of the first, physical cosmos, even in the absence of the endowments of the new, spiritual creation which were offered to Adam. That is how Adam, in his failure, remains "the man of the earth, earthy,"[10] and yet fully human. His fault is not in being natural, but that though he was chosen from among natural mankind to bring it into far more than that, he and his descendants carry *unnatural* baggage from his willful failure.

The image of God has carried various different interpretations over the centuries. Penman's hypothesis of a relatively *recent* endowment with the image focuses our thinking, by excluding a number of older concepts of "image," of which reason is one. Archaeology reveals imaginative and sophisticated art, music, and technology, and even ritual, tens of thousands of years, or more, in the past.

In more recent understandings, "image" has been interpreted as "temple image," given the cosmic temple picture of Genesis 1, or as the related concept of royal images set up by ancient kings in distant provinces to represent their presence. This view I favor myself. In a pagan temple, the image is not necessarily seen as an accurate representation of the god. It could be a meteorite, as the sacred image of Artemis at Ephesus was said to be.[11]

In his reinterpretation of the myth of Cupid and Psyche, *Till We Have Faces*, C. S. Lewis's character, Queen Orual, discovers how the ancient image of their goddess Ungit, a shapeless stone that pushed itself up from the earth, has more spiritual power than the classical Greek statue enlightened people had recently made to replace it.

> "Do you always pray to that Ungit," said I (nodding toward the shapeless stone), "and not to that?" Here I nodded towards our

9. Walton, *Lost World of Adam and Eve*, 89.
10. 1 Cor 15:47.
11. Acts 19:35.

new image, standing tall and straight in her robes and (whatever the Fox might say of it) the loveliest thing our land has ever seen.

"Oh, always this, Queen," said she. "That other, the Greek Ungit, she wouldn't understand my speech. She's only for nobles and learned men. There's no comfort in her."[12]

He captures an important fact about such potent images. What mattered was not their resemblance, but that they were *designated* as the locus for the god's worship and communion. One of the glories of Genesis 1 is that it takes the pagan idea of a world created by and for the gods, who are to be served and fed by a human race created as slaves and worshipped in temples containing sacred images, and transforms it into a cosmos created by Yahweh as his temple in its entirety, with the earth created for the benefit of mankind as his temple image and vice-regent, operating as it were in the outer court of the cosmic temple.

On this understanding the *imago dei* is a question of divine designation more than of particular endowments—yet that designation is part and parcel of humanity's creation, as we have seen. It seems that the goddess Ungit was sacred from the very time she first pushed herself out of the earth, though her appearance was only that of a rough boulder. So because humanity's creation need not be linked to any specific human attribute, we will not necessarily be able to detect true humanity's origin by archaeology or biology, any more than the new creation of a believer is evident physically.

Indeed, Brian Brock considers that only such a story of designation by God for the *imago dei* gets the relationship of creature to Creator right:

> The core point to keep in mind is that the cause and motor of *this* history is the divine impingement on creatures; it is not the capacity of these creatures to have this relationship that is the motive force of this history.[13]

Brock, in this, echoes the important truth that divine grace supplies what it demands. In Augustine's words,

> "Give me the grace to do as you command, and command me to do what you will!"[14]

---

12. Lewis, *Till We Have Faces*, pt. 2, ch. 2.
13. Brock, "Jesus Christ the Divine Animal?," 66.
14. Augustine, *Confessions* 10.29.

Clearly divine appointment requires a suitable vessel: a cactus is not an appropriate creature to be God's viceroy. For the "image" to mean anything, mankind must have had some rational awareness of it (which a cactus cannot), though in Penman's scenario this would fall short of a living relationship with Yahweh, for Adam was intended establish that, as the representative "federal head" of the race.

Might we, therefore, expect to find any signs of a change in universal human awareness in archaeology, demonstrating the presence of the image of God? Remember that it need correspond to no clear biological changes. The principal thought expressed in Genesis 1 is actually that of *rule*. One cannot be appointed to "subdue" the earth (extending the work of God in creating order from chaos) and to "rule" it (on God's behalf, remember, both governing and stewarding the world's resources) without a concept of humanity as in some way *above* creation. We take that for granted now, because we have great technical mastery in many areas of life.

The Mesolithic hunter-gatherer, it would appear, saw himself as part of nature, rather than in any sense above it. Can we find, in history, a transition from that to a sense of being rulers of the world? Klaus Schmidt, the excavator of Göbekli Tepe in Eastern Turkey, certainly regards the monument as the first sign that people were shifting from "seeing themselves as part of the natural world to seeking mastery over it."[15] It is similarly the standard view that the Neolithic megaliths in my own country, the United Kingdom, most famously Stonehenge, reflect both the first deliberate imposition of human will on the landscape and an apparent transition to the worship of actual gods.

In Mesopotamia itself the naming of, and sacrifice to, gods appears at around the same time. The early mythic literature there speaks of the imposition of order on the earth and, at the level of human city-state activity, to "the descent of the kingship from heaven." That, rather than megalomania, explains the Mesopotamian kings' self-designation as "king of heaven and earth." The early Egyptian literature too carries the idea of man's duty, and the king's especially, to preserve the order of creation through correct ritual and wise rule.

These ideas of rule are not inherent in the key concept of an obedient relationship of service to Yahweh described in Genesis 2. But they are intrinsic to the *imago dei* in Genesis 1, which becomes accentuated,

15. Mann, "Birth of Religion."

though only implicitly, in the calling of Adam and Eve to a greater kind of rule. What changes in the Garden of Eden is that the duty and privilege of rule are taken to a new level; in extent, to the whole cosmos, including the angelic realm, as well as the earth; in duration, to eternity through the tree of life; and in scope not only to subduing, but to transforming creation so that Yahweh's glory is all in all. I will explore this more later.

Soul, Image, and Bestiality

One of the perennial objections to any *Homo divinus* model of anthropology, and one that has been raised frequently in connection with Genealogical Adam, is of newly ensouled, rational humans of Adam's line interbreeding with irrational, soulless, "pre-Adamic" brutes, a concept that seems to critics both distasteful and bizarre, not to mention bestial. But once again, this is to have an unclear concept of what "human" means in this context. In this section I examine what similarities and differences Scripture may teach between Adam's line and others outside the garden.

This problem is often raised by Roman Catholics, for whom a key concept is the "rational soul" of Thomistic theology. That anthropology seems to depend on Aristotelian concepts of what constitutes humankind, more than biblical ones. Genesis says that Adam "became a living soul (*nephesh*),"[16] and that indeed overlaps to some degree with the Thomistic concept of hylemorphic dualism, in which the "soul" is the formative, or perhaps "informational," principle of a human, and not some separate entity.

But Genesis makes no comment on what constitutes the particular "form" or "nature" of Adam, as opposed to the animals, or to Neanderthal, or (in Genealogical Adam scenarios) of those people outside the Garden of Eden. To the Bible, the "soul" of a creature is simply its life principle. "Rational" is a philosophical addition.

Purely evolutionary models, and others that deny an historic Adam, tend to regard all human endowment—such as cognition, abstract thought, moral consciousness, developing awareness of the spiritual and even of God—as emergent from natural processes.

But in the model above, humankind is created in Genesis 1 to be his image, his representative to rule the earth, at some time of God's choosing and in some way he does not specify. But in Genesis 2, Adam is appointed

16. Gen 2:7.

to a greater rule and destiny, within an intended new creation, through special relationship with Yahweh.

Even were we to dispense with the historical Adam and Eve, a division of the race through such a relationship would be inevitable. At *some* point in historical time someone received revelation from God, a command, and the knowledge of accountability and, subsequently, faced judgement both on earth and in eternity. None of that could have emerged gradually, least of all through evolution. And it could not, plausibly, have come to all in the world at the same time.

One has to accept that certain key things were discrete, historical events, different in kind from any evolutionary process. Creation in the *imago dei* is one—but quite separate are the first self-revelation by Yahweh to Adam, his appointment over even the angels, the gift of access to eternal life, the decree of accountability to God, the institution of godly marriage; and, subsequently, the loss of much of that by sin.

The strong scientific evidence is that there was a scattered, but interbreeding, world community of at least several thousand individuals, and often millions, throughout the entire lengthy period we could possibly consider for Adam, from 300,000 BCE in Africa to 3,000 BCE in Mesopotamia.[17] So it seems almost inevitable that, in some way, some form of "humankind in the image of God" would have coexisted with "divine but fallen humanity." And those two populations must have interbred, because there is only one "blood" of mankind today, all of whom are commanded by God to repent and be saved to eternal life.

Just as Genesis 1 is interested in the cosmos constituted as God's temple with man as his image, rather than with humanity's material ontology, so Genesis 2—3 are also more interested in man's covenant relationship with God than with his biological, or even his intellectual, capacities.

If we take Genesis 1 and 2 as sequential, and chapter 1 as describing the creation of mankind *en masse*, including those who lived before and alongside Adam, then we have a human race created in the image and likeness of God which possesses all the intellectual, artistic, and cultural attainments that scientific and historical research has revealed to be

---

17. Recent work by S. Joshua Swamidass, Richard Buggs, Steven Schaffner, Ann Gauger, and others has shown that a two-person bottleneck is genetically possible, but not more recently than about 500,000 years. See Swamidass, Buggs, et al., *Adam, Eve and Population Genetics*.

ubiquitous from prehistoric times. We do not, in any sense whatsoever, have brutes.

But in Scripture we have an Adam and Eve with significantly *more* than that—they have a personal, intimate covenant relationship with the true God, Yahweh, and a commission to bring about a new creation in which God's glory would be all in all. Greg Beale sees this as the high calling of Adam, albeit he failed so catastrophically:

> The OT storyline that I posit as the basis for the NT storyline is this: *The Old Testament is the story of God, who progressively re-establishes his new-creational kingdom out of chaos over a sinful people by his world and Spirit through promise, covenant, and redemption, resulting in worldwide commission to the faithful to advance this kingdom and judgment (defeat or exile) for the unfaithful, unto his glory.*[18]

On this he sees the whole narrative of Scripture to be based. The glory of God is what Adam and Eve began to receive in the garden, and it is that which they were expected to spread through the whole earth, and indeed the whole cosmos, as they began to expand the boundaries of the garden to exceed the Genesis 1 creation ordinance to fill the earth, and subdue it. It was the glory of God that was the core of what was lost by the fall, and which is really only seen in humanity today by our inarticulate longing for it.[19] As the Psalmist says:

> 3 When I consider Your heavens, the work of Your fingers,
> The moon and the stars, which You have ordained;
> 4 What is man that You take thought of him,
> And the son of man that You care for him?
> 5 Yet You have made him a little lower than God,
> And You crown him with glory and majesty!
> 6 You make him to rule over the works of Your hands;
> You have put all things under his feet, . . . [20]

Let me, then, return to the objection with which I started this section—that intermarriage between Adamic man and those from outside the garden would constitute bestiality of some kind. This "yuk factor"

18. Beale, *New Testament*, 16.

19. Though the witness of members of the inaugurated kingdom of God must be understood as the revelation, in humble form, of God's glory.

20. Ps 8:3–6.

comes from considering those outside as "nonhumans," in a way that does not correspond to any identifiable definition of "human," as I showed above, but is imagined, and often expressed, as equivalent to Charlton Heston's liaison with the nonrational Noma in the original *Planet of the Apes* film.

It ought rather, though, to be seen as more comparable to Abraham's relationship with Hagar or Keturah, or that of Boaz with Ruth. Those women acquired new problems by attaching themselves to a stiff-necked and backsliding people—but they also came under the blessing of God's covenant, and crossed over from the limited life of this world and the flesh, to the life of heaven and the spirit. Arguably, that is when they became fully human.

Conclusion Relative to Genealogical Adam

There is every reason to believe that humankind was created in the image and likeness of God before the call of Adam, whose main distinctive was his covenant relationship, not his essential nature. We are therefore able to recognize and accept, without difficulty, any level of cultural achievement, and even spirituality, in those "outside the garden." By focusing on the unique features of Adam's calling, we are able to see his scriptural role as entirely different from that of "first human," and so begin to integrate his significance into an overarching biblical theology is a way that other schemes tend to miss. I will begin to explore this in more depth in chapter 12.

9.

THE SPECIAL CREATION OF ADAM?

When Is Transformation Creation?

IN CHAPTER 1, DISCUSSING the genre of Genesis, I mentioned the Evangelical pastor, Tim Keller, and the non-negotiability of the special creation of Adam in his view of Genesis. Keller is not only sympathetic towards theistic evolution, but wrote a lengthy essay[1] for the Evolutionary Creation organization BioLogos, to which I shall refer again. In the video discussion I referenced previously,[2] Keller says that the question of Adam's historicity is one he would discuss more with Christians than with unbelievers, but he goes on to endorse the view that Adam and Eve were specially created. I *précis*:

> Not only was there an Adam and Eve . . . it sure seems like the text says that God created Adam and Eve, and didn't just adapt a human-like being; it says he created him out of the dust of the ground.

Keller's BioLogos essay shows that he is not simply taking Genesis 2 naïvely as historically literal, being fully aware, and happily accommodating within the faith, all the available views. He gives much space to the tentative hypothesis proposed by Derek Kidner, in his Genesis commentary. As Keller quotes him, Kidner wrote:

1. Keller, "Creation, Evolution, and Christian Laypeople."
2. Keller, "Non-Negotiable Beliefs."

Man in Scripture is much more than *homo faber,* the maker of tools: he is constituted man by God's image and breath, nothing less. . . . [T]he intelligent beings of a remote past, whose bodily and cultural remains give them the clear status of "modern man" to the anthropologist, may yet have been decisively below the plane of life which was established in the creation of Adam. . . . Nothing requires that the creature into which God breathed human life should not have been of a species prepared in every way for humanity . . .[3]

If this . . . alternative implied any doubt of the unity of mankind it would be of course quite untenable. God . . . has made all nations 'from one' (Acts 17:26). . . . Yet it is at least conceivable that after the special creation of Eve, which established the first human pair as God's vice-regents (Gen 1:27, 28) and clinched the fact that there is no natural bridge from animal to man, God may have now conferred His image on Adam's collaterals, to bring them into the same realm of being. Adam's "federal" headship of humanity extended, if that was the case, outwards to his contemporaries as well as onwards to his offspring, and his disobedience disinherited both alike.[4]

Keller adds:

Here Kidner gets creative. He proposes that the being who became Adam under the hand of God first evolved but Eve did not. Then they were put into the Garden of Eden as representatives of the whole human race. Their creation in God's image and their fall affected not only their offspring, but all other contemporaries. In this telling, Kidner accounts for both the continuity between animals and humans that scientists see, and the discontinuity that the Bible describes. Only human beings are in God's image, have fallen into sin, and will be saved by grace.[5]

Kidner seems to suggest an evolved Adam being "upgraded" (as it were) in order to maintain mankind's solidarity with the earth and the animal kingdom, yet in order to preserve the "heavenly" aspect, Adam's wife is created directly from him, rather than being recruited from Kidner's "pre-Adamites" to whom, incidentally, he allows all the intellectual and cultural attributes known to archaeologists.

3. Kidner, *Genesis,* 28.
4. Ibid., 29.
5. Keller, "Creation, Evolution, and Christian Laypeople," 11.

Kidner offered his ideas, back in 1967, for others to improve upon. He proposed Adam's legacy as federal head of the race to be mediated to the rest of mankind in some kind of immediate supernatural way. I suggest that the genealogical model we are discussing does the job equally well, and in a less mysterious way.

But I wish to draw your attention to the way that, despite his sympathy for Kidner, the evolution-friendly Keller nevertheless appears to go beyond him in affirming some kind of special creation for Adam (as well as for Eve) as the fountainhead of the human race. I want briefly to explore why he might consider this supernaturalism necessary, though accepting evolution, apart from the obvious reason that he believes it is taught in Scripture.

As shown in the last chapter the biblical picture stresses the essential *unity* of man: he is not an animal with an added soul, nor even an animal with an added mind, but (as Genesis puts it) "a living soul," a created unity. That unity is expressed in the central hope of the gospel, which is the resurrection of the body on earth, rather than the ascension of the disembodied soul to heaven.

Likewise, in orthodox theology sin "came into the world by one man," as Paul teaches in Romans 5, so that sin is a fall from the heavenly creation, not a residuum of the animal creation (even though its effect is often to make us more like "brute beasts"[6]). As Keller points out, no scholar seems to have managed to extricate Paul from teaching an historical Adam in Romans 5 without also implicating him in fundamental error—a body blow to the doctrine of inspiration, despite the "so what?" attitude of some who deny an historical Adam.

No doubt Keller has other reasons too for, in effect, exempting Adamic humanity from the evolutionary process, as he seems to do by saying that God "didn't just adapt a human-like being."[7] Such a special creation poses no problems for the Genealogical Adam hypothesis. A specially created Adam and Eve would have been, we may assume, biologically-speaking identical with the existing race, as was fitting since Adam was to become their federal head and archetype. This makes the finding of a wife by Cain and, arguably, the intermarriage of the "sons of

6. 2 Pet 2:12.

7. Even evolutionary aspects need to be considered in theological terms. As N. T. Wright puts it: "A fully Trinitarian vision of God, Jesus, and the Spirit goes with the vision of a theistic, that is, non-Epicurean, evolution." Wright, "Christ and the Cosmos," 105.

God" with the "daughters of men" in Genesis 6 quite natural. Adam and Eve's exact genotype is unknowable, but no doubt it was as comparable to their neighbors' as the wine at the marriage of Cana was comparable to any good Galilean vintage.

Nevertheless, "creation" as used in the Bible is a far more flexible term that the *ex nihilo* creation of systematic theology. On the one hand, as the Hebrew word *bārā* it is only ever used with God as subject. On the other, it is not the *only* word used of God's creation, even in Genesis. The word "make" (the generic artisan word *'asah*) is a virtual synonym in Genesis 1, but we should not forget his acts also include "separating," commands for the earth to "bring forth" and for the water to "teem." Adam in chapter 2 is "formed" (*yatsar*), a word also mostly used of God's creation in Scripture, but also of people making images, for example.

Although "create" may be a useful *technical* term in systematic theology, for example in describing what God does *ex nihilo*, in Hebrew Scripture it seems simply to be used, with several other verbs, in a non-technical way for anything new that God brings about. Its use in Genesis is not so much about saying that certain parts of the work required *bārā* and others not, but about the attribution of divine will and causality to the whole account. The word *bārā*, like certain other key words, is mentioned seven times from 1:1 to the linking verse 2:4, thus expressing completeness or perfection. The Genesis account is constructed almost as carefully as creation itself, but the meanings of the words for "create" are somewhat interchangeable.

John Walton may be right or wrong in suggesting that the particular nuance of *bārā* is about functional organization,[8] but it is certainly not necessarily about "*pffing*" something from nothing in an instant. David in Psalm 51:20 asks God to create a clean heart in him—meaning the transformation of the old one, and morally rather than physically at that. In Psalm 54:16 God says that he creates the smith, which is as much as to say that the skills, training, and vocation for a trade come to actual existing men ultimately from God. Israel is described as being "created" (from a rabble in Egypt) in Isaiah 43:1, and so too, prophetically, the new nation of the church (from sinners like us) in Psalm 102:18. God creates evil in Isaiah 43:7, meaning "disaster" rather than "sin," and the context

---

8. Walton, *Genesis 1 as Ancient Cosmology*, 127–33. He emphasizes the *functional*, as opposed to *material*, connotation of *bārā*, but the distinction need not concern us here.

is the destruction of empires by war and similar quite familiar events. He even creates darkness (the mere *absence* of light) in that same verse.

In all these the common meaning is not "causing to exist *ex nihilo*," but "designing" or "intending." God's specific intentions come to be, whether that be from nothing, or from something already existing; and the result may be a situation as much as something material.

So *bārā* is a general and adaptable, not a technical, word—but nevertheless we should not understand it as indicating merely "natural causes." The whole point of all its uses, and its synonyms and analogues, is to point to God's bringing about of what would otherwise *not* happen.

Perhaps, then, it would still be possible see Keller's special creation as a *transformation*—what Thomas Aquinas would call a substantial change rather than a mere "adaptation" (which would be an "accidental" change in Thomist terminology)—of the whole nature of an existing human. I agree with Aquinas that creation is always, properly speaking, an immediate act of God apart from means. "God uses evolution to create" is a misunderstanding of the biblical doctrine of creation, unless that use of creation is seen as no more the *occasion* for creation. And yet Israel the nation was *created* by God from ordinary people (Isa 43:1), and every Christian is a "new creation" whilst remaining to all appearances thoroughly human. But those appearances mask a true change of nature, in the Aristotelian sense. Perhaps the same was true for Adam.

The Nature of Adam and Eve's Creation

Genesis 2 describes the formation of Adam from dust (*'adamah*),[9] and breathes his breath, or spirit, into his nostrils. Eve is made from Adam's rib, or perhaps better, his side.[10] Now, from the point of view of divine power, clearly neither of these was necessary: God could easily create both Adam and Eve *ex nihilo*.

Conversely, from the "scientific" point of view, God was not manufacturing products from raw materials at all in these texts. Dust is not only organizationally, but chemically, dissimilar to human flesh. And mass was apparently not conserved, or Adam's genetic makeup retained, in the creation of Eve. So why should Yahweh do it that way?

9. Gen 2:7.
10. Gen 2:21–22.

Jesus' miracles are instructive not merely by being miracles, but by being instructive. When Jesus turned water into wine, he flouted all we understand about nature. Wine is not chemically derived from water, and there is no potential power in water to become wine (only the power in grapes, yeast, and so on to incorporate water into a far more complex product when organized by people). Likewise, two dead fish have no inherent potential to go forth and multiply under any circumstances, and still less five loaves, yet the Lord chose to feed 5,000 men, as well as women and children, in that way rather than by turning stones into bread (as Satan had once reminded him he could).

The reason he acted in these ways is clearly the theological meaning taught by these things. The wine at Cana represents the new wine of the gospel replacing the old water of the ritual law. The bread and fish taught the disciples that their apparently meager resources were, in Christ's power, sufficient to feed the whole kingdom of God, and in John's Gospel, led to his teaching that in the kingdom the real food he would give would be his own body.[11]

The dust of Adam's origin is, throughout Scripture, used as a metaphor for humanity's humble earthly origin and, indeed, for his commonality with the animals over which he has been given rule.[12] This is made, by Paul, the point of contrast between the old "natural" creation in Adam, and the new spiritual creation in Christ.[13] I would suggest that it is this origin from the earth that Genesis 2 is concerned to teach, and not the precise mode of events.

Granted, the life-giving *ruach* of God breathed into Adam may be taken as our "spiritual constituent," and this may indeed be significant in teaching that there is something of heaven in Adamic man's nature, too. But this cannot be pressed too far because in Genesis 7:15, *all* animals are said to have the breath of life. From this very fact arises the doubt in Ecclesiastes about whether man's spirit has any different destiny from that of the animals.[14]

Similarly Eve's origin from Adam is used in Scripture to show the complementarity of the sexes that makes up humanity only jointly and, sometimes though not at all fashionably, to show woman's derivation

11. John 6.
12. Eccl 3:19–21.
13. 1 Cor 15:42–50.
14. Eccl 3:19–21.

from the man.[15] These latter passages appear to make a stronger case for the literal truth of Eve's special creation from Adam than for Adam's from dust, which may be one reason why Benjamin Warfield was happy to accept an evolutionary origin for Adam, though not for Eve.[16]

The more significant feature in Genesis, perhaps, for special creation is that Adam is not mentioned as having parents, and that is unusual for major biblical figures. Yet this too, as I have shown from the Mesopotamian *Adapa* myth in chapter 4, is not unprecedented: Adapa was a leader *amongst* other men, yet was described as created directly by the god Ea.

In that case I suppose the reason was to indicate Adapa's "chosenness," the very thing I have marked out as significant about Adam. The role of an archetype is "mythical," in the positive sense that Adam is being used in Genesis as a figure of Israel's failure, and in Romans 5 as our precursor, and that with which Christ is contrasted. I would argue that using creation language about him, rather than stating his genealogy from nonelect ancestors, would mirror the creation of Israel as a nation, which is far more significant than their ancestry.

So, to return to Adam as an actual man, can we infer that there was there anything exceptional about him before his admission to the garden (for whatever his creation from dust means, it occurred in the world outside the garden)?[17] It is of course not impossible that the language of creation in 2:7 indicates some *de novo* spiritual capacity for relationship with God, but that isn't clear from the text. Israel, after all, was an extraordinary nation but comprised of ordinary folks.

There is certainly no suggestion in Genesis that Adam was endowed for the first time with "an eternal soul." Eternal life is to be found only in the garden, in communion with God, and expressed, perhaps metaphorically, and perhaps sacramentally, by eating from a tree. Rather, it is his solidarity with the whole human race that seems to be stressed afterwards. He takes the image of God *into* the garden with him, and the image departs from God's presence when he is exiled. It seems to me, then, that Adam becomes "first father" of the human race, seen in its spiritual dimension, by dint of his covenant relationship, not because of his special creation. Or that this relationship constituted his special creation.

15. 1 Cor 11:7–8, 1 Tim 2:11–14.

16. Noll and Livingstone, *B. B. Warfield,* 130.

17. Gen 2:7–8.

Command, Relationship, and Freedom

It was Yahweh's command to Adam and Eve that, although it proved fatal to them, also constituted the intimate relationship they had with him, which is the most important distinctive between them and any humans outside the garden. Claus Westermann writes that it was only this command that made relationship possible, and that in this way it constituted the gift of freedom:

> The freedom of this relationship arises only from the command; without the command there would be no freedom.[18]

Now this is a particularly bold statement in that Westermann has just quoted Gerhard von Rad's words about the preceding permission to eat from any tree of the garden:

> God begins by allowing man complete freedom.[19]

It is true that the first words of God's address, about freedom to eat from any tree, give the man his first taste of "autonomy"—and autonomy is how most people nowadays regard "freedom." But Westermann argues that because this permission is so utterly reasonable in freeing the man from any risk of privation, it is not freedom at all. It is the "unreasonable" command to abstain from the tree—only intelligible through trust in God that eating it will, in fact, lead to death with no understanding of why or how—that actually creates a meaningful relationship with God. And that is because obedience must be based on trust, with freedom either to bestow that trust on Yahweh or not. And the basis of the trust is that it is placed in the same God who created both Adam and the tree. It is faith.

This is profound, when Adam is compared to the new Adam, Jesus Christ, whose radical freedom consisted in being entirely committed to obeying his Father in everything. Westermann is right in saying that relationship with God is built on obedience and that this obedience brings true freedom, and that was as true of Jesus as it would have been of Adam, and as it should be of us.[20]

18. Westermann, *Creation,* 90.

19. Ibid.

20. "O God, who art the author of peace and lover of concord, in knowledge of whom standeth our eternal life, whose service is perfect freedom," wrote Thomas Cranmer, in the Anglican *Book of Common Prayer.*

Westermann distinguishes three kinds of societal restriction on people: the taboo, the command, and the law, of which only the second is truly personal, making command "something essentially different from law." "There can only be command where there is speech" (and so, properly speaking, freedom is confined to rational beings), and "the voice of him who commands must be there so as to command."[21]

Command is, necessarily, in the second person, and therefore relational. This gets to the heart of the Eden narrative as, necessarily, bespeaking a new and personal encounter between human and God, in which God speaks, as Yahweh, to the man. Paul addresses this in Romans 5:17–21, distinguishing the breaking of a command by Adam from the sin and death that reigned, without such a command, between Adam and Abraham. Perhaps Paul also makes a similar distinction to Westermann between "law" and "command," not only in that passage, but in Romans 2:17–29, where he speaks both of Jewish disobedience to the Law of Moses and gentile disobedience to the "law" of conscience as rendering them without excuse. Yet law is not the personal command that, in the garden, established a true covenant relationship with Adam for the first time, distinguishing him fundamentally from anyone else who may have lived at that time.

Perhaps it also establishes why it is Adam who is held accountable to God for the consequences of the first sin, rather than Eve, although she first ate the forbidden fruit. She had not received the command directly from God, but only through Adam (and Genesis 3:16 shows how that relationship was thereafter marred). Westermann sums up his argument thus:

> The command in the Creation narrative has a completely positive meaning. It is an act of confidence in man in his relationship to God. It takes him seriously as man who can decide in freedom and it opens to him the possibility of loyalty.[22]

Such relationship is profoundly different to even the most sophisticated system of religion. I suggest that Adam was called to be the first instance of such a personal relationship with God, from an existing human race which might well have had all the features of a culture, and even of religious worship, though based on nature rather than revelation. These appear both in the archaeological record and the ancient texts.

21. Ibid.
22. Ibid.

But valuable to people though such worship is, and even at that time glorifying to God, it is not relationship of the kind that came to Abraham through the voice of God, to Moses through the burning bush, and to every born-again Christian through the conviction of the Holy Spirit. These must be distinguished from religion, as such, in order to understand the special, new, role of Adam.

Such true relationship could not come to the Israelites after they delegated Moses to receive laws, commandments, and ordinances on their behalf at Mount Sinai,[23] except in the most attenuated way, as Israel's subsequent history of faithlessness shows. And it could not come through any conceivable evolutionary process, or any "natural" development, for faith comes only from hearing the voice of God:

> How then will they call on Him in whom they have not believed?
> How will they believe in Him whom they have not heard? And
> how will they hear without a preacher? . . . So faith comes from
> hearing, and hearing by the word of Christ.[24]

And sin comes only through disobeying that voice and breaking relationship, though sin's effects of death and evildoing might well, in the right circumstances, be a consequence, as Paul says in Romans 5, of *another person's* broken relationship, if that person was a representative head. The Garden of Eden then, on Westermann's reasoning, was a unique and very important place.

Special Creation and Deception

One objection often raised against the special creation of Adam, and indeed any direct involvement of God in the world, is that God could be accused of being deceitful. In this case, it is suggested, for God to create Adam *de novo* with characteristics like the people outside the Garden of Eden, and yet with his own unique genomic makeup, would be to give him an appearance of continuity with humanity that is false.

Were we to have access to his genome, it is said, it would give us a spurious history of Adam's ancestry not only from particular, non-existent, parents but from previous species. This genus of complaint is a common cavil against both Creationists and Intelligent Design proponents:

23. Exod 20:19; see Sailhamer, *Meaning of the Pentateuch*, 392.
24. Rom 10:14, 17.

"Why would God give things the appearance of arising by evolution or by chance if he actually created them ex nihilo and by design?"

The argument is intrinsically weak, because the rejoinder could simply be, "Why would he make things look designed, if they are not?" The *appearance* of design is undeniable in nature. And so the argument shifts to who is interpreting the phenomena rightly. Yet it is not unique to this issue. The question of what false evidence of provenance the wine at Cana would show is another example, but less central than the fact that Jesus, born of a virgin, presumably had the full genome of a Jewish male, divinely rather than naturally endowed.

Under Genealogical Adam, this problem is purely academic. The science shows that most of our distant ancestors are what is called "genetic ghosts," that is to say, we inherit no actual genes from them at all, as they have been "diluted out" over the generations. This would be true of an Adam or Eve created *de novo* several millennia ago. It is very unlikely that unique genes from such individuals would have survived to the present, still less be identifiable. No "deceptive evidence" exists now.

This, however, does not satisfy the critics, because the deception would have been happening at the time, even if no geneticists were around to document it, just as a large tree created instantly in Eden (they say) would have given a deceitful appearance of age even if nobody counted the rings.

This "divine deception" argument is actually a prime example of how our enculturated "soft scientism"[25] gives us a quaintly parochial view of human experience. The fact is that, taking mankind as a whole over history, nothing has been more pervasive and normal than the attribution of divine (or other nonmaterial) agency within the processes we now choose to call "Nature," altering them at will.

The classical civilized pagan religions, including the Mesopotamian, Egyptian, Norse, Greek, and Roman systems—and even South American belief systems—all saw the gods as active in controlling nature, often through minor deities associated with the phenomena as well as directly (remember the Greek dryads and nymphs). In more intellectual systems (and also in more primitive systems—see chapter 10), a supreme divinity

25. There are two extremes of scientism: hard scientism and soft scientism. Hard scientism believes that science alone will solve nearly all human problems or science will eventually explain or describe everything. If a belief is not "scientific," then it is meaningless. Soft scientism says that theological statements must be subjected to scientific scrutiny in order to have any intellectual credibility.

might be involved, as in Platonism or Hinduism. Even in the Hellenistic ivory towers where radical new ideas were spawned, for every rational-ist atomist like Democritus[26] there was a Chrysippus[27] who affirmed the governing activity of God over inanimate, and even human, events.

In the Genesis creation account, polytheism is stripped away to make God the ultimate Creator of a crafted cosmos that appears super-ficially rather like the modern concept of a Nature operating apart from God. Very little space is given in Scripture to secondary personal causes in nature, apart from anomalies like the delegation to Satan of Job's afflic-tion from "natural" causes.

But that biblical separation of God from nature is illusory. Although other deities have been abolished, and even angels are largely unmen-tioned in natural happenings, the gap is filled in the Bible not with a self-sufficient nature, but with God's providential government of an *instrumental* creation. Nothing did more than the Bible to establish the reality of secondary causes (against occasionalism or pantheism), but it established them as tools in God's hands, not as a world independent of God's ongoing control by virtue of its created natures or fixed "laws."

The biblical picture is, then, that of the world as an instrument on which God plays. A guitar or a trumpet is a true secondary cause in music, and may be examined and studied without a trace of animism (though even that may be alive and well amongst real people whilst violinists still talk about the "soul" of a Stradivarius violin). Yet although instruments are real causes in the world, we are not deceived into thinking they will produce anything musical without a player.

The view that God may act directly in nature continues uninter-rupted into the Christian era, whether one takes the Patristic injunction to treat every circumstance as being from God's hand,[28] St. Benedict be-ing protected by a raven from poisoning in Umbria,[29] or the preaching in the Middle English *Piers Plowman* that the recent Black Death and famine were undoubtedly judgements of God.[30]

It is true that material secondary causes were treated as investigable in their own right long before Bacon: Bede in the seventh century had

26. Democritus, b. Abdera, Thrace, c 460 BCE, d. c 390 BCE.

27. Chrysippus, b. Soli, Cilicia, c 279 BCE, d. c 206 BCE.

28. Epistle of Barnabas 19; Didache 3 (Staniforth, trans., *Early Christian Writings*, 188, 192).

29. White, trans., *Early Christian Lives*, 176.

30. Attwater and Attwater, trans., *Piers Plowman*, Passus V, 114–22.

a high view of divine providence but investigated the natural causes of tides. Natural causes and remedies were sought alongside spiritual causes during the Black Death. But whilst in the thirteenth-century universities those like Jean Buridan were initiating the independent investigation of secondary causes, it was always within the context of theological work in those same universities, developing the doctrine of universal providence and divine concurrence as a necessary correlate to it.

We have to go forward a few centuries to Francis Bacon, Descartes, and their heirs for the attempt to create a new kind of science, based on the methodological assumption that worthwhile conclusions could be drawn from empirically investigating only material efficient causes in nature, whilst denying formal causes (by dint of adopting "the mechanical philosophy" of atomism) and ignoring final causes, which were held to be hidden within God and therefore not amenable to science.

It should be remembered that at least part of the motivation for this change, in the religious milieu of the times, was a conscious extension of the de-sacralization of nature. It was felt that by denying agency within nature, and particularly Aristotelian internal teleology, God's sovereignty would be glorified. The sovereignty of God over nature's actions was not seriously called into question, though it came to be seen in the polarized terms of "miracle" *versus* "nature."[31] Nevertheless, even in Francis Bacon's utopian novelette, *The New Atlantis*, allegorizing the more pious and rational age he was hoping to introduce, the plot starts with the providential rescue of lost sailors after prayer by the stilling of a storm and bringing to a safe destination.[32] Even for Bacon, God controls nature providentially.

Still, the new view of science brought in its wake a new view of nature, at least in academic circles, culminating in the Deism that saw God's detachment from nature as a rational virtue, or even as a rational necessity. But we should remember that, as Deism increasingly occupied the rarefied academic high ground, ordinary people still had no difficulty assuming God's providential control of nature either within the old ecclesial traditions or in popular movements like that of Wesley. That is, they accepted God's right to do what he liked with nature until it was educated out of them by those who, having imbibed deistic ideas at universities,

31. "The creation of the cosmos, celebrated in the vivid imagery and multi-layered stories of the biblical texts and especially the New Testament's vision of Christ as the agent of that creation, seem a far cry from the picture of 'nature' and 'supernature' over which cultural wars are still waged." Wright, "Christ and the Cosmos," 97.

32. Bacon, *New Atlantis*, 1.

increasingly occupied the pulpit and the master's desk—and in a later century, of course, the newspaper editor's office, the TV studio, and even the recording studio.

The belief in nature as a closed system of causes seems to depend on constant rules and reminders, rather than on human instincts. Yet despite all this most ordinary people worldwide still feel no sense that God is deceiving them by working in and through nature to govern his world. Most of them think it is only logical that the King of the world should also govern it.

God owes scientific methodology nothing. And so if he decided that it was appropriate for Adam and Eve to be specially created, and yet fully biologically conformed to those arising by some other, "natural" means outside Eden, nobody has any legitimate cause to complain.

Conclusion Relative to Genealogical Adam

In Scripture, the concept of creation has a broad range, and is not to be simply equated with systematic theology's category of "*creation ex nihilo.*" And yet whether we are considering the creation of humankind in general, or of an especially called Adam and Eve in the Garden of Eden, creative activity over and above what we are accustomed to calling "natural causes," must be involved.

The existence of creation language in both Genesis 1 and 2, then, does not require that the two chapters are describing the same event, that is, the creation of the first human. A "non-Adamic" humanity outside the garden would be both in continuity, and in discontinuity, with the rest of the animal creation. The discontinuity would primarily consist of the *imago dei.* Adam is distinct in other ways, whether he be created from dust, but biologically identical to the rest of humankind, or whether the "formation from dust" and "breath of God" are intended metaphorically.

10.

RELIGION BEFORE ADAM

Primitive Religions of the World

GENEALOGICAL ADAM, AS A paradigm, is open to a number of understandings of the status of those outside the Garden of Eden. In itself, it merely predicts that whatever their status was, interbreeding with Adam's line would, within two to four millennia, have merged all their descendants into Adam's lineage.

So how we picture "non-Adamic" man depends, for example, on where Adam is placed in history for other reasons. It also depends on how the text itself is interpreted. For example, C. John Collins, on exegetical grounds, considers the creation of humanity in Genesis 1 to refer to the same event as that of Adam and Eve in Genesis 2.[1] In that case, of course, we would have no reason to suppose the *imago dei* to exist outside the Adamic line. In fact, Scripture would be silent about non-Adamic people, except in the hints of their existence in the Genesis text, as laid out in chapter 2. This leaves such "outsiders" in something of a theological vacuum, whereas we would expect some account of their spiritual situation to appear in the Bible.

In my view, because this raises doubts about the status of humankind apart from Adam (a problem that archaeology appears to demand we answer at some stage in history), and consequently confuses the special role of Adam, I prefer a sequential to a parallel reading of the two

1. Collins, *Did Adam and Eve Really Exist?*, 52–55.

chapters.[2] This also makes more sense to me in literary terms, as I will explain in chapter 15.

The suggestion made by James Penman, cited in chapter 8, that humankind outside the garden was fully "in the image of God" in its "God-consciousness," invites us to consider seriously how a humanity that was before Adam, but which was created in the image of God, would look in religious terms. We seem generally to default to an evolutionary idea that primitive religion, without special revelation, would be at best idolatrous and polytheistic, or quite possibly "pre-religious" in the sense of spirit worship, ancestor worship, nature worship, totemism, or shamanistic magic. And this leads to all kinds of questions about God's apparently allowing idolatry before there was even sin, and similar difficult issues.

The assumption that true religion is the end of a slow evolutionary process is furthered by the still popular interpretation of Paleolithic cave art as shamanistic. However, this common view is in fact highly problematic, as a 2010 paper on cave art by anthropologist Homayun Sidky argues. He wonders "why so many anthropologists, archaeologists, and scholars in other fields subscribe to these views," despite the "paucity of any concrete testable and falsifiable evidence for any of these assumptions."[3] It appears, according to Sidky, that the shamanistic theory depends on proponents, particularly one influential figure in the field, Mircea Eliade (1907–1986), taking for granted poorly evidenced nineteenth-century views based on evolutionism.

> Eliade (1961) took the inadequately documented and mis-construed subject of shamanism, which initially referred to a geographically limited phenomenon, or even a mental illness, gave it the trappings of a legitimate topic of scholarly inquiry, and transformed it into an investigative category with global application.[4]

This easy acceptance of evolutionary explanations on inadequate evidence appears to be something that has dogged the whole study of ancient religion, for as linguist and anthropologist Wilhelm Schmidt

---

2. It also, in my view, poses problems for correctly understanding the temple imagery of Genesis 1: see chapter 16.

3. Sidky, "Antiquity of Shamanism," 68.

4. Ibid., 73.

records, it "dominated almost the entire nineteenth century . . . the whole
earlier period of ethnology."[5]

Not only is the reading back of modern shamanistic practices from
Siberia, or the Sami of Lapland, into the Paleolithic highly speculative, but
the nineteenth-century evolutionary anthropologists failed to consider
that even behind the modern examples was often a hidden stratum of an
almost certainly more primitive theism, and specifically the belief in a
Creator sky-god, a belief found ubiquitously amongst the most primitive
cultures of the world.

Among the Arctic people, such as the Sami, the sky-god has a special concern for the welfare of animals:

> It is particularly characteristic of the Arctic primitives to differ-
> entiate a divine protector of beasts, both wild and tame. Origi-
> nally it was none other than the Supreme Being who was Lord of
> the beasts they hunted, these being one of their most important
> sources of food.[6]

So when we see the proliferation of prey animals in ice-age European cave art, why should we assume it represents shamanistic hunting
magic, when intercession, or thanksgiving, to a high God for hunting
success is no less possible? The latter will inevitably be less visible, because it is more spiritual.

The development of religion was naturally one of the interests of
early anthropology as new, often primitive, cultures were discovered.
Travellers' and missionaries' reports were frequently incomplete or in-
correct, but from the early days indications of belief in a high God were
found from far afield. For example:

> The celebrated traveller, Mungo Park, who visited Africa in
> 1805, had good opportunities of understanding the natives. He
> did not hurry through the land with a large armed force, but
> alone, or almost alone, paid his way with his brass buttons. "I
> have conversed with all ranks and conditions upon the subject
> of their faith," he says, "and can pronounce, without the smallest
> shadow of doubt, that the belief in one God and in a future state
> of reward and punishment is entire and universal among them."
> This cannot strictly be called monotheism, as there are many
> subordinate spirits who may be influenced by "magical ceremo-
> nies." But if monotheism means belief in One Spirit alone, or

5. Schmidt, *Origin and Growth*, 220.

6. Ibid., 262.

religious regard paid to One Spirit alone, it exists nowhere—no, not in Islam.[7]

Describing half a century later:

> Wilson's observations on North and South Guinea religion were published in 1856. After commenting on the delicate task of finding out what a savage religion really is, he writes: "The belief in one great Supreme Being, who made and upholds all things, is universal." The names of the being are translated "Maker," "Preserver," "Benefactor," "Great Friend." Though compact of all good qualities, the being has allowed the world to "come under the control of evil spirits," who, alone, receive religious worship.[8]

Various theories, natural or revelatory, were proposed to explain this, but evolution now began to be in the ethnological air, as evidenced by the fact that one of the major writers on the subject was Herbert Spencer. His philosophical evolutionism had done much to popularize Darwinism, even inducing Darwin to adopt the word *evolution*, a term he had at first avoided. Evolutionary theory was applied to everything, and not least religion. The most influential works in this field were those of Edward Tylor from 1865 onwards.[9]

In biblical studies Tylor's work led *via* Julius Wellhausen (consciously under Tylor's influence)[10] to the eventual dominance of the history of religions school (*Religionsgeschichtliche Schule*[11]) in both Old and New Testament Studies, leading to assumptions, still current today, that Israelite monotheism must have evolved from polytheism (and that in turn from the animism in the mists of time),[12] and that Christianity must originally have been simple monotheism until influenced by pagan mystery religions.[13]

In anthropology,

---

7. Lang, *Making of Religion*, 142–43, Kindle ed.

8. Ibid.

9. Tylor, *Researches into the Early History of Mankind*.

10. Schmidt, *Origin and Growth*, 192–93.

11. "History of Religions," *Wikipedia*. https://en.wikipedia.org/wiki/History_of_religions_school.

12. Kitchen, *Reliability*, 485–86.

13. Hurtado, *Destroyer of the gods*, 193–96.

All the other theories, however, came into being after the out-
break of materialism and Darwinism, and their work was all
done on the lines of Evolutionist natural science. This puts all
that is low and simple at the beginning, all that is higher and of
worth being regarded only as the product of longer or shorter
processes of development.[14]

As a more recent writer observes of this period, occupying much of
the nineteenth and all of the twentieth centuries, in some quarters:

> To comprehend what now seem to be obviously faulty inter-
> pretations and explanations, we would have to write a treatise
> on the climate of thought of their time, the intellectual circum-
> stances which set bounds to their thought, a curious mixture
> of positivism, evolutionism; and the remains of a sentimental
> religiosity.[15]

The first to react against this academic consensus was folklor-
ist Andrew Lang, in 1898, who reviewed the same reports used by the
anthropological evolutionists (like them working from his study rather
than in the field) and found that they had uniformly neglected a mass
of evidence that didn't fit their theories. This evidence suggested that the
primitive peoples ubiquitously acknowledged a sky-god who is above all
things—and the more primitive the culture, the more free was their religion from the supposedly more rudimentary elements of nature worship,
spirit veneration, and so on:

> It is a positive fact that among some of the lowest savages there
> exists, not a doctrinal and abstract Monotheism, but a belief
> in a moral, powerful, kindly, creative Being, while this faith is
> found in juxtaposition with belief in unworshipped ghosts, to-
> tems, fetishes, and so on. The powerful creative Being of savage
> belief sanctions truth, unselfishness, loyalty, chastity, and other
> virtues.[16]

The failure of others to notice this lay, apart from their commitment
to evolutionism, in the sometimes subtle nature of such beliefs, and their
increasing dilution the more advanced the culture:

> Now, it is mere matter of fact, and not of assumption, that the
> Supreme Being of many rather higher savages differs from the

14. Schmidt, *Origin and Growth*, 13.
15. Evans-Pritchard, *Theories of Primitive Religion*, 5.
16. Lang, *Making of Religion*, 165.

Supreme Being of certain lower savages by the neglect in which
he is left, by the epicurean repose with which he is credited, and
by his comparative lack of moral control over human conduct.
In his place a mob of ghosts and spirits, supposed to be potent
and helpful in everyday life, attract men's regard and adoration,
and get paid by sacrifice—even by human sacrifice. Turning to
races yet higher in material culture, we find a crowd of hungry
and cruel gods.[17]

Lang gives the example of the Zulu nation, which seemed to be in
the very process of forgetting the high God, who was thought too inscru-
table to be "useful":

"In process of time we have come to worship the Ama-
dhlozi (spirits) only, because we know not what to say about
Unkulunkulu."[18]

The change must have been relatively recent, for,

A very old woman was most reluctant to speak of Unkulunkulu;
at last she said, "Ah, it is he in fact who is the Creator, who is in
heaven, of whom the ancients spoke."[19]

Lang speaks of near-mockery in this woman's tone. He attributes the
change to the Zulus' rise to militant imperialism, and their desire for gods
who would bring power rather than challenge ethics, and he accounts for
the process of, apparently, promoting the high God either into merely
ceremonial rule or nonexistence thus:

All this attests a faint lingering shadow of a belief too ethereal,
too remote, for a practical conquering race, which prefers intelligible serviceable ghosts, with a special regard for their own
families.[20]

Lang's intellectual reputation ensured that he must be heard, but his
work was either ignored or criticized without being refuted. He was succeeded in time by Wilhelm Schmidt, who sought in a monumental series
of volumes (fortunately supplemented by a more accessible "primer," *The
Origin and Growth of Religion*) to consolidate similar conclusions with a
huge mass of better field data. He critiqued Lang's adoption of the rather

17. Ibid.
18. Ibid., 134.
19. Ibid.
20. Ibid.

scattergun anecdotal approach of his predecessors, and in particular his easy assumptions about which societies were more primitive. But Lang's general conclusion that the more remote and unreached peoples were more likely to preserve primeval beliefs was sound, and those beliefs concurred on the existence of the sky-god who created all things, cares for all things, and (in many cases) requires no offerings and cannot be known.

Schmidt sought to use consistent methodology in order to understand how different religious practices had developed in different groups. But he was as certain as Lang—and on more rigorous grounds—that the sky-father was a truly indigenous phenomenon, and not, as critics had countered, a result of the teachings of missionaries. He concludes:

> Of this we may be fully confident, for by the methods of the history of culture we can establish two connected propositions, firstly, that these high gods are found among, and only among, the peoples ethnologically oldest, and secondly, that all these ethnologically oldest peoples have such gods.[21]

After this, in 1965, the celebrated anthropologist Edward Evans-Pritchard re-examined the state of play, observing first of all how little work had been done since Schmidt in the thirties. Secondly, he pointed out that the discussion had often been driven by scholars whose evolutionary agenda was not purely dispassionate:

> They sought, and found in primitive religion, a weapon which could, they thought, be used with deadly effect against Christianity.[22]

Thirdly, he offered a sympathetic critique of Schmidt, ironically on the basis of Schmidt's commitment to theories of development that were, themselves, open to question:

> Schmidt wished to discredit the evolutionary ethnologists, according to whose schemata of development these same peoples should be in the lowest grades of fetishism, magism, animism, totemism, and so forth. Undoubtedly he proved his case against them, but only at the cost, as with Lang, of accepting their evolutionary criteria, giving historical chronology to cultural levels.[23]

21. Schmidt, *Origin and Growth*, 14.

22. Evans-Pritchard, *Theories of Primitive Religions*, 15.

23. Ibid., 103–4.

What this all means, in effect, is that we have high certainty that the primitive cultures studied right across the world have an ancient form of theism that involves creation, ethical loftiness and government (usually through nature), and benevolent providence. Sacrifice is seldom offered, but where it is the thank-offering of firstfruits.[24]

What we can be far less sure of reconstructing from the evidence itself is how and why it developed, and the processes that led, in various places and times, to its degeneration into what are more familiarly seen as "primitive" religious and magical practices. In particular, we can be much less sure than the earlier writers were of a direct connection between the sky-god and revealed monotheism:

> I quote Pettazzoni: "What we find among uncivilized peoples is not monotheism in its historically legitimate sense, but the idea of a Supreme Being. And the erroneous identification, the misleading assimilation, of this idea to true monotheism can give rise only to misunderstandings."[25]

In other words we know that uncivilized people believe in a Supreme Being, but we cannot say when that belief arose, although it is extremely ancient, and we cannot be certain of the causes. These conclusions refute the "history of religions" approach:

> The first error was the basing of [the interpretations of primitive religion] on evolutionary assumptions for which no evidence was, or could be, adduced. The second was that, besides being theories of chronological origins, they were also theories of psychological origins; and even those we have labelled sociological could be said to rest ultimately on psychological suppositions of the "if I were a horse" sort.[26]

Although Evans-Pritchard warns against the "high God" beliefs being equated simplistically with "monotheism," I will finish this assessment of modern "primitive religion" by showing that, to those whose people embrace it, the belief maps readily to the monotheism of the gospel of Jesus Christ. Don Richardson popularized this aspect for Christians in a book of 1981.[27] He gave many examples from around the world of tribes which, when first reached by missionaries, were astonishingly, and

24. Schmidt, *Origins and Growth*, 207.
25. Ibid.
26. Ibid., 108.
27. Richardson, *Eternity in Their Hearts*.

widely, receptive to the gospel compared to those belonging to the more sophisticated world religions.

This openness was usually because, often submerged beneath the daily practice of animist or other practices, there was a persistent belief that the original Creator was a distant, invisible, and benevolent Being who dwells in the heavens. It was as if this belief prepared them to receive the gospel.[28] They were ready to accept that it was possible to know this God personally.

We occasionally see such peoples in the news, when we read of minority ethnic groups steadfastly holding on to Christianity in the face of persecution from the major national religion—notable examples being the Karen people of Burma, or the Santal of Bangladesh. It is apparent from this that their Christianity stems from very deep roots.

Primitive Religions Before Adam

This picture of world religions, so seldom brought to our notice, is naturally intriguing with respect to Genealogical Adam. We must, of course, be cautious about what may be inferred about the past from present beliefs, and have already seen the dangers of trying to conclude too much from the data, whether that be in Schmidt's overconfident methodology for constructing a historical narrative from a single body of information (all too reminiscent of Wellhausen's documentary hypothesis and its successors down to present-day historical Old Testament minimalism), or in reading a stable 40,000-year tradition of shamanism into cave art when direct observation shows shamanistic practice even changes from year to year.[29]

Nevertheless, the consistency of the basic theme of the sky-god, from Tierra del Fuego, via the African Bushmen and Asiatic tribes, to the most primitive of the Australian Aborigines and even the Andaman Islanders, is highly significant. For our purposes, it is also important that in the more accessible parts of the globe, and in those more civilized, these beliefs are at their weakest, or altogether absent.

---

28. In some cases, a more immediate preparation in the form of recent or ancient prophetic messages from this God seems to have occurred.

29. "As Kehoe (2000: 48) has pointed out, there is an abundance of cross-cultural evidence demonstrating the fact that nowhere do magico-religious traditions remain unchanged." Sidky, *Antiquity of Shamanism,* 72.

From the biblical perspective, it is notable that sky-god beliefs more closely match the situation of Genesis 1 than they do that of Genesis 2 and 3, and that in a number of ways. Genesis 1 is about the creation of a cosmic temple, in which God dwells in heaven, and humanity is created in God's image to rule on earth. God is in heaven, but humankind is on earth. There is a great distance between them, though no enmity—God is Creator and Father, as well as moral guide, and he governs nature in response to human need and behavior.[30]

If we can imagine people with beliefs like this spreading, or being already scattered, across the world, then we will see something like the deepest stratum of our primitive sky-god religion. The religion is natural, or at least aboriginal, sincere, trusting, and unaffected, lacking priest-craft or elaborate ritual—but it is also somewhat distant. God watches all and cares for all, but he does so from the holy of holies in the heavens far above. Lang records a Greenlander explaining his belief in a Creator Being to a missionary:

> He then stated the argument from design. "Certainly there must be some Being who made all these things. He must be very good too . . . Ah, did I but know him, how I would love and honour him."[31]

But although Paul, like the Greenlander, speaks of the argument from design in Romans 1:19–20, his context is not why people believe in the true God, but why sinners have no excuse (because of the argument from design) for disbelief. Rather, belief in the sky-god appears generally to be what Alvin Plantinga calls a "properly basic belief."[32] People "in the image of God," (and we have no way to be sure exactly when that image became characteristic of humanity) believe in that God by nature, not by argument, as surely as they believe in the existence, and humanness, of other souls. Argument is, in fact, what tends to suppress that natural belief, not what gives rise to it.

Genesis 2 is not like that, and neither is Genesis 3. The characteristic of the garden is the intimacy Adam and Eve have with God. He is far from remote, but he is also more demanding. He gives a specific command, and as we have seen, it is that command that initiates a covenant

---

30. For God's government of nature in Scripture, see Garvey, *God's Good Earth*, ch. 1.

31. Lang, *Making of Religion*, 118.

32. Plantinga, *Where the Conflict Really Lies*, 42–43.

relationship. The *reason* for that covenant relationship, as biblical theologians like Beale, Middleton, or Sailhamer have pointed out, was to bring God's glory *down to earth*, filling everything as Adam and his offspring spread the close relationship to Yahweh through the world—and ultimately through the whole cosmos. The joining of heaven and earth in a new creation, described as the culmination of the work of Christ as the new Adam in Revelation 22, is in fact the commission first given to Adam in the garden.

The actual effect, though, was to bring sin into the world. What we see in Genesis 1—11 is mainly the spread of tyranny and false religion, not of God's glory. This is amply demonstrated by the ANE parallel to the Genesis protohistory: the *Eridu Genesis*, and *Atrahasis*, and the *Epic of Gilgamesh* all show the fully developed polytheism, idolatry, and priestcraft that the ethnologists discussed in this chapter have found to be associated with the later, degenerate stages of religion.

This decline accords closely with Paul's description of the pattern of degeneration of religion through the first sin, in Romans 1:18–32. Paul, here, is basing his entire argument on the aftermath of the fall in Genesis. He is talking about Adamic man, which is the only kind of human with whom he is concerned in proclaiming the gospel.

So how might this state, the religious reality we find in the world today, be explained by the Genealogical Adam model? Starting from my token Ussherian "4004 BCE Adam," Genealogical Adam predicts that no human being in the world now is genealogically unrelated to Adam. All men are descended from Adam, though not exclusively. The more remote from the center of radiation in Eden, the more fortuitous, and so the less cultural, we would expect the connection with Adam to be after a few thousand years.

The Table of Nations describes peoples apparently culturally dominated by Adam's descendants. We may see this in history through the close cultural ties, and even through the shared religious vocabulary and practice, of these peoples. It is as if Seth's line are preserving, in a somewhat more pure form than their neighbors, the knowledge of Yahweh, which degenerates elsewhere into the human sacrifice of Molech, or the sexual license of the Canaanite pantheon. Outside Israel (and sadly, sometimes inside it) El acquires Ashtoreth as a wife, and Baal as a son, the temples acquire prostitutes, and the role of Israel, as it emerges, is a constant struggle for purity of religion. For both good and ill, Adam's line calls on the name of Yahweh, though in increasingly debased knowledge, and they influence those around them. As Lang put it:

> The Old Testament is the story of the prolonged effort to keep Jehovah in His supreme place. To make and to succeed in that effort was the *differentia*, of Israel.[33]

That, however, is not how things are likely to have worked in Australia, or South America, or New Guinea. Here we may imagine individual traders, captives or shipwrecked sailors, from peoples in contact with distant cousins of Adam, marrying into a primitive culture—one, in my scenario, that is following the natural religion of Genesis 1, the worship of the sky-Father.

Genealogically, all that people would, before too long, inevitably become genealogically related to Adam. And sin, or anything else peculiar to Adam's line by descent, would surely have affected them. But the same is not necessarily true culturally. One insignificant or nonresident parent could leave the primordial religion largely untouched. And so we would find the least corrupted, Genesis 1, form of religion, the natural fruit of the image of God in mankind, in the most remote regions.

In contrast we would expect the greatest perversion of religion to exist where Adam's sinful people had most influence. But there we would also expect, mixed in with corruption, to find the remnants of the truth about God's glory and the way to eternal life. We would find pagan idolatry, magic, and true Yahwism in the Levant, and sincere but unfocused belief in a Supreme Being in remote, untravelled regions. For the methodological reasons which I cited from Evans-Pritchard above, it is impossible, in such a scenario, to say that some aspects of primitive religion may have not come from the inheritance of Adam. I name two here.

The first is the quite common belief amongst undeveloped peoples that God is so distant from mankind, and so little known by him, because of some fault on man's part in the past. Did this belief come through contact, at some stage, with those who knew of the fall, or in some other way? One way or another, it is an awareness of universal sin. The second is that, according to Schmidt,

> All primitive peoples without exception believe in another life. As to what it is like, they cannot all say ... but the great majority

---

33. Lang, *Making of Religion*, 130.

of them recognise such a distinction of good and bad in a future life.[34]

This is interesting, because one would conclude from Genesis that awareness of (and therefore desire for) eternal life came from only the experience of the Garden of Eden. So, given the difficulties of dating the development of religious beliefs, it might be, once more, that eternity was put into the hearts of these primitive tribes through the heritage of Adam. This would demonstrate that, indeed, there are no truly primitive, in the sense of non-Adamic, peoples alive today.

On the other hand, we might suppose that the longing for eternity was actually an aspect of the *imago dei*, which would raise the likelihood that, in some way, the blessings promised to Adam were intended to act retrospectively to those outside the garden, who already had the desire for immortality, especially those who had died in ages past. Such a conclusion weakens any charge that God was being "unfair" to those outside the garden, but at the cost of a significantly more complicated theology.

Primitive Religion and a Good Creation

Although such questions appear unanswerable, I would suggest that those outside the garden would have done very well with no inkling of immortality, if that is how God organized things. Even now, there are many people who have lost any obvious desire to survive death, and state, apparently in all honesty, that life is for living now, and death provides a suitable and welcome end to that. Such an attitude is only a problem if, as Christian doctrine teaches, it is mistaken, and there is indeed a judgement and an eternal outcome to be faced. But bear in mind that all such outcomes exist in the context of the new creation of imperishability, for nothing in the old was created to last forever.

The lesser glory of the first creation[35] *includes* its perishability, which God nevertheless deemed "very good."[36] As Augustine wrote:

> . . . for these creatures received, at their Creator's will, an existence fitting them, by passing away and giving place to others, to

34. Schmidt, *Origin and Growth*, 275.

35. 1 Cor 15:40.

36. Gen 1:31.

> secure that lowest form of beauty, the beauty of seasons, which
> in its own place is a requisite part of this world.[37]

There seems no reason why human beings created as the crowning glory of that perishable first creation might not have possessed a nature just as comfortable with their impermanence as the other animals evidently are with theirs. Their particular glory would have been to worship the Creator in heaven rationally, and to receive his guidance in the way they should lead their lives, both practically and morally.

Such a situation could have continued quite satisfactorily for as long as such humans existed. There seems no reason why our Paleolithic cave dwellers might not have been glorifying the true God back in 40,000 BCE, or even before. Their lives would have been fruitful, enjoyable, and—most significantly—lived with true reference to their Creator.

That sounds rather idyllic, and in the sense that it would have been a sinless existence, in line with the will of God, it was. But this ignores what Genesis 2, in my view, seeks to teach us: that there was a time, not long ago in the scheme of things, when God decided to take such human beings, created in the image of God, and glorify them through a closer relationship with him, enriching and renewing the whole creation thereby.

The good creation, in other words, was intended to get better through Adam. But instead it got worse. This should be no surprise, because that is the whole message of the fall, and why the human condition has such a tragic element. And yet that whole drama, according to Scripture, is encompassed in the overarching purpose of maximizing the glory of God through Christ, the "Lamb slain before the foundation of the world."[38]

Conclusion Relative to Genealogical Adam

Ethnology reveals that the most primitive religion is a "natural" belief in a Supreme Being in heaven. On the other hand, less primitive peoples closer to where we would expect to find the Garden of Eden have suffered the kind of religious and moral degeneration we find described, for Adam's race, in Romans 1.

The more primitive state appears closer to what we find in Genesis 1, which, if its events precede those of the Garden of Eden, offers anthropological support to the scenario suggested by Genealogical Adam theory.

37. Augustine, *City of God* XI 22.
38. Rev 13:8.

11.

THE IMPORTANCE OF GENEALOGY

Genealogies and Adam

IN THIS CHAPTER I will consider the biblical genealogies originating from Adam not only in Genesis, but in 1 Chronicles and in Matthew's and Luke's gospels. The issue concerning me here is not directly how these support, or otherwise, the Genealogical Adam framework, but their purpose. What may be said of these will, perhaps, cast light on the other pieces of genealogical information scattered throughout the Bible, and so on the role of genealogy in the biblical metanarrative.

If Genealogical Adam focuses our attention on the scientific importance of genealogy, rather than genetics, to understanding human origins, then perhaps we ought to focus more than we do on the genealogies in the Bible, all ultimately deriving from Adam. They are likely to be more important to the story if the writers were chronicling a particular lineage rather than mankind in general.

When my mother was tracing her family history, she visited an ancient, and staunchly Christian, aunt in a care home far across the country, and asked her what she knew. "All I know is that I'm descended from Adam and Eve," Aunt Grace replied. This was highly frustrating to the would-be genealogist after a long journey, but quite sufficient, on reflection, for any purpose related to one's membership of the human race. Why would the biblical authors require more than that?

Both anciently and now, genealogies are not, in fact, merely about descent, but about convergences and divergences abstracted from what is actually a meshwork of birth relationships—the irrefutable fact on which the Genealogical Adam hypothesis depends. A couple of generations ago British genealogy was all about trying to show royal, or aristocratic, lineage. I suppose that in a class-based society, although a grocer was never likely to inherit a title, still less the throne, nevertheless descent from the Duke of Norfolk on the distaff side gave one some sort of connection to *Debrett's Peerage*, and a feeling that one was on the same playing field as one's social superiors.

During the Peasants' Revolt of 1381, the Lollard priest John Ball quipped:

> When Adam delved, and Eve span,
> Who was then the gentleman?[1]

The answer wasn't "Adam"! His point was a good one—if we are all of one family, why are some considered socially inferior? Nowadays the aspirations of genealogists are, apparently, closer to Ball's, in our more egalitarian society. A prosperous businessman or politician might like to increase his street credentials by claiming working-class ancestry, or even descent from slaves. Continuing the connection to the Peasants' Revolt, my mother's Non-Conformist family fancied, not too implausibly, that they had direct descent from its other leader, Wat Tyler. But when Adam delved and Eve span, nobody was an oppressed minority, either. Even the exploited are the children of Charlemagne.

No genealogist is interested in what everyone shares: heirs to a millionaire's fortune might wish to prove how they are descended from him, but would not expend research effort on his obscure great-aunt.

Perhaps we can see this clearly from Matthew's genealogy, which explicitly places Jesus' ancestry in relation to his descent from Abraham, as the recipient of the covenant of salvation, from David as recipient of

---

1. *"Whan Adam dalf, and Eve span, Wo was thanne a gentilman?*

"[A]b initio omnes pares creatos a natura, servitutem per injustam oppressionem nequam hominum introductam, contra Dei voluntatem; quia, si Deo placuisset servos creasse, utique in principio mundi constituisset quis servus, quisve dominus, futurus fuisset."

"When Adam delved and Eve span, Who was then a gentleman?

"From the beginning all men by nature were created alike, and our bondage or servitude came in by the unjust oppression of worthless men. For if God would have had any bondmen from the beginning, he would have appointed who should be bond, and who free." Sermon preached at Blackheath (Walsingham, *Historia Anglicana*, 32–33), + translation.

the covenant of kingship, and from the exile as a reminder both of Israel's continued estrangement from God, and of the promise of restoration through Messiah. And for those purposes, Matthew has no reason to go back beyond Abraham, or to include every generation.[2]

Now, if Adam in Genesis is assumed to have a universal significance as the "very first human being," then his genealogy in Genesis 5 may appear to be, in effect, a history of humankind's spread. To assume this, though, one needs to see the Table of Nations of chapter 10 as implying a belief that it covers *all* nations, and that it supposes the flood to have been worldwide. Neither is necessarily what Scripture wishes to imply, as I discussed in chapter 6.

Rather, in the context of the Pentateuch it seems that the main purpose of the Genesis 5 genealogy is to trace Seth's line ("in [Adam's] own image and likeness," a phrase not used of Cain or Abel), which clearly continues to revere Yahweh,[3] down to Abraham, and thus eventually to Israel. The question to investigate is why this matters. It can scarcely be simply to prove that Israel belongs to the human race, nor even that it worshipped Yahweh, for the text suggests that outsiders had come to do that too.[4] Surely it has something to do with the story of Adam itself, whether Adam is seen as the archetypal progenitor of humanity, or primarily of Israel.

One link that has sometimes been drawn between Adam and Israel in the context of *Torah* is the way that Israel is called by God, as Adam was, to live in a land "flowing with milk and honey"[5] in the presence of God. Not only does this echo the Garden of Eden, but also the triple promise to Abraham—of people, land, and blessing—reflects God's original creation ordinance in Genesis chapter 1 for 'ādām to multiply, fill, and rule the earth, and (by implication) to do so on God's behalf. As we have seen, Adam's line received this commission in an enhanced,

---

2. Matthew's stylized use of three cycles of fourteen generations (Matt 1:17) is variously interpreted, but may represent 6X7, that is a stylized six days of creation leading to the new creation sabbath in Christ. Don Carson prefers the explanation that "14" is the numerical value of David's Hebrew name, repeated thrice (Carson, *Matthew 1–12*, 69). Whatever the explanation is, it is certainly not gratuitous.

3. Gen 5:24, 29.

4. Gen 4:26.

5. Exod 3:8.

relational, and covenantal way in the garden, and Yahweh renewed it to Noah's line after the flood.[6]

The *Torah* records numerous rebellions of Yahweh's "stiffnecked people,"[7] and Deuteronomy leaves the people on the brink of the promised land, with the question still open of whether they will actually inherit it, amid dark warnings that, like Adam and Eve, they might be exiled from it if they are unfaithful to the covenant. Thus the *Torah* ends by challenging Israel with a great hope based on obedience, like that following the command in the garden, and with a warning based on the example of Adam's expulsion.[8]

This makes good literary sense, but only really works if Adam has some real connection with Israel. Like Israel, Adam was called for a special purpose of service to God, but the genealogical bloodline traced back to him in Genesis makes the connection more than thematic. In its direct application, at least, the *Torah* does not take Adam as "all humanity" in his relationship to God and in his disobedience, for both Israel's covenant and the penalties for breaking it are unique amongst humanity. If this line of interpretation is correct, the message of the Genesis genealogy is either, "You are called to Adam's role—don't mess up as he did" or, more pessimistically, "Like father, like son."

Something of this is possibly recalled in the Chronicles genealogy too, in that the book starts with "Adam, Seth, Enosh . . ."[9] This long genealogy at the beginning of 1 Chronicles is the bane of generations of young Christians attempting to plough through their Bibles from end to end, but it is there for a purpose. The work ends with the reality of the exile, expressed in Genesis-like terms as exact retribution for the non-observance of Sabbath years,[10] that is for rebellion from the government of God established at creation in Genesis 2:2.[11]

And yet though we will spot such a connection between the Babylonian exile and the Eden exile if we are alert, it is not actually pointed out explicitly in the text: it is the genealogical descent from Adam that demonstrates its relevance, and that in connection with the covenant.

6. Gen 9:1, 7.

7. Deut 31:27.

8. Deut 29–32.

9. 1 Chron 1:1.

10. Adam's sin similarly disrupts God's Sabbath of creation's seventh day, Gen 2:2–3.

11. 2 Chron 36: 17–22.

The Table of Nations is glossed over, in First Chronicles, as are the non-Israelite tribes descended from Abraham (though they are there). The greatest emphasis is on the line of David and on the priestly descendants of Levi, and on their joint failure after the pattern of the priest-king Adam. In other words, Adam's failure is being connected, by the genealogy, to the failure of Israel.

Yet it is also significant that the genealogy of the royal line is continued after the exile in 1 Chronicles, and that the genealogies of some returning exiles are also given. The story of Israel and its kings is therefore not yet over, and in some way their hope, like their disaster, harks back to their descent from Adam. Surely it must be what is *special* about both Israel and Adam that explains the genealogy, and not that Israel is human like everybody else, even though other descendants of Adam are named in passing. It seems that just as not all descendants of Abraham are Davidic kings, so not all descendants of Adam are Israel, though both ancestries somehow validate their respective ministries.

If we now turn to Luke's genealogy of Jesus, unlike the others it goes from the present, in the ancestral direction, towards "Seth, the son of Adam, the son of God."[12] Now, the idea that Luke intends to prove Jesus' divinity by tracing his ancestry to God really does not work. In the first place, it would actually prove that *every* person descended from Adam is the Son of God, which removes any special significance regarding Jesus. Secondly, the genealogy starts with Jesus being son, "as was thought," of Joseph,[13] suggesting that the genealogy is as much legal as biological. Thirdly, Luke has already stated[14] that what establishes Jesus as Son of God is his virgin birth (we needn't spend time here on exactly what Gabriel meant by that claim), so that the genealogy would be superfluous.

A second explanation is that, by this genealogy, Luke means to establish Jesus' solidarity with the human race, in its estrangement from God. This is possible, but it seems to me that a genealogy back to Adam is an unwieldy way of showing Jesus' true humanity, especially when, in the first place, the genealogy begins with a kind of "legal fiction," and secondly, when the genealogy goes back not to Adam himself, but to God. "Born of Mary" would prove the point equally well. Perhaps this explanation becomes a little stronger if we note that Luke has already expressed

12. Luke 3:38.
13. Luke 3:23.
14. Luke 1:35.

some interest in the Gentiles, though most of his concern has been with Jesus as the king and saviour of Israel:

> 30 "For my eyes have seen Your salvation,
>
> 31 Which You have prepared in the presence of all peoples,
>
> 32 A Light of revelation to the Gentiles,
>
> And the glory of Your people Israel."[15]

Even so, I return to that niggling detail that the genealogy goes from Jesus to Adam as "son of God," not as "origin of sin." The genealogy is therefore not pointing to Jesus as the "solution" to Adam. Adam is nowhere else in Scripture referred to directly as God's son. He was, after all, created from mere dirt, albeit enlivened by God's breathing his Spirit into him. Perhaps Luke, here, is extrapolating from an interpretive choice concerning that mysterious passage in Genesis 6 in which the "sons of God" fall for the "daughters of men," marry them and have children.

I discussed this passage in chapter 2,[16] and also its two commonest interpretations, either that the "sons of God" were angelic beings who interbred with humans, their offspring being the demons that plagued mankind, or that the "sons of God" were Seth's line, and the "daughters of men" people not descended from Adam (such as Cain's wife).

If Luke followed something more like the second of these, then Adam's sonship would have been in relation to his appointment to a specific role, like Seth's line, and like the anointed king of Israel, who was also known as "son of God."[17] Such a view would tie together the genealogies we have looked at not only in Luke, but in Genesis and 1 Chronicles. It would have to do with the purpose for which Adam was called, in which he failed, but whose future fulfilment was entrusted to his descendants in God's wisdom. That would include the roles of Israel, her priesthood, and the Davidic kings, all of whose exile also demonstrated their failure to fulfill Adam's intended function.

Greg Beale avoids invoking Genesis 6 in discussing this because of its disputed meaning, but on other grounds strongly affirms Adam as an archetypal "son of God," and Jesus as inheriting that role, in a long section entitled *Jesus as the Adamic Son of God*.[18] Beale begins with the close

---

15. Luke 2:30.

16. "Marriage, Sons of God, and Daughters of Men."

17. Ps 2:7, 12.

18. Beale, *New Testament*, 401–23.

parallel between the "image and likeness" phraseology applied to Seth's birth,[19] and the equivalent imagery in Genesis 1. In this he assumes that Adam and Eve are the subject of Genesis 1:26–28, that is the first humans, but the passage need not be understood this way, since if it has a wider human race in view, then just as Eve shrinks from view in Beale's analysis, so once Adam has become the federal head, or archetype, of the race, it is *Adam's* sonship that becomes the focus. Beale's discussion is well worth reading for the other evidence he adduces for Adam as a son of God.

Luke's genealogy therefore affirms, by one means or another, the Pauline concept that "a second Adam to the fight, and to the rescue came."[20] Jesus comes as the son of David the king, whose "kingdom will never end,"[21] but also in the line of Adam's kingship. He comes to restore Israel, "to be merciful to Abraham and his descendants forever, even as he said to our fathers."[22]

And he comes, as we have already seen in Luke, as "a light for revelation to the Gentiles"—that is, as king of the whole race of mankind, with a universal calling analogous to that of Adam. On this understanding, then, Luke's genealogy from Adam primarily relates to the royal role, one of sonship, that God first intended for Adam in history, a role transferred, and expanded with each human failure, in a convoluted genealogical succession right down to Jesus. It works if Adam is seen as the founder of the entire human race. It works, too, for federal headship models. But it also works, and perhaps by closer analogy, for an Adam called to a role for a race that already existed (under Genealogical Adam theory), just as Jesus was. What will *not* work is if Adam is seen as:

- *Fictional*, in which case Scripture is just lying or misled. Whatever may be its varying conventions, genealogy is about real relationships. Even in these postmodern times, for a white person who identifies as a black to invent a family tree leading back to Africa would be considered illegitimate. The Jews were very particular about genealogy: the latter part of the 1 Chronicles genealogy says that ancestry was recorded even at village level,[23] a significant allocation of resources in a semi-literate society. And in Ezra we read

19. Gen 5:1–3.
20. John H. Newman, "Praise to the Holiest in the height" (1865).
21. Luke 1:33.
22. Luke 1:54–55.
23. 1 Chr 9:22.

that lack of solid genealogical evidence rendered returning priests ineligible for service.[24]

- *Typological,* that is if Adam is *only* a mythic representation of "Everyman." In that case any genealogy is as good as any other, and no genealogy at all is more economical and less misleading.

- *Biological,* if one sees Adam as representing some first member of the species, back in the mists of prehistory. Then the genealogies are simply absurd: to skip a few generations (as Matthew does, consciously) may be legitimate, but to represent 60,000 or more years by ten generations or so is simply meaningless, as I have pointed out before.

If, then, the principal purpose of the genealogies is to indicate the transmission of a hereditary role given by God, then literal descent is important for those to whom that role is transferred. The necessity for *universal* human descent from Adam is less pressing in these particular passages, although questions about how both the knowledge of God and the curse of sin spread to mankind leave that a significant matter in its own right, depending on the model being considered. But that is a separate question.

It could be pointed out that pedigree collapse implies that not only Jesus, but the whole of Israel, would probably be descended from David a thousand years after his time, just as all Europeans are proverbially descended from the Emperor Charlemagne. "Pedigree collapse" is the phenomenon noted in the introduction to the book, on which Genealogical Adam depends: the more generations one goes back in a family tree, the more whole populations become descendants of particular ancestors. Yet even so Jesus was, in his own time, acknowledged to claim descent from David is a special way, as indeed (as one second-century writer records) were the grandchildren of Jesus' brother Jude, who were, for a while, viewed with suspicion as possible revolutionaries by the Emperor Domitian.[25]

So the descent of all mankind from Adam is a separate issue, to which scientific genealogical studies certainly contribute insights. But the biblical genealogies, it seems to me, are all about *calling*—a calling

24. Ezra 2:62–63.

25. They were named Zoker and James, and came under imperial suspicion because of their royal lineage, but showed they were only simple farmers, according to Hegesippus, quoted in Eusebius, *History,* 3.19.1–3.20.7; 3.32.5–6.

to hereditary royal rule and priesthood, originally of Adam, leading to repeated failure until the one came to whom it rightly belonged, as recorded prophetically by the author of Genesis:

> The scepter will not depart from Judah, nor the ruler's staff from between his feet, until he to whom it belongs shall come; and the obedience of the nations shall be his.[26]

Genealogy, Adoption, and Culture

The 2017 Nobel Prize for Literature was awarded to Kazuo Ishiguro. The Nobel Press Release said:

> The Nobel Prize in Literature for 2017 is awarded to the English author Kazuo Ishiguro, "who, in novels of great emotional force, has uncovered the abyss beneath our illusory sense of connection with the world."[27]

That description "English author" might surprise some unfamiliar with him, when they see the name, but his "Englishness" was stressed with pleasure by an erudite interviewer on the BBC at the time of the award.

Ishiguro is actually a fellow townsman of mine. He came to England from Japan when he was only six, his father being an oceanographer, and once he overcame the exoticism of the surroundings in which he found himself (the Saxon commuter and market town of Guildford, Surrey), he more or less forgot his origins. His best-known novel, *The Remains of the Day*,[28] is both brilliant, and utterly . . . English. I was a second-generation Guildfordian, and (if my mother's family is to be trusted) have a genealogy going back to the other leader of the Peasants' Revolt, Wat Tyler. But which of us is more English? It is Ishiguro, not I, who has the Nobel Prize for his quintessentially English prose.

The question therefore arises of how much the Bible describes human inheritance in terms of *adoption*, rather than simply physical descent, and how this relates to its understanding of genealogy. After all, even modern genealogy, as ordinary people practice it, very much includes other relationships than natural generation as significant. For

---

26. Gen 49:10.

27. *The Nobel Prize.* https://www.nobelprize.org/prizes/literature/.

28. Ishiguro, *Remains of the Day*.

many adopted people, especially when their adoption was early in life, both emotionally and in terms of their characteristics they often owe more to their adoptive parents than to their birth family, despite stories of separated twins choosing the same hobbies or clothes.

Consider the importance of adoption in the New Testament. The believer's relationship with God is sometimes described in such terms, as we become adopted children of God in Christ.[29] And that gives us, we read, the same privileges and, ultimately, even the same character as the family into which we are "reborn."

It is rather harder to think of direct Old Testament parallels to that, and of course that is the context for thinking about an historical Adam, and inheritance "in the flesh." And yet in the New Testament, Paul retrospectively describes Israel's relationship to God in the very same, adoptive, terms:

> 3 . . . my kinsmen according to the flesh, 4 who are Israelites, to whom belongs the adoption as sons, and the glory and the covenants and the giving of the Law and the temple service and the promises, . . .[30]

It is intriguing that all these terms, in their essential form, may also be applied to Adam. Erin Heim explains that the absence of adoption language in the Old Testament merely reflects the lack of such a cultural convention amongst the Jews. The New Testament writers, then, recognize the theological value of a Greco-Roman practice, in describing what The Old Testament usually speaks of as "sonship" in relation to God:

> Therefore, what we have in the New Testament adoption metaphors is a *recasting* of the Jewish sonship tradition that primarily functions to highlight its *elective quality* [my italics].[31]

There is, as we have seen, a great stress on genealogy in the Old Testament, to the extent that after the return from exile, some were excluded from the Levitical priesthood because they could not prove their bodily descent from Aaron. And yet a little reading between the lines shows that that is not the entire story. When Israel came out of Egypt, a good number of non-Hebrews came out with them, a "mixed multitude,"[32]

29. Rom 8:15; Gal 4:5; Eph 1:5.
30. Rom 9:3–4.
31. Heim, "In Him and Through Him," 133.
32. Exod 12:38.

throwing in their lot with the new would-be nation. And as far as we know, they became part of the covenant community, which would entail their being adopted by one or other of the twelve tribes.[33]

Then, too, it is clear from the Pentateuch as well as from archaeology that the occupation of Canaan was far more a matter of cultural infiltration and intermarriage than it was of military conquest, still less genocide.[34] It should be no surprise, therefore, that we find that the core genetic makeup of Jews nowadays is pretty close to that of the Levantine population as a whole, just as "Anglo-Saxon" England's genetic profile is, in the greater part, that of the founder population after the ice age. We too experienced a conquest that was more cultural than genetic.

Nationality is a very different concept from "race," being so much to do with enculturation rather than simply descent. In God's estimation, adoption—or election—to a tribe or culture appears to be a real aspect of the genealogy that is so important in the Bible. In Matthew's genealogy, Ruth the Moabitess is specifically mentioned as Jesus' ancestor, as is Rahab, the Canaanite innkeeper of Jericho. Adopted Israelites founded the Davidic royal line, from which Jesus came.

Genealogical science shows that Adam would have become, within a couple of millennia or so, a universal common ancestor. But apart from that the Table of Nations indicates Adam's cultural influence on the world, and Genesis 4:26, when "men began to call on the name of the LORD," even specifically mentions his positive religious influence.

The link Erin Heim makes between adoption and election takes us back to the concept of *calling* stressed in the previous section. Even within Adam's line, election was a significant factor in genealogy: Seth's line was chosen over Cain's (and remained elect as the sons of Noah spread out); Abraham's over Lot's; Isaac's over Ishmael's; and Jacob's over Esau's, as Paul discusses in Romans 9. On the one hand:

> 7 [N]or are they all children because they are Abraham's descendants, but: "through Isaac your descendants will be named." 8 That is, it is not the children of the flesh who are children of God, but the children of the promise are regarded as descendants.[35]

33. My erstwhile medical partner, who had been a missionary in Zaire, reported that the locals did not know how to relate to him and his wife until they had gained honorary membership of a tribe.

34. Kitchen, *Reliability*, 168–79.

35. Rom 9: 7–8.

On the other hand:

> 25 As He says also in Hosea,
>
> 25 "I will call those who were not My people, 'My people,'
>
> And her who was not beloved, 'beloved.'"
>
> 26 "And it shall be that in the place where it was said to them, 'you are not My people,'
>
> There they shall be called sons of the living God."[36]

So if we consider that there were human beings, created in the image of God, outside the Garden of Eden, then the contribution of Adam and his descendants to the human race as we now have it may be, in biblical terms, even more extensive than what is supposed by the Genealogical Adam hypothesis, and yet somehow still encompassed by the Bible's concept of genealogy, which includes adoption. By the same token, conventional population genetics might be even more marginal a consideration in that regard than in the matter of Adam as a universal ancestor.

Conclusion Relative to Genealogical Adam

Not long ago a scientist, who is a Christian, suggested to me that genealogy is really of little or no significance to *anything* important, let alone original sin or a metaphysical connection to Adam.

Others have implied that genealogy, in Scripture and doctrine, is an accommodation to primitive thought that is no longer relevant, because we have now science showing the complex genetic relationships of human groups. Outside the hobby of family history, the view is quite general now that genealogy is about nothing real, but just accidents of birth.

And yet genealogy was never considered anything but self-evidently crucial by the Bible writers and by two millennia of earlier theologians. As I have discussed, genealogy forms the core of the biblical narrative, from Adam's genealogy in Genesis to Christ "the root and offspring of David" in Revelation 22, and much is lost if it is ignored.

If, in some way, what differentiates fallen Adam from anyone who may have existed before were some new substantial nature conferred in the garden (and we are so ignorant of the laws of form that it is hard to make sense even of that under current patterns of thought), and if original sin were a fundamental corruption of that form, then the transmission of

36. Rom 9:25–26.

sin in the human race might still be by natural generation. Like royalty or family estates, form is entirely heritable, and genealogical, but not necessarily or entirely genetic.

Nevertheless, the complex use of genealogy in the Bible discourages us from placing all the significance of Adam on even genealogical biology, just as genealogical science shows us that genetics gives too limited an understanding of humanity. If Genealogical Adam becomes embedded in the way we think of Bible origins, then there is still much work to be done on the *theology* of genealogy.

§4: Generations of Glory

(New Creation)

". . . but indeed, as I live, all the earth will be filled with the glory of the Lord."

NUM 14:21.

12.

ORIGINAL SIN

Preserving the Family Inheritance

IN THE CHAPTERS OF this section I reach the core of my argument, which is that Genealogical Adam theory fits into, and even refines, a biblical theology metanarrative of the whole Bible, thus making a significant contribution to our understanding of God's purposes in the world. I commence by discussing the question of inherited sin.

One of the strengths of Genealogical Adam theory is that it allows the traditional set of teachings known as "original sin" (in the West) or "ancestral sin" (in the East)—that is, the inheritance by the whole human race of ill effects from the sin of our first father, Adam—to be held together with the findings of science.

One objection that has frequently been made is that there is no need to maintain such a doctrine in the first place, making a literal Adam, and our descent from him, irrelevant. Whether or not that is the case, some form of baleful inheritance from Adam, whether in the form of shared guilt in his sin, liability to death (which, in Genesis 3, was the penalty for Adam's sin anyway), or corruption of nature has from early times been a mainstream doctrine of the major branches of Christianity East and West.

It cannot be required of a theory that simply confirms that we are all descended from Adam that it either defends or explains the doctrine of original sin. But it can be worthwhile to show that the issue is not irrelevant, and perhaps even to speculate, in the kind of world to which Genealogical Adam points, how the doctrine might be understood and refined.

The name that comes up most often in the discussion of original sin is Augustine. For many, the whole question may be dismissed by pinning it on that one man, and then dismissing him as a theological aberration. But as a recent article on Augustine's writings on original sin[1] shows, Augustine did not invent the idea, though he developed it significantly in various directions. The article also suggests that there is very little real depth of knowledge of his true views amongst many of those who criticize him.

In fact, Augustine started his argument from a long-established church practice, the baptism of infants:

> The practice was not especially controversial, because a general consensus held that infants who died without receiving baptism were unable to enter the kingdom of heaven (*C.Jul.* III.12.25)— although Christians disagreed about the precise nature of infants' final destination. Augustine's rationale for this practice is straightforward: God would not keep little ones from heaven unless they were sinners and merited such treatment. Infants need exorcism and baptism because they need the medicine of Christ, who saves people from sin (*Gr.et pecc.or.* 2.24.28; *C.Jul. imp.* I.50). Moreover, Augustine notes, the creed straightforwardly states that baptism is for the forgiveness of sins.[2]

Further evidence of this long-standing belief comes from the local Council of Carthage of 251, comprising sixty-six bishops, which as Cyprian writes, concluded that an infant should not be denied baptism,

> . . . who, being lately born, has not sinned, except in that, being born after the flesh according to Adam, he has contracted the contagion of the ancient death at its earliest birth, who approaches the more easily on this very account to the reception of the forgiveness of sins—that to him are remitted, not his own sins, but the sins of another.[3]

Moreover, Augustine pointed out that for God to allow (as he clearly does) infants to suffer deformities, disease, mistreatment, and death

1. Couenhoven, "St Augustine's Doctrine."
2. Ibid., 361.
3. Cyprian, "Epistle to Fidus," 198.

would be unjust if they were not subject to sin in some way, since death was given as a penalty for sin. In his thinking Augustine acknowledged his debt to Cyprian, Ambrose, and Hilary, and from the start of the controversy with Pelagius he was supported by notable orthodox contemporaries like Jerome.[4] So he was by no means clambering out on a new limb.

As far back as the second century Irenaeus had argued against the Gnostics that Adam was redeemed, basing his argument *on the assumption*, presumably already extant and normal in the church, that death, and possibly corruption, had come to the race through Adam's sin. He writes of Adam's descendants as "begotten in captivity,"[5] and goes on to expand:

> If a hostile force has overcome certain [enemies], has bound them, and led them away captive, so that they begat children among them; and somebody, compassionating those who had been made slaves, should overcome this same hostile force; he certainly would not act equitably, were he to liberate the children of those who had been led captive, from the sway of those who had enslaved their fathers, but should leave these latter . . . the children succeeding to liberty through the avenging of their father's cause, but not so that their fathers, who suffered the act of capture itself, should be left [in bondage]. For God is neither devoid of power nor of justice, who has afforded help to man and restored him to His own liberty.[6]

What kind of bondage does Irenaeus have in mind? A majority of the Eastern church has taken it to mean "liability to death," rather than sin or guilt. But apart from the fact that a punishment inflicted by God on the children, as Augustine argued, must surely imply some guilt in order to be just, Irenaeus goes on to discuss the curse on the ground. This I have argued elsewhere to be of limited duration,[7] though still lasting ten generations until after the flood, but by Irenaeus it is (more conventionally) applied to all men *as a punishment*, implying hereditary guilt:

> But man received, as the punishment of his transgression, the toilsome task of tilling the earth, and to eat bread in the sweat of his face, and to return to the dust from which he was taken.[8]

4. Ibid., 389.

5. Irenaeus, "Against Heresies," III.XXIII.2, 363.

6. Ibid., 363–64.

7. Garvey, *God's Good Earth*, 25–30.

8. Irenaeus, "Against Heresies," 364.

It is, of course, the guilty who are punished. I will turn to Paul's teaching, especially in Romans 5, later, but it has often been noted how little teaching on Adam, and particularly on Adam as the author of sin, there is in the Old Testament. In fact the earliest clear sources for original sin in Judaism date from after the destruction of the second temple in 70 CE, apparently independently of Paul's writing, in the form of 4 Ezra (or 2 Esdras) and 2 Baruch.[9] Both include the idea that death and sin originate in Adam. And so in 2 Baruch:

> Therefore the multitude of time that [Adam] lived did not profit him, but brought death and cut off the years of those who were born from him. Wherein did Moses suffer loss in that he lived only one hundred and twenty years . . .

> And I answered and said: "He that lighted has taken from the light, and there are but few that have imitated him. But those many whom he has lighted have taken from the darkness of Adam and have not rejoiced in the light of the lamp."[10]

And in 2 Esdras, death is also mentioned first:

> "You gave [Adam] one commandment to obey he disobeyed it, and thereupon you made him subject to death, him and his descendants."[11]

But then Ezra speaks of corruption of heart:

> "But you did not take away their wicked heart and enable your law to bear fruit in them. For the first man, Adam, was burdened with a wicked heart; he sinned and was overcome, and not only he but all his descendants. So the weakness became inveterate. Although your law was in your people's hearts, a rooted wickedness was there too; so that the good came to nothing, and what was bad persisted."[12]

An angel later replies in confirmation of Ezra's understanding:

---

9. N. T. Wright, in Walton, *Lost World of Adam and Eve,* 171–72.

10. 2 Bar 17–18, *Wesley Center Online.*

11. 2 Esd 3:7, *New English Bible.*

12. Ibid., 3:20–22.

> "A grain of the evil seed was sown in the heart of Adam from the first; how much more godlessness has it produced already! How much more will it produce before the harvest!"[13]

In fact, even the word *fall* occurs in this book, as Ezra bewails the extent and finality of the coming judgement:

> "O Adam, what have you done? Your sin was not your fall alone; it was ours also, the fall of all your descendants."[14]

It may be no accident that both these apocalypses, composed in the aftermath of the destruction of Jerusalem, are set after its first destruction, by Babylon in 587 BCE. N. T. Wright has pointed out how no Jew at the time of that exile could possibly have read the Eden account without identifying with it:

> [C]ertainly the Jews of the Second Temple period would have no difficulty in decoding the story of Adam as an earlier version of their own story: placed in the garden; given a commission to look after it; being the place where God wanted to be at rest, to exercise his sovereign rule; warned about keeping the commandment; warned in pazrticular that breaking it would mean death; breaking it and being exiled. It all sounds very, very familiar.[15]

This leads me to conjecture that, despite our lack of any literary sources for it, Paul, 4 Ezra, and 2 Baruch may have been tapping into some strand of existing tradition on the fall within the Jewish consciousness.[16] Be that as it may, all three sources suggest something more than simply similarity to Adam in universal sin and death—it is something to do with inheritance by his offspring.

Augustine's scattered teaching actually contains several propositions,[17] but the most difficult for our worldview, perhaps, is the

---

13. Ibid., 4:30.

14. Ibid., 7:48.

15. Wright in Walton, *Lost World of Adam and Eve*, 177.

16. Modern Judaism is said to deny original sin, yet Seth Postell reports that the modern Israeli Jewish scholar Tvi Erlich regards the Sinai theophany and the tabernacle as intended to be the solution to Adam's sin. See Postell, *Adam as Israel*, 34.

17. "In brief, the five elements of the doctrine of original sin are as follows: (1) the source of original sin is a primal sin in the Garden of Eden. (2) All human beings share in this sin because of our solidarity with Adam, the progenitor of the race. The results of the primal sin are twofold. (3) From birth, all human beings have an inherited sin

concept of our solidarity with Adam. This is more than the "federal head-ship" concept of the sixteenth century Reformers like John Calvin:

> In Augustine's view, solidarity with Adam is more than a legal matter of a covenant between God and the human race, in which Adam, as our representative, has the power to ratify or break the treaty for all of us. Solidarity with Adam, for Augustine, is both social and ontological. As Augustine says,

> We were all in that one man, seeing that we all were that one man who fell into sin. . . . We did not yet possess forms individu-ally created and assigned to us for us to live in them as individu-als; but there already existed the seminal nature from which we were to be begotten. . . . when this was vitiated through sin . . . man could not be born of man in any other condition (*Civ.Dei* XIII.14).[18]

We find this idea of "solidarity" rather difficult. But Couenhoven records that it was difficult for Augustine as well, which is why he never attempted to spell it out fully:

> Some sort of invisible and intangible power is located in the secrets of nature where the natural laws of propagation are con-cealed, and on account of this power as many as were going to be able to be begotten from that one man by the succession of generations are certainly not untruthfully said to have been in the loins of the father. They were there . . . though unknowingly and unwillingly, because they did not yet exist as persons who could have known and willed this (*C.Jul.imp.* VI.22).[19]

In fact,

> he tells his opponent Julian, "if you cannot understand this, be-lieve it" (*C.Jul.imp.* IV.104; cf. Mendelson 1998).[20]

(original sin itself), which comes in two forms: common guilt, and a constitutional fault of disordered desire and ignorance. (4) In addition, Augustine holds that the hu-man race suffers a penalty because of sin—human powers are weakened, and we will experience death. (5) Finally, Augustine speculates about how both sin and penalty are transmitted from generation to generation." Couenhoven, "St Augustine's Doctrine," 363.

18. Ibid., 367.

19. Ibid., 368.

20. Ibid.

Why, then, does Augustine insist on the idea? Simply because he finds it stated unequivocally in the analogy Paul draws between our being "in Adam" and subsequently "in Christ."[21] Augustine characteristically placed the authority of Scripture above his own understanding of it. A similar concept exists in Hebrews 7:9–10 (which in Augustine's day was thought to be written by Paul). Here Levi is said to have been, in some sense, present "in the loins" of Abraham when he paid tithes to Melchizedek, thus acknowledging his superiority.

Later Reformers like Calvin, with his humanist training, were even less comfortable with Paul's language of participation, preferring a forensic model for our solidarity with Adam. But it is the way that Paul frames the whole argument of Romans 5, and to some extent that of 1 Corinthians 15, that continues to persuade scholars and laypeople alike that the link to Adam by genealogy is a vital component of the human problems of sin and death.

I discuss this matter of participation briefly in the section *Three meanings of adam* in chapter 7. I will close the present section with a quotation from Owen Barfield, whom I referenced there. Very briefly, his thesis is that a primitive sense of participation was gradually lost, not least through the Hebrew monotheism that radically separated God from his creation, but that in the gospel a new, purified, sense of participation must be, and is, regained, for the Triune God participates in humanity through the incarnation, and we in turn participate in God through Christ. So toward the close of his book, following a section on the Enlightenment's near-total loss of the sense of participation, from which we all still suffer, Barfield writes:

> For instance, a non-participating consciousness cannot avoid distinguishing abruptly between the concept of "man," or "mankind," or "men in general" on the one hand and that of "*a* man"—an individual human spirit—on the other. This difficulty did not arise to anything like the same extent as long as original participation survived. Therefore our predecessors were able, quite inwardly, to accept the sin of Adam as being *their* original sin also. And therefore we are not—because, for us, Adam (if he existed) was after all—somebody else! This has brought with it the loss of the whole concept of the "fallen" as an essential element in the make-up of human beings; which in its turn is

21. Rom 5:12–21; 1 Cor 15:20–22.

responsible for the devastating shallowness of so much contemporary ethics and contemporary psychology.[22]

Thus we see that what was a natural mode of thought for Paul or the writer to the Hebrews was a mystery to be accepted by faith to Augustine in the fourth century, and an irrational nonsense to some of his contemporaries and their modern followers. Augustine at least had the humility to subordinate his knowledge of how the world works to the authority of Scripture.

Given, though, that of themselves the facts of our aboriginal participation in Adam, through genealogy, and our latter-day participation in Christ, by new birth and adoption, are at least mutually analogous, perhaps we should regard the concept of such participation or solidarity as a feature of the new creation, whose story begins with Adam, rather than as the residuum of a primitive mind-set, as I discuss from this chapter onwards.

Is Another Will Hidden Somewhere?

As I mentioned above, the teaching of Irenaeus was pitched against that of the Gnostics, who, as systematic theologian Louis Berkhof records, regarded evil as inherent in matter, and as such, a product of a Demiurge. Of this belief Berkhof points out that,

> [t]his theory naturally robbed sin of its voluntary and ethical character. [23]

In effect it renders our creation, and therefore ultimately God, the origin of our sin, and that is why, at least in the West, the view of Irenaeus prevailed. However, in the third and fourth centuries the Eastern Church tended to discount the inheritance of sin, and this culminated in Pelagianism, which denied any connection between Adam's sin and ours.[24]

To Pelagius, our wills are radically free and sin is entirely voluntary, being primarily the result of the imitation of the example of others. Although part of his motivation was to remove the sense that Adam's sin was punished in those not to blame (Pelagius, unlike Augustine, evidently could not live with a concept of solidarity or participation), amongst

22. Barfield, *Saving the Appearances*, 183–84.

23. Berkhof, *Systematic Theology*, 219.

24. Ibid.

other problems it leads to another issue of theodicy. Since sin is, in fact, found to be universal, the freedom of our wills turns out to as prone to moral failure as the inherent evil of matter in Gnosticism. Once again the fault lies in God's creation of our nature, which leads to an individual fall in every case. As in Gnosticism our sin seems to arise from our lower nature under Pelagianism, needing therefore to be constrained by the higher, spiritual nature with its free will.

In our own times, attempts have been made to rehabilitate Pelagius, even though his teaching was condemned by two ecumenical councils, at Carthage in the West in 418, and at Ephesus in the East in 431. But the commonest position now amongst those who reject a hereditary aspect to sin, and who therefore see no need for a historical Adam, is to attribute sin to evolution, usually through the idea of evolution's "selfishness" being the very means through which humankind came into existence, so that such selfishness is inevitable, or at least in practice unconquerable by any higher aspect of our nature.

This actually relies on a false view of science, for there is nothing intrinsically (or even extrinsically) selfish about evolution, even in its classical Darwinian forms, as I discussed in my previous book.[25] But it is a theology almost as old as the theory of evolution itself. Berkhof cites Frederick Tennant's Hulsean lectures of 1901–2, delivered in Cambridge. Animals are incapable of sin, Tennant reasoned, but their behaviors are determined by the selfish "survival of the fittest" in evolution.

> This means that the impulses, propensities, desires, and qualities which man inherited from the brute cannot themselves be called sin. In his estimation these constitute only the *material* of sin, and do not become actual sins until the moral consciousness awakens in man, and they are left in control in determining the actions of man, contrary to the voice of conscience, and to ethical sanctions.[26]

Such a theory seems to differ from Pelagianism only in that humanity begins its moral activity already weighed down by several billion years of ingrained behaviors for its indeterminate free will to overcome. The will does not, in his model, simply imitate nature—it has to rise above it. This view has the additional disadvantage of the lack of any mechanism to explain how humanity gained an unconstrained free will through

25. Garvey, *God's Good Earth*, 131–37.
26. Berkhof, *Systematic Theology*, 225.

"selfish" evolution. And if, in some variants, the will is given directly by God rather than through nature, its impotence against the lower nature is shown by the universality of sin, and once again God must be account-able for the weakness not only of his original mode of creation, but of his special endowments for humanity.

"Free process creation" claims to get around this by conceiving evo-lution, or nature, to be a quasi-personified entity granted "autonomy" by God. "Freedom," seen as autonomy, is said to be a necessary condi-tion of God's self-giving love, and hence the resulting evils in evolution (and consequently humanity) are not his own responsibility. The flaws in this are multiple: neither nature nor evolution is, in fact, a volitional be-ing, except in pan-psychic process theology, so they can possess neither freedom, nor sin. Since God created the process through which the very possibility of life has arisen, then it is squarely his responsibility if the creative process necessarily involves evil and selfishness.

In any case, if nature or evolution *did* possess such a free will capable of erring, why cavil at the possession of such a facility in a real primordial human, Adam, who undoubtedly was a moral being, rather than in a primordial physical process, which undoubtedly is not?

In the Augustinian scheme, in contrast, the one sin of Adam is seen as a monstrous aberration, a *negation* of nature, which whilst mysterious as to cause other than the cunning of Satan, is a contingent event in actual history, rather than an essential feature of nature.

If the history I have begun to lay out in this book is correct, though, sin is not a feature of mankind's animal nature, a primitive hangover which the higher nature of mankind seeks to overcome, albeit unsuc-cessfully. If Adam and Eve were those chosen to be the fountainhead of the new creation from an existing human race (and a spiritually innocent one at that, as discussed in chapter 9), then sin is a product of the *higher* nature of humanity—it is truly a fall from a position of high privilege.

What does Genesis imply about this? The first sin was committed by a couple dwelling in direct communion with Yahweh, in a kind of covenant relationship with him, which was endowed with sage-like wis-dom for Adam to name the creatures, and which had access to the tree of eternal life. It is at least implicit that the role to which they were called would leave even the angels subject to them. They were, in fact, adopted as children (sons) of God.[27]

27. Luke 3:38.

According to Augustine's reasoning, the root of their sin was spiritual pride, but even if that particular interpretation is contested, it was a disobedient desire to equal God in wisdom on their own terms. The heinousness of sin, as has been recognized throughout church history, is that it is the corruption of the *higher* nature of humanity.

In 1954 Martin Luther King Jr. preached a sermon based on Psalm 8, "What is Man?"[28] This makes the same point about the source of sin in humanity well. In his interpretation of the psalm, humankind becomes the center of creation through participation in Christ. Although King says nothing about the origin of humanity either in its biblical description or evolutionary science, he nevertheless has something to contribute in that context.

In first addressing the importance of seeing humankind's physical animality, he does not in any way treat that as a problem, but instead stresses the need for the due recognition of meeting our physical needs. This perhaps addresses his time more than ours, for then much Evangelical Christianity had somehow become persuaded that the gospel is only about the salvation of the soul (seen as spiritual), and that the body is something to be despised or even escaped after death. Dr. King's dichotomizing of man may, perhaps, tend to draw attention away from our created unity, but actually he assumes that unity in his critique of pietistic neglect of the body and of human society and politics.

In transitioning after that to the spiritual aspect of humanity, in which, he says, lies man's greatness, he briefly mentions the old adage that the chemical constituents of a human are worth less than $1. This was always a little misleading (carbon or sulphur may be cheap, but in 1954 a single bottle of insulin would have cost over double that—now it costs in the hundreds, which is presumably considered progress by somebody). Yet his point is completely valid for all those nowadays who dismiss humankind in materialistic terms as "a fortuitous cosmic afterthought"[29] because "biology took away our status as paragons created in the image of God."[30] King responds to such thinking:

> Can we explain the literary genius of a Shakespeare in terms of 99 cents? Can we explain the artistic genius of a Michelangelo in terms of 99 cents? Can we explain the musical genius of a

28. King, *What is Man?*
29. Gould, *Dinosaur in a Haystack*, 327.
30. Gould, *Ever Since Darwin*, 267.

Beethoven in terms of 99 cents? Can we explain the spiritual genius of Jesus of Nazareth in terms of 99 cents? Can we explain the ongoing processes of our own ordinary lives in terms of 99 cents? My friends, there is something in man that cannot be calculated in materialistic terms.[31]

This underlines his point that the greatness of humanity—and to King that includes both its capacity for goodness and its capacity for evil—arise from that spiritual (and therefore, we may deduce, non-biological) aspect of humankind. That, at least in principle, potentially separates the biological origins of humanity from its exceptionalism, subject to what Scripture teaches on specifics.

Although King does not refer to Genesis directly, he does attribute this greatness in humanity to the image of God, which is of course a Genesis 1 concept. One interesting insight is that he describes that image not in terms of any "reflection" of God in the makeup of humankind, so much as in its appointment and capacity for relationship with God. Now in truth there must be some overlap there, in that something in humankind (such as rationality, will, and so on) must correspond to analogous capacities in God if there is to *be* any relationship. The actual biblical phrase is, after all, "image and *likeness*." But the emphasis on God's appointment of humankind to its relational role is sound.

By locating humanity's capacity for greatness in the spiritual aspect of its nature, King thereby clearly shows sin to be a product of the supernatural will, rather than the natural animal instincts:

Animals follow their natures. But man has the power of acting upon his own nature almost as if from without, of guiding it within certain limits, and of modifying it by the choice of meaningful ends. Man can be true or false to his nature. He can be a hero or a fool. Both possibilities, the noble and the base alike, indicate man's greatness.[32]

Two implications follow from this in connection with, and in contrast to, many evolutionary understandings of humanity. The first is that since it is humankind's unique greatness to be, like God, possessed of a rational will, this is what alone permits the possibility of evil. In that case the common idea in theistic evolution of inanimate nature being "free" from God's despotic control, so that evolutionary outcomes might fall

31. King, *What is Man?*
32. Ibid.

outside God's will and even be positively evil, must be mistaken. Augustine rightly recognized that evils must arise from wills, not natures, to be evil.

Secondly, it also follows that (as King clearly shows) human sin cannot be regarded as a product of the "selfish" biology of evolution, as so many evolutionary theologies have claimed since the nineteenth century. It is not the created animal part of our natures that is "red in tooth and claw" and needs quelling by God-given reason. Rather, as Genesis teaches, it is our higher, rational nature that is the source of sin, and hence of not only physical death (in a creature intended for eternity) but spiritual death, the breach of relationship with God. So sin is, as has always been taught, a fall from innocence to be corrected, not a primordial shortcoming to be improved:

> Whenever a man looks deep down into the depths of his nature
> he becomes painfully aware of the fact that the history of his life
> is the history of a constant revolt against God "All we like sheep
> have gone astray." Every nation, every class and every man is a
> part of the gone-wrongness of human nature. Of all the silly,
> sentimental teachings which have ever characterized any gen-
> eration the denial of human sin is one of the worst.[33]

Perhaps you will regard Martin Luther King's teaching on humanity as bread-and-butter fare, theologically speaking. If so that is actually to the good. His diagnosis of humankind's condition is what the Bible teaches, and what the gospel of Christ has always addressed. Inasmuch as that diagnosis is tragic (whether that is judged in the pastoral and personal terms King uses in the sermon, or in the light of world events like the battle for civil rights of the sixties or the culture wars now), understanding how humanity is created causes us, like King, to say, "Man is not made for that."

I suppose it was partly this understanding of human greatness— the greatness we owe to our creation by God himself, however it came about—that made Martin Luther King such a powerful force for good, and which generated the reaction of hatred that led to his murder. I leave the last word in this section to him:

> "What is man that thou art mindful of him, and the son of man,
> that thou visitest him? For thou hast crowned him with glory
> and honour. Thou madest him to have dominion over the works

33. Ibid.

of thy hands, thou hast put all things under his feet. All sheep and oxen, yea and the beasts of the field, the fowl of the air, and the fish of sea, and whatsoever passeth through the paths of the sea." This is man's kingly prerogative. Who this afternoon will rise out of the dark and dreary valleys of sin and evil, realizing that man's proper home is in the high mountain of truth, beauty and goodness, yea even where God the eternal dwells forever?

Conclusion Relative to Genealogical Adam

Genealogical Adam places the concept of original sin, as historically conceived in the early and Western church, back on the table. There is no real doubt that the key teaching on original sin, that of Paul in Romans 5 and 1 Corinthians 15, regards human descent from Adam as the root of our need for Christ, as the remedy for sin and death.

Because genetic science may no longer be marshalled to claim ancestral sin is impossible, we have to grapple again with concepts like "participation" and "solidarity," which given this language is used of our union with Christ, we should never have conceded to Enlightenment metaphysics as we have.

Since Genealogical Adam also recognizes the creation of Adam and Eve as a distinct phase of human history, rather than a restatement of the creation of humankind at the dawn of existence, human sin therefore becomes a truly historical event. Adam's high calling strongly suggests, as Martin Luther King's theology affirms, that sin comes from the higher part of our nature, through the election of Adam by God. It is, like the failure of Israel, a breach of a specific covenant, rather than a fault of created nature.

13.

THE TRANSMISSION OF SIN

Is Inherited Sin Really Implausible?

IT IS ALL BUT impossible now to accept Augustine's always speculative mechanism for the transmission of the sin-nature (as opposed to guilt for Adam's first sin). He worked from the plausible classical belief that one's situation at the time of conceiving a child might well affect the nature of the conception, and from the conclusion that sin was a defect in the higher, rational nature. Since experience shows that the sexual act is now, at one stage or another, no longer under the control of the rational faculties but of "concupiscence" (lust), it was reasonable for him to suggest that this concupiscence became transferred to the life so created, just as other situational elements were widely believed to be, only more universally.

Nowadays we might call such factors "epigenetic," but what we know of epigenetics does not allow such an immediate, or universal, effect. Augustine seems to have been wrong in this suggestion—but we should remember that it *was* only a suggestion, and that Augustine was rare amongst classical writers in publishing retractions of all the ideas in his writings that had been shown to be wrong.

Ignorance of Augustine's actual ideas has led to a shorthand that he taught the genetic transmission of sin, which is impossible because neither genes nor genetics were known to him. In *The Genealogical Adam and Eve* Joshua Swamidass is at pains to explain how unreliable genetic transmission is. Most of our ancestors, even a relatively few generations ago, are "genetic ghosts," in that we carry not a single one of their genes. Hence no "sin gene" could plausibly come to affect the whole species.[1]

This contrasts, Swamidass explains, with genealogical ancestry, which is utterly reliable. We can know for certain that we have two biological parents, four at the second generation, 1,028 at the tenth, and so on, even if we know nothing of their genetic makeup. Furthermore, genealogical population genetics can make us quite certain that the whole race has universal common ancestors beyond calculable points in history, of which an Adam at any realistic time in history is more than likely to be one.

However, these facts tell us nothing about *how* we might inherit the sin of Adam. Biologically, it currently seems impossible, on genetic grounds. But that may not be the whole story, for up until the last decade or so, when the science behind Genealogical Adam was published, genetics seemed to preclude the existence of Adam and Eve, too. The reason for this was that it was asking the wrong questions, and drawing conclusions based on false premises that it took as the final word, namely that genetics tells the whole story of inheritance.

I wish briefly to suggest here—even more tentatively than Augustine suggested in his theory of the transmission of sin—that science may be moving towards an understanding of inheritance of form, and of embryological development and evolution, that are not entirely genetic.

A number of well-credentialed, if not mainstream, biologists, have presented an increasing weight of evidence that organisms are not passive recipients of a "genetic blueprint," but have some global capacity to direct their own development, and even their own evolution, to some extent.

For example, molecular biologist James Shapiro[2] has described the genome as a "read-write storage system," used and adapted by organisms for what he terms "natural genetic engineering," rather than determining them.

In a completely different field Michael Levin, interested in the possibilities of organ regeneration, suggests in a review article of his discipline that there is evidence that cells do not "execute genetic programs" in embryological development, so much as guide development according to

1. Swamidass, *Genealogical Adam and Eve,* 51–54, 84–85.
2. Shapiro, *Evolution.*

some "map" of the intended end-state.[3] This might mean, for example, that it not always genetic mutations that lead to cancer, but failures in the mechanisms of preserving the "normal form" that cause such mutations secondarily.

Oxford physiologist Denis Noble has been propounding physiological mechanisms as a major component of evolution for a number of years.[4] Noble is much cited in a recent press article on the current state of "the gene" by Ken Richardson, who writes about the increasing realization that living things work by interactions between all their components:

> . . . it was slowly appreciated that we inherit just such dynamical systems from our parents, not only our genes. Eggs and sperm contain a vast variety of factors: enzymes and other proteins; amino acids; vitamins, minerals; fats; RNAs (nucleic acids other than DNA); hundreds of cell signalling factors; and other products of the parents' genes, other than genes themselves.
>
> Molecular biologists have been describing how those factors form networks of complex interactions. Together, they self-organize according to changing conditions around them. Being sensitive to statistical patterns in the changes, they anticipate future states, often creating novel, emergent properties to meet them.
>
> Accordingly, even single cells change their metabolic pathways, and the way they use their genes to suit those patterns. That is, they "learn," and create instructions on the hoof. Genes are used as templates for making vital resources, of course. But directions and outcomes of the system are not controlled by genes. Like colonies of ants or bees, there are deeper dynamical laws at work in the development of forms and variations.[5]

Disrupt the usual pathways, and somehow organisms will do their best to reach the same goal by whatever means they can devise. This is astonishingly different from the genetic determinism we have grown used to assuming. In a gene-centred age, it is easy to forget that we do not simply inherit genes that build our bodies: we inherit a body, in the form of a fertilized egg-cell, part of a continuous chain of protoplasm and all the

---

3. Levin, "Morphogenetic fields in embryogenesis, regeneration, and cancer."
4. Noble, *Music of Life.*
5. Richardson, "End of the Gene."

other cellular constituents that stretches back into the distant past at least to the first human being, but logically, in an evolutionary framework, to our earliest ancestors.

This book takes the particular form it does partly because of the contents of my library and my online sources, which make up the bibliography. But given all the comparable literature that there is out there, which I do not have available, I might have written much the same book had I worked in the Cambridge University Library instead of at home, using different sources. That is because my library did not determine my thought, but rather my thought process determined which books I would consult, subject to availability. What if our genome, thought by Watson and Crick to be "the secret of life," should turn out instead to be the partly arbitrary library that some as yet undefined "we" use to help us build our bodies?

These new ideas are not yet sufficiently explored, still less universally accepted, to enable us to draw any real conclusions about how they might inform Genealogical Adam, and particularly the question of original sin. But they raise sufficient questions to allow the possibility that, as in the case of genealogical science, the limitations of current knowledge might lead to conclusions based on false premises. Perhaps there are more scientific truths to be uncovered from genealogy. Time will tell if this is so, but meanwhile there are also other ways of thinking about the transmission of sin from Adam.

Tentative Thoughts on Culture and Sin

In the last chapter, I looked at the way that biblical genealogy is more complex than mere descent, since biblically it also encompasses adoption into God's people. As well as the more personal examples like Ruth the Moabitess, I pointed to the biblical and archaeological evidence for the absorption of Canaanites into Israel, and suggested that the Table of Nations implies cultural infiltration rather than the occupation of virgin territories.

The discussion so far in this chapter has been vague on how sin, and particularly the corrupted nature rather than imputed guilt, might be transmitted down Adam's line. Augustine's attempt at an explanation, through the concupiscence of the act of procreation, finds little support nowadays, and the new ideas in biology are tentative and highly contested.

Can we nevertheless make headway on understanding how the propensity for sin might spread universally from a historical individual among others, "in accordance with the Scriptures"? I believe we can, tentatively. It helps guide our thinking if we don't start from the surprisingly common assumption that "everyone knows what sin is," apart from the Bible's teaching. We must instead define sin as Genesis defines it, and as Paul refines it. In Genesis 3, sin was rebellion against a command of God, and not selfishness, disobedience to a moral law, and so on.

If Adam was the first man to be called into covenant relationship with God, then the breaking of that covenant-trust by eating the fruit of the tree of the knowledge of good and evil (probably an idiom for "the tree of wisdom"[6]) accounts for sin coming into the world. Adam, then, became corrupted from his true (but incomplete) knowledge of God, by his own illicit version of wisdom seized through that knowledge. He could not go back either to ignorance of God, or to his previous naïvety, and he could no longer go forward into learning God's wisdom, as no doubt God had planned in the first place.

That such a thing would become a canker in his soul leading to all the other perversions of sin is easily comprehended.[7] Adam's case then is closely parallel (and intentionally so, within the structure of *Torah*) to the chosen nation of Israel whose breaking of their covenant loyalty led them to become, according to the prophets, worse than the pagan nations around them and therefore exiled.[8] Rebels who have known God can be worse than those who never knew him, like the parable of Jesus about the cast-out devil who comes back with his friends, so that "the last state of that man is worse than the first."[9]

But that does not, in itself, account for Adam's sin becoming the universal problem of mankind. Paul in Romans 1 comments on the Genesis progression: from disregard of the known God, through idolatry, to sin in ever more perverse forms. But he makes no comment on just *how* it spread from Adam and Eve themselves, except to say in Romans 5 that

6. Walton, *Genesis*, 170–72.

7. Rom 1:18–32.

8. 2 Kgs 21:9–13.

9. Matt 12:45.

consequently "death spread to all men, for all sinned."[10] This could be, and has been, interpreted in many ways.

Nowadays the general idea of the inheritance of a corrupted nature tends to be understood according to Neo-Darwinian scientific ideas as necessarily "genetic"—and it is therefore rejected as impossible on the grounds of population genetics, for genetic inheritance is never reliable, quite apart from the bizarre corollary that gene therapy could be an answer to sin apart from the work of Christ. But we saw in the last section that this is, perhaps, too limited a view of inheritance.

Genealogical Adam suggests Adam to be a common ancestor of the whole present race, even if he appeared as one man amongst many in third- or fourth-millennium Mesopotamia, as Genesis implies when interpreted in an historical manner. This negates the genetic problem, but does not in itself offer a theory for the transmission of sin. Yet even in biology, descent is not only genetic—our protoplasm, too, is inherited from our parents. But let us leave aside this inheritance aspect for now, and consider only what it tells us about the *cultural* connections of the human race.

Culture is, and always has been, worldwide. Take the example of the bow and arrow, quoting Wikipedia:

> The bow and arrow appears around the transition from the Upper Paleolithic to the Mesolithic. After the end of the last glacial period, use of the bow seems to have spread to every continent, including the New World, except for Australia.[11]

It appears, from other anthropological research, that bows were not adopted in Australia for purely local reasons concerning size of prey animals and the like, and not because of lack of contact. Aborigines simply preferred the spear and spear-thrower, and the throwing stick.

In Africa the earliest evidence for archery dates to 71,000 years ago. The earliest extant bow is from Denmark, and is dated to c 9,000 BCE, just a millennium after the Mesolithic began there, but evidence exists that by then the technology had already reached Japan and the Americas. Obviously other examples could be given of the worldwide spread of good ideas, but the bow demonstrates that even before my default

---

10. Rom 5:12.

11. "Bow and Arrow," *Wikipedia*. https://en.wikipedia.org/wiki/Bow_and_arrow #History.

putative chronological setting for Adam (4004 BCE!) culture could and did encompass the world.

Amongst the early Christian writers, only the heretical Pelagius denied original sin and saw people as blank slates, born as innocent as Adam, and therefore entirely individually responsible for being sinful or righteous. Evolution has made Pelagianism seem a viable option again to many, against the mainstream of historical theology, though as I have discussed above it has often been turned on its head to make *sin*, rather than innocence, the original state.

Pelagius believed that sin spread merely through imitation, and since his clear implication was that it could be overcome (in theory) simply by a refusal to imitate, his views were decisively rejected as inadequate to account for the universally entrenched and intractable nature of sin. When the Council of Trent used the phrase "by propagation, not by imitation"[12] it was only quoting from Augustine's detailed rebuttals of Pelagius:

> Since, however, these are actually the words of the apostle, to whose authority and doctrine they submit, they charge us with slowness of understanding, while they endeavor to wrest to some unintelligible sense words which were written in a clear and obvious purport. "By one man," says he, "sin entered into the world, and death by sin." This indicates propagation, not imitation; for if imitation were meant, he would mention the devil as the object of the imitation. But, as no one doubts, [the apostle] refers to that first man who is called Adam: "And so," says he, "death passed upon all men."[13]

But both Pelagius's trivialization of sin as mere imitation (and of grace as, for example, God's provision of the Law to give a better model to imitate), and its rejection by the orthodox, depend on a rather individual concept of a human being. To Pelagius the individual is born, matures to the age of being able to choose, and then makes his choice for good or evil. To Augustine and most well-taught Christians before and since, man is born corrupt by inherited nature, and so is bound to choose the way of sin unless grace prevails.

But a greater understanding of man's fundamentally social nature (perhaps reverting somewhat accidentally to a more biblical world

---

12. Trent, Fifth Session, 3.

13. Augustine, *On the Merits*, I.9.

view) now enables us to see that it is only possible to become human at all through the absorption of our parents', and community's, culture. Our nature is not exclusively "from our genes," and in fact genetics has a relatively minor role in the inheritance of complex behavior. It is not even just from our cells. We inherit speech by absorbing in infancy the language of our society, to express the world view of our society. And so there is a level at which our first enculturation, though a social rather than a genetic affair, is in a real sense the propagation of our very humanity from, first, our parents and then our society. As philosopher Roger Scruton reminds us:

> Communities are not formed through the fusion or agreement of rational individuals; it is rational individuals who are formed through communities.[14]

But I might also quote leading British philosopher (the late) E. J. Lowe:

> Selves as persons are not created through biological processes but rather through socio-cultural forces, that is, through the co-operative efforts of other selves or persons. Persons create persons, quite literally.[15]

If we were isolated from our culture—and especially from speech— as babies, we would fail to become real people at all. Even in evolutionary terms the importance of this has been increasingly realized: Eva Jablonka, for example, regards culture as a driver of evolution that is of equal importance to genetic change, in animals as well as mankind.[16] The philosopher of biology Elliott Sober goes further, particularly in the case of humans with speech and literature:

> Cultural selection can be more powerful than biological selection. . . . [T]houghts spread faster than human beings reproduce.[17]

Discussing this Conor Cunningham adds, citing Henri de Lubac:

> There is no pure nature . . . just as there is no pure culture.[18]

---

14. Scruton, *Modern Philosophy*, 494.
15. Cited in Cunningham, *Darwin's Pious Idea*, 375.
16. Jablonka, *Evolution in Four Dimensions*.
17. Cunningham, *Darwin's Pious Idea*, 126.
18. Ibid.

In that context "imitation" in the sense of enculturation is far more than Pelagius's morally neutral human being making a free choice between alternatives: it is the restriction of his alternatives to those of the milieu that made him a human being in the first place. It is impossible to choose the philosopher's life in a culture lacking philosophy. You will never become an accomplished safecracker in tribal Amazonia. In other words, cultural inheritance can be as hard and pervasive as genetic inheritance (perhaps more so, given what we are discovering about the disjunction between genotype and phenotype). And it is quicker, and does not depend on any genes becoming fixed in the whole population: just on the spread of a strong idea or a habit. We might paraphrase Scruton:

It is culpable sinners who are formed through sinful communities.

Sin is as broad as culture, and culture as broad as the human race. So perhaps one could compare the spread of sin from Adam with the analogy of Christian mission. However strong the message of the love of Jesus is, experience shows that it can't be communicated at all apart from the *culture* of the missionary. That's why the best practice toils endlessly to enculturate both missionaries and message to the host culture, to avoid the gratuitous imposition of the missionary's own cultural prejudices. But in practice, it is impossible to quarantine culture absolutely. There is some kind of dialectical fusion between the missionary's culture and the host's culture, with the gospel as the medium between them. The same is true of any cultural contact whatsoever, and cultural interaction can never be artificially prevented for long.

If Adam were indeed the first person to have a true relationship with God, it would have affected every subsequent relationship of his. There can be no more powerful idea than the possibility of personal knowledge of God, even had his commission not been to spread the knowledge of such a possibility to the whole creation. Such communication happened willy-nilly, down the line of Seth, by intermarriage and no doubt in other ways. But though it would not be by genetic descent, yet it would truly be propagation from Adam.

At the same time, if Adam were also the first to become corrupted by rebellion against God, then all his communication, and especially that about God, would also be tainted by sin. Adam's cultural contribution to the world would be the knowledge that there is a God who seeks communion with people and in whom is eternal life, but also the knowledge that one can assert one's own wisdom against such a God and maintain

Promethean independence. And thereby would have been born mankind as we know it—*Homo divinus peccatum*—"divine (but sinful) man."

It is a far more potent and universal influence than that achieved by the inventor of the bow and arrow. And like the latter, though rather more like the opening of Pandora's box, it could not be undone once it had been done. It would become as much an integral part of "human nature" as the power of speech, or fire, or the human genome.

And if it would take a miracle to replace the human genome without losing humanity in the process, then the restoration of a person to the full image and likeness of God requires a similar miracle. It requires a new creation, even, into a new society.

Conclusion Relative to Genealogical Adam

Both the latest developments in biology, and considerations of socialization in the making of human beings, provide backing to the possibility of the transmission of the sin nature from Adam to his descendants. Genealogical science provides an understanding of the way that any such inheritance would become universal, whilst being consistent with the history of humankind provided by secular studies.

With the sole exception of Augustine's speculative theory of transmission of sin "through concupiscence," Genealogical Adam is entirely compatible with Augustinian, Irenaean, and all other historical models of original or ancestral sin.

14.

ADAM AND THE NEW CREATION

History and the Bible's Metanarrative

HAVING EXAMINED VARIOUS WAYS in which the Genealogical Adam theory can place Adam and Eve into human history and the sciences, I must now extend the case for why, and how, it is *important*. The basic answer to this is "biblical theology," understood not simply as an overall theology of the Bible, nor even as the story the Bible tells, but as the unfolding *history* of God's dealings with the real world, and of humankind in particular.

In chapter 1 I showed that "salvation history" has always been a special feature of Christianity, and of the Reformed tradition in particular, though even the historic Creeds are irreducibly historical in their content. This is supremely seen in the fact that the only begotten Son of God became a particular man for our sake. Erin Hein points out in her essay on adoption in the Bible:

> In the incarnation, the historical particularities of Jesus revealed the personhood of the eternal Son. In the resurrection and the ascension, these historical particularities were taken up into the divine life. The eternal Son bears the scars of the crucifixion, retains the lineage of David, and is recognizable in form as Jesus. Thus it is plain that Jesus's bodily redemption *includes* the particularities of his embodiment.[1]

1. Heim, "In Him and Through Him," 147.

When individuals are incorporated into Christ by faith and new birth or adoption, it is as people with individual characteristics and histories that they become part of the same historical narrative as that of Jesus of Nazareth. And so it is utterly appropriate that this concern for individual lives, rather than simply universal truths, should also mark the very beginning of the drama the Bible describes. As I quoted in chapter 1, "Adam is placed at the beginning of the Sacred Scripture so that love might bear a human face and a name, so that it might be 'personal.'"[2]

A greater appreciation of the importance of this overarching story, together with an increasing awareness of its shape, have been developing in recent years, with the failure of the old critical consensus on the supposed literary disunity of the Old Testament. In relation to that came the challenges within Old Testament studies to the emphasis in biblical studies on tracing supposed sources, and instead seeking better to elucidate the message of the only documents we actually have—the completed books of the Bible, and particularly the Pentateuch. The death knell was first sounded for the long-dominant Documentary Hypothesis back in the 1970s through work done by Rolf Rendtorff, and carried on by various scholars such as Norman Whybray, John Van Seters, Norman Wagner, George Coats, H. H. Schmid, and, notably, by David Clines in Sheffield, who helped develop an entire "school" of scholarship treating the Pentateuchal text as a single literary product, with its sources deemed irrelevant (without denying that there were sources).[3]

Consequently many Evangelical scholars have sought to renew the quest for a truly biblical theology by approaching its books, and often the whole canonical *Tanakh*, as finished, unitary, compositions. Richard Bauckham adapted the term "metanarrative" from postmodernism for this in 2003.[4] Since Evangelicals have a strong sense of the divine authorship of Scripture alongside that of the human authors (and editors), it has been easier for them than for some to see the Eden narrative as a deliberate element in the literary composition of Genesis 1—11, and as the perspective is widened, of Genesis *in toto*, the *Torah*, the *Tanakh*, and finally the entire Christian Bible.

The result of this search for a unified "compositional strategy" (to use John Sailhamer's terminology) has been to find a unified narrative

2. Riches, "Mystery of Adam 1."

3. Clines, "Response to Rolf Rendtorff."

4. Bauckham, "Reading Scripture as a Coherent Story." The fact that he redefines the term in the process of appropriating it is appropriately postmodern!

structure across the whole Bible. For example, writing as a New Testament historian N. T. Wright said in 2011:

> One word, in particular, about the big story of Scripture—the story which is presupposed throughout the NT. How much clearer can I make this? The big story is about the Creator's plan for the world. This plan always envisaged humans being God's agents in that plan. Humans sin; that's their problem, but God's problem is bigger, namely that his plan for the world is thwarted. So God calls Abraham to be the means of rescuing humankind. Then Israel rebels; that's their problem, but God's problem is bigger, namely that his plan to rescue humans and thereby the world is thwarted. So God sends Israel-in-person, Jesus the Messiah, to rescue Israel, to perform Israel's task on behalf of Adam, and Adam's on behalf of the whole world. He announces God's kingdom, and is crucified; and this turns out to be God's answer to the multiple layers of problems, as in the resurrection it appears that death itself has been overcome.[5]

Notice how Wright's summary is only secondarily about "salvation history," for the problem of sin arises as the "thwarting" of God's original plan for the world. Returning us to the theme of each believer's participation in this story, John Collins describes the metanarrative from the point of view of Israel's self-understanding:

> The OT is thus the story of the one true Creator God, who called the family of Abraham to be his remedy for the defilement that came on the world . . .
>
> This overarching story serves as a grand narrative or worldview story for Israel: each member of the people was to see himself or herself as an *heir* of this story, with all its glory and shame; as a *steward* of the story, responsible to pass it on to the next generation; and as a *participant*, whose faithfulness could play a role, in God's mysterious wisdom, in the story's progress.[6]

G. K. Beale takes this unification of the Bible's theme further than most, as I quoted in a previous chapter:

> The OT storyline that I posit as the basis for the NT storyline is this: *The Old Testament is the story of God, who progressively re-establishes his new-creational kingdom out of chaos over a sinful*

---

5. Wright, "Justification," 52.
6. Collins, "Theology of the Old Testament," 30.

*people by his world and Spirit through promise, covenant, and
redemption, resulting in worldwide commission to the faithful
to advance this kingdom and judgment (defeat or exile) for the
unfaithful, unto his glory.*[7]

Beale's analysis, taking up one thousand pages, emphasizes how
the overarching concept of "new creation" occupies every movement of
the unfolding narrative, though with the key points being the victory
of Christ in its achievement, against the failure of Israel, which in turn
was called to remedy the failure of Adam. Beale's thesis, then, is actually
rather radical: the new creation is not simply a New Testament theme,
but *the* major subject of the whole Bible from Genesis 2 onwards. The
Bible, then, can actually be described as the book of the new creation.

Other scholars have also recognized the story that links Adam
to Israel and then to the work of Christ, such as John Collins,[8] John
Sailhamer,[9] and Seth Postell, who lists a number of others.[10] Postell, in his
book *Adam as Israel*, builds on Sailhamer's thesis—that the Pentateuch
is actually the story of Israel's failure, which foresees dimly that God
would one day provide a remedy—and applies it particularly to the early
chapters of Genesis, notably to the Eden narrative. Adam, like Israel, is
taken from his place of origin into a sacred space where Yahweh may be
encountered. But like Israel, through disobedience and rebellion, he fails
and is exiled back to a place where, though Yahweh may still be worshipped, the intimate relationship of grace is lost, together with the hope
of eternal life. Many other, subordinate parallels are drawn by Postell, not
only in the Pentateuch, but elsewhere in Scripture, demonstrating that
the Eden story is considered foundational by the biblical authors. Once
one is alerted to the typology, the links between Adam and Israel are hard
to miss.

Since Jesus is also portrayed as the "true Israel," Daniel 7 being the
most crucial passage, then his mission, like Israel's, has its ultimate root
in that of Adam. But Beale goes beyond most of these writers by viewing the intended, but failed, role of Adam not as a complication of the
creation of the world, but as the first, apparently abortive, movement of a
story of *new* creation. It is this view on which I hope to expand.

7. Beale, *New Testament*, 16.
8. Collins, *Did Adam and Eve Really Exist?*, 41–42.
9. Sailhamer, *Meaning of the Pentateuch*, 306–23.
10. Postell, *Adam as Israel*, ch.3.

Adam as the New Creation

The thought of Adam as not simply the man who blights creation soon after its completion, but as the failed appointee of something beyond the Genesis 1 creation, is not entirely novel. In fact it may be found in the work of the first great post-apostolic theologian, Irenaeus, who lived in the second century (c 120–200). He has always been an important early source because he learned his Christianity from Papias, who learned it in turn from the apostle John.

Irenaeus certainly did not believe in an old earth, or in humans not descended from Adam living outside the garden, for both of which I argue in this book. Yet he does draw an important distinction between what we may recognize as "old creation" and "new creation" events in humanity's story.

In his *Proof of the Apostolic Preaching*, two chapters cover Genesis 1 and Genesis 2—3, respectively:

> 11. But man He formed with His own hands, taking from the earth that which was purest and finest, and mingling in measure His own power with the earth. For He traced His own form on the formation, that that which should be seen should be of divine form: for (as) the image of God was man formed and set on the earth. And that he might become living, He breathed on his face the breath of life; that both for the breath and for the formation man should be like unto God. Moreover he was free and self-controlled, being made by God for this end, that he might rule all those things that were upon the earth. And this great created world, prepared by God before the formation of man, was given to man as his place, containing all things within itself. And there were in this place also with (their) tasks the servants of that God who formed all things; and the steward, who was set over all his fellow-servants received this place. Now the servants were angels, and the steward was the archangel.[11]

Although the human creations of Genesis 1 and 2 are conflated here, the "creation ordinance" is clearly that of Genesis 1:26–28, and angels and an archangel are ministers in the task, but not subordinate to humanity. But in the next chapter:

> 12. Now, having made man lord of the earth and all things in it, He secretly appointed him lord also of those who were servants

11. Irenaeus, "Proof of the Apostolic Preaching," 11.

in it. They however were in their perfection; but the lord, that is, man, was (but) small; for he was a child; and it was necessary that he should grow, and so come to (his) perfection. And, that he might have his nourishment and growth with festive and dainty meats, He prepared him a place better than this world, excelling in air, beauty, light, food, plants, fruit, water, and all other necessaries of life: and its name is Paradise. And so fair and good was this Paradise, that the Word of God continually resorted thither, and walked and talked with the man, figuring beforehand the things that should be in the future, (namely) that He should dwell with him and talk with him, and should be with men, teaching them righteousness. But man was a child, not yet having his understanding perfected; wherefore also he was easily led astray by the deceiver.[12]

Now, what I want to point out is the clear contrast expressed between these two chapters. In the first, the man is created to rule the earth, with the angels to help (as in Psalm 8 or Hebrews 2), and the archangel (an as yet uncorrupted Satan[13]) to organize this assistance. This is a public role, and works well.

The problem occurs with a *change* in that situation, which Irenaeus expresses as a "secret" plan of God's to make Adam the lord of the angels too—which effectively means making humankind God's co-regent for the whole cosmos. Paradise, an area apart from the rest of the created earth, is set aside for this, and the man is taken *from* his original setting and placed there. The personal tutelage and fellowship of the Son as *Logos* was, to Irenaeus, what the garden was about. The end of my quotation introduces Irenaeus's particular understanding of the fall of mankind, which occurs in his chapter 16, as being due to immaturity. And it is certainly the case that, as far as being a ruler of the universe is concerned, the naked ape had a lot less experience than the archangel.

Now for Irenaeus Adam was the first man. There is no evidence that he had any notion of other men existing, to exercise the limited rule of the earthly creatures, before Adam. And in fact his opinion was that Adam sinned by nightfall of the very day of his creation. But there is no doubt that he saw the commission of mankind as having two separate stages; the first being to rule the earth by dint of being the highest of the "animal" creation of Day 6; and the second, the purpose within God's secret

12. Ibid., 12.
13. Ibid., 16.

counsel (but guessed by Satan, perhaps?) that this lowly physical being, because created in God's image, should go on to rule even the angels.

Where does Irenaeus get this sequential reading of Genesis 1 and 2? It seems to me that he probably read the text carefully in the light of the later scriptural commentary on it, and particularly Psalm 8, interpreted through the exposition of Hebrews 2:5–15:

> 5 For He did not subject to angels the world to come, concerning which we are speaking. 6 But one has testified somewhere, saying,

> "What is man, that You remember him? Or the son of man, that You are concerned about him? 7 "You have made him for a little while lower than the angels; You have crowned him with glory and honor, And have appointed him over the works of Your hands; 8 You have put all things in subjection under his feet."

> For in subjecting all things to him, He left nothing that is not subject to him. But now we do not yet see all things subjected to him.

> 9 But we do see Him who was made for a little while lower than the angels, *namely*, Jesus, because of the suffering of death crowned with glory and honor, so that by the grace of God He might taste death for everyone.

> 10 For it was fitting for Him, for whom are all things, and through whom are all things, in bringing many sons to glory, to perfect the author of their salvation through sufferings. 11 For both He who sanctifies and those who are sanctified are all from one *Father*; for which reason He is not ashamed to call them brethren, 12 saying,

> "I will proclaim Your name to My brethren, In the midst of the congregation I will sing Your praise."

> 13 And again,

> "I will put My trust in Him."

> And again,

> "Behold, I and the children whom God has given Me."

> 14 Therefore, since the children share in flesh and blood, He Himself likewise also partook of the same, that through death He might render powerless him who had the power of death,

that is, the devil, 15 and might free those who through fear of
death were subject to slavery all their lives.

A superficial reading of this passage may give the impression that
the writer is saying, "Psalm 8 only makes sense when you see 'man' as
meaning Christ." But in fact his argument is far more subtle than that.

The psalmist is certainly being prophetic in the eschatological
sense, but is talking about God's intentions for mankind *as a whole* (as
one would assume from a simple reading of the psalm) and, I suggest,
is referring back to Eden. Here, then, is a naked ape, mere dust, who
by rights ought to be beneath the regard of God compared to the starry
heavens where he reigns with his divine council. And yet in God's view
man's humble state below the "angels" (in Hebrews' Greek—"*elohim*," or
"gods/divine beings" in the original Hebrew) was to be temporary: many
commentators and translators prefer "for a little while lower than the
angels" to "a little lower than the angels," if only because it is hard to see
ourselves, as perishable and limited beings, being by nature anything but
hugely lower than the angels.

But God's intention, in the view of the writer of Hebrews, was always
that humankind, as his very image (or the image of the Son, the "exact
image" of God's nature, in Hebrews 1:3), should reign together with him.
Although at the very beginning of that elevation in the calling of Adam,
it was thwarted by the fall and Adam's expulsion, yet the plan was never
abandoned by God. We may see the same ultimate aim in the covenant
with Abraham,[14] and hence both in Israel's call and in the gospel which
Paul identifies with Abraham's call.[15] Hebrews assumes that the psalmist
was aware of that high purpose (the "secret appointment" of Irenaeus's
text), and clarifies the meaning in verse 8:

> For in subjecting all things to him, He left nothing that is not
> subject to him.

So God's ultimate purpose for man was more than simply to be top
dog (or better, perhaps, chief steward) on earth, subduing and ruling the
creatures here. As Hebrews 1:14 says of angels:

> Are they not all ministering spirits, sent out to render service for
> the sake of those who will inherit salvation?

14. Gen 12:1–3.
15. Gal 3:8.

So then, even the mighty spiritual *elohim* of the divine council, who one reads about in Job or Revelation, were created to become servants to mankind. Hence the psalmist's wonder at comparing and contrasting humanity with the heavens: even the moon and the stars are part of what God subjects to mankind. It is also worth noticing Paul's statement, in Romans 4:13, that God's promise to Abraham and his seed was to inherit the *kosmos*, all things in heaven and earth, when he could have used *ge* (earth as opposed to heaven).

But of course, there is a rather big problem with this glowing assessment of humanity's greatness, to which Hebrews draws attention at the end of verse 8, and that is that the psalmist didn't actually *see* anything *like* that going on around him, but only people in sin, weakness, and subjection to death:

> But now we do not yet see all things subjected to him.

That, says Hebrews, is exactly the same a thousand years on in his own time, as of course it is also true two thousand years after Hebrews was written. We do not see humanity's righteous rule over all things. But, he goes on:

> 9 But we do see Him who was made for a little while lower
> than the angels, *namely*, Jesus, because of the suffering of death
> crowned with glory and honor, so that by the grace of God He
> might taste death for everyone.

The point is not simply that Psalm 8 is only true if you apply it prophetically to Jesus rather than to "humankind" *simpliciter*, but that Jesus is the means by which the psalm's words about humankind as a whole, gleaned from the Genesis account, become true. Jesus recapitulates the Adam story by stepping down from divine glory to become a mere man, he suffers death *"for everyone,"* i.e. on behalf of everyone, and *as 'ādām* (i.e. as the second Adam), he is crowned with glory and honor at God's right hand. But we may be confident this would have been the case for humankind in due course anyway, had Adam and Eve learned obediently from the Lord rather than falling into sin.

The passage in Hebrews goes on to plumb the mystery of the achievement of Christ's suffering, but also to say how our spiritual union with him, or participation in him, by faith, makes his own glorification to be ours also—and in this way the psalmist's words are fulfilled in us, and our sense of humility and wonder should match, or exceed, his, because we *do* begin to see the hope in fulfillment and not merely in promise.

And so we can now see that Irenaeus was speaking, in effect, of the difference between the old, earthly creation and the new, spiritual creation, making the same distinction that Greg Beale develops at book length. The transition begins in Adam.

The creation ordinance of Irenaeus's chapter 11, which is that of Genesis 1, is perfectly good as far as it goes. But in his extremely brief, young earth, time-scale, it gives Adam no time to settle to the task before his transfer to the Garden of Eden, and rapid disaster. However, the same chain of events appears far more rational and plausible in the Genealogical Adam model, in which Adam is a *representative* taken, as in chapter 8 above, from the existing race of natural humankind, which is already fulfilling God's creation ordinance.

What we actually learn about mankind from ancient history and archaeology completely fits the picture Irenaeus paints of natural humanity. From Paleolithic times humankind began to gain mastery over both its fellow creatures and its environment, a mastery which by the Neolithic becomes very marked—witness Çatalhöyük, the Indus Valley culture, Stonehenge, and so on.

Remember that the description that the end of the creation account gives is of God reigning unopposed in his "Sabbath rest," but in the heavenly "Holy Place" of the cosmic temple: his *shekinah* glory does not fill the world. Remember also the account I gave in chapter 10, from anthropology and ethnology, of the nature of the most primitive religion known, worshipping a righteous, but distant sky-god without priest-craft or, usually, sacrifice. This was the crowning glory of the old creation, a creation which is still in existence because, as theologians have pointed out from antiquity, there is no evening to the seventh day.

But *within* that successful old creation, which modern science suggests continued for billions of years without humanity, and for hundreds of thousands of years with it, God chose to begin a better work—a work of *new* creation. That work started in Eden, with Irenaeus's "secret appointment" of Adam and Eve, intending that the new, eternal, and spiritual creation should come through humankind. There is, therefore, something quite new happening in Genesis 2, and it is *not* just another way of describing the creation of Genesis 1. With that Irenaeus appears to agree.

A Word From the Westminster Confession

The Reformed Westminster Confession of 1646, like Irenaeus, seems to hint at the difference between "natural man" as first created, and humanity in special relationship to God. In chapter VII, section I, "Of God's covenant with man," the Confession reads:

> The distance between God and the creature is so great, that although reasonable creatures do owe obedience unto him as their Creator, yet they could never have any fruition of him as their blessedness and reward, but by some voluntary condescension on God's part, which he hath been pleased to express by way of covenant.[16]

In the following section it goes on to describe the first covenant as that with Adam (which it describes as a covenant of works):

> The first covenant made with man was a covenant of works, wherein life was promised to Adam, and in him to his posterity, upon condition of perfect and personal obedience.[17]

I think the emphasis on "works" in the Confession's understanding of the covenant with Adam misunderstands the fullness of the grace and faith involved, and the relational nature of obedience. But its point is well made that a covenant must be, and was in this case, a personal interaction. Adam was not in such relationship by creation, but by a specific calling and command.

Under the Genealogical Adam paradigm I am suggesting that humankind outside the garden, by nature, did indeed render "obedience unto him as their Creator," at just the kind of great distance which the Westminster Assembly rightly deduces. In contrast covenant was, historically, a feature of the calling of Genesis 2, rather than the creation of Genesis 1. The calling, though, as well as constituting a covenant, also was a call to inaugurate a new creation, which was the very "fruition, blessedness and reward" of the covenant, applied both to humanity and, eventually, the whole cosmos as humanity's intended realm.

16. Shaw, *Exposition*, 84.
17. Ibid.

The New Creation through Christ

Before spelling out in more detail what that new creation was intended to achieve, I will first stress that, had Adam never sinned, it would still have been through Christ that it would have come about. In its innocence, humanity was created after the image of the true image of God, the Son. As Philip Edgcumbe Hughes reminds us,

> The authentic identity of man can be grasped only through the knowledge of man's relationship to Christ—a relationship which, far from having its beginning with the incarnation of the Son of God at Bethlehem, extends right back to the creation itself, and even beyond that to the eternal distinction within the unity of the Godhead between the persons of Father, Son and Holy Spirit.[18]

In part, at least, that distinction has to do with the fact that as the Word, the *Logos* of God, or that which goes out from God, the Son is God as he relates to his creation. This means that there is an ontological *correspondence* with, and perhaps even a *participation* in, Christ by the whole of creation. As Murray Rae puts it,

> We might say that Christ is the inner logic of creation, the one in whom its origin, its order, and its telos are revealed.[19]

As the only element in the creation made in the image and likeness of God, humanity has a further, unique, ontological affinity with the *Logos*, however that image is perceived. Furthermore, in the garden the economy of the Trinity requires that it was as the Son that Yahweh had communion with Adam and Eve, perhaps as a theophany.

Since Christ *is* wisdom, to know him is to receive wisdom. It would appear, then, that the grasping at wisdom from the tree of knowledge was not in any way forbidden because God wished to deny humanity wisdom. On the contrary, wisdom is highly prized in Scripture, not least in Christ, who is not only described as "the wisdom of God,"[20] but "wisdom *for us*."[21] As Richard Middleton writes:

18. Hughes, *True Image*, 3.
19. Rae, "Jesus Christ, the Order of Creation," 29.
20. 1 Cor 1:24.
21. 1 Cor 1:30.

It was God's purpose, from the beginning, to bring the cosmic temple to its intended destiny by human agency, in cooperation with God. So humans (as image of God) were to fill the earth with descendants (Genesis 1:28) who would represent God's rule in their cultural pursuits and flourish in accordance with God's wisdom. The human race was created to extend the presence of God from heaven (the cosmic holy of holies) to earth (the holy place) until the earth is filled with the glory of God as the waters cover the sea.[22]

It was because Eve saw that it would make her wise that she was tempted to take what had been forbidden. But did Adam and Eve actually gain God's wisdom by eating the fruit? The testimony of the story, and of teaching on wisdom throughout the Bible, is that they did not: they acquired only a *semblance* of wisdom, which was why God had forbidden the fruit in the first place. As Proverbs stresses,

> 7 The fear of the Lord is the beginning of knowledge;
> Fools despise wisdom and instruction.[23]

It is only a fool who does not desire wisdom. But only in relationship with God can true wisdom (for the task given to mankind) be gained:

> 10 The fear of the Lord is the beginning of wisdom,
> And the knowledge of the Holy One is understanding.[24]

It had been the Lord's intention, without doubt, to endow them with such wisdom (beyond price, according to Proverbs[25]) in his own time and his own way. But wisdom must grow in an orderly way, as even human educators know, and as even the human nature of Jesus experienced.[26]

This is the root of Paul's denigration of human wisdom in 1 Corinthians 1—2, which is not a condemnation of any particular system, Greek or otherwise, but of *all* wisdom not gained through knowledge of God, wisdom's only true source. Romans 1, Paul's exposition of sin and God's wrath, is a commentary on the early chapters of Genesis, but particularly on the Eden story. Human decline starts with the disregard of God, with the claim to wisdom (the degenerate wisdom taken from the tree) leading

22. Middleton, "Further Thoughts on the Imago Dei.
23. Prov 1:7.
24. Prov 9:10.
25. Prov 8:10–11.
26. Luke 2:52.

to idolatry.[27] Somewhat to our surprise, it is in just punishment of this that God gives all men over to moral sin—this defacement of nature is itself, in Paul's teaching, the "due penalty of their error [in the true worship of God]."[28] Sexual perversion is the paradigmatic example Paul gives, but it is paralleled by every human evil:

> 28 And just as they did not see fit to acknowledge God any longer, God gave them over to a depraved mind, to do those things which are not proper, 29 being filled with all unrighteousness, wickedness, greed, evil; full of envy, murder, strife, deceit, malice; *they are* gossips, 30 slanderers, haters of God, insolent, arrogant, boastful, inventors of evil, disobedient to parents, 31 without understanding, untrustworthy, unloving, unmerciful; 32 and although they know the ordinance of God, that those who practice such things are worthy of death, they not only do the same, but also give hearty approval to those who practice them.[29]

All these arise from "a depraved *mind*," note, which is as much as to say "from the damage caused to our reason by the false 'wisdom' gained at the fall."

The upshot is this: that the fall is about the radical failure of human wisdom by humankind's seizure of autonomy through the archetype, Adam. This affects both his ability to live practically as God intended and his moral compass apart from the instruction of Christ. It must inevitably affect our science as well as our religion, and our judicial and political systems as well as our personal behavior.

At the feet of the pre-incarnate Christ, an obedient Adam and Eve would have learned the true wisdom of God, and so the new creation would have been from Christ, through humankind. It still is, of course, except that through the incarnation, the Son himself became the new human archetype.[30]

27. Rom 1:22–23.
28. Rom 1:27.
29. Rom 1:28–32.
30. See Isa 59:15–21; 63:1–6.

New Creation Narrative Constituents

At this point I will seek to summarize what seems to constitute the new creation narrative implicit in Genesis 2. At one level, this is a case of recognizing that the work of Christ fulfills that very narrative, to which has been added his soteriological role. For as N. T. Wright tells us in the quotation near the head of this chapter, Jesus overcomes the thwarting of Yahweh's original plan (by the defeat of Satan and the redemption from sin and death) before he goes on to fulfill that original plan—which was, in short, to achieve his new creation through humanity.

Greg Beale describes what Adam and Eve were intended to receive in the garden—the content of the new creation—as "escalated blessings," escalated, that is, beyond the creation mandates of Genesis 1, which were still part of their role, and achieved through obedience to the command.[31]

Victory over evil: His first element is victory over the "evil serpent." Adam's role as a priest-king included the exclusion of unclean things from God's sacred space. I find something of a conundrum here, especially if the serpent is taken (as I have suggested previously) as a legitimately present "archangel" (in Irenaeus's terms) of the divine council, whose sin only arose through jealousy and pride *in* the garden. In narrative terms, this would make his "evil" just as aberrant as Adam's sin. Nevertheless, we can know (because Jesus was set apart as sacrificial Lamb even before creation[32]) that Satan's perversion and temptation of Adam was within God's secret knowledge, and so Beale is correct to include the overcoming of attempted deception as a potential victory blessing for Adam, as it was for Christ in the wilderness temptation.

The glory of God: Beale's second blessing is the participation in, and spreading of, the glory of God throughout the cosmos:

> Although the word "glory" is not found in Gen 1–3, it is likely conceptually included in the notion of Adam and Eve as image-bearers of God's attributes . . .[33]

He supports the case through Psalm 8 and other Scriptures. There is indeed a persistent strand of teaching through the Bible that the core of eschatological hope is the pervasive glory of God.

14 "For the earth will be filled

31. Beale, *New Testament,* 34–43.

32. Rev 13:8.

33. Beale, *New Testament,* 37.

With the knowledge of the glory of the Lord,
As the waters cover the sea."[34]

It is important to see that this glory, expressed fully in Revelation 21—22, is already inherent in the Eden narrative, just as it was also at the core of Israel's intended role.

Eternal life: Thirdly, Beale points to the gaining of eternal life, a blessing which increases the scope of the other blessings massively, for it suggests a transformation of the whole created order, for that order to be commensurate with imperishable humans. One suspects these blessings, without the fall, would eventually have found their fulfilment christologically in the concept of adoption, which I covered generally in chapter 11 ("Genealogy, Adoption, and Culture"), but which Erin Heim explores in depth in her essay in *Christ and the Created Order*:

> When considered together, the adoption metaphors in the New Testament point to Christ as the *locus* of adoption, and present adoption as the *telos* of human existence.[35]

As even the ancient theologians noted, eternal life was not of the original order of creation, but of grace, in Christ—which is what either a metaphorical or a sacramental tree of life would stand for. Adoption into Christ became the ultimate goal of mankind through Adam in the garden, not by the original nature of humanity. St. Athanasius wrote:

> This, then, was the plight of men. God had not only made them out of nothing, but had also graciously bestowed on them His own life by the grace of the Word. Then, turning from eternal things to things corruptible, by counsel of the devil, they had become the cause of their own corruption in death; for, as I said before, though they were by nature subject to corruption, the grace of their union with the Word made them capable of escaping from the natural law, provided that they retained the beauty of innocence with which they were created. That is to say, the presence of the Word with them shielded them even from natural corruption, as also Wisdom says:
>
> "God created man for incorruption and as an image of His own eternity; but by envy of the devil death entered into the world."[36]

---

34. Hab 2:14.
35. Heim, "In Him and Through Him," 129.
36. Athanasius, "Incarnation," 1.5.

Beale lists several other "possible" escalated blessings, but these three are sufficient for my purpose here, which is to show that what Christ achieved was not a return to Eden, as the pristine state of the Genesis 1 creation before sin, but the completion of what Eden was intended to achieve as a "new thing" initiated within that creation: that is, an entirely new creation through humankind in Adam, as it were expanding the borders of Eden to include, ultimately, the whole cosmos within the presence and glory of God.

If this be so, then the first creation was always intended to be provisional, though of long duration, humanly speaking—*and was perceived by the author of Genesis to be so.* This is actually further demonstrated by two specifics of the creation account: the darkness, and the deep (Heb. *tehom*; Gk. *abyss*).[37] These two major constituents, representing jointly the primordial "empty and functionless" state, *tohu wabohu*, are first pushed aside by God, and then incorporated as useful, if ambiguous, elements of his *good* creation.

Thus the darkness is alternated with light to become the night, and the deep is first separated by the firmament to make the upper waters (from which come both the blessing of rain and, on Day 4, the birds), and then is separated from the dry land to become the seas, once again the source of fish, over which humanity is given rule.

Throughout Scripture, however, these two elements remain emblematic of *tohu wabohu* in their danger to mankind, though they are always under God's ultimate control. "Darkness" is represented as a source of dread, of the hiddenness of God, and even as a major metaphor of sin. The sea represents the forces of chaos (for example, as the medium in which Jonah fled from God, or as the waves which Jesus stills in the storm on the Lake of Galilee, or of course as the flood of Noah).

They are *not* products of sin, but are necessary constituents of God's good creation. And yet when the final kingdom is consummated in Revelation 21, we read that "there was no longer any sea"[38] and "there will be no night there."[39] These words do not necessarily say anything literal about the new creation lacking a diurnal cycle or oceans. Rather it is all about the conscious resolution of the Genesis symbolism of a residual

---

37. Gen 1:2.

38. Rev 21:1.

39. Rev 21:25.

primordial deficiency of human utility, together with the long-delayed filling of all things with God's glory.

In fact that whole chapter of Revelation, closing the witness of Scripture just as Genesis opens it, is more about the transformation of old creation to new than it is about the ending of sin's interruption to that transformation. Verse 4 says not simply that the old order has passed away (as the 1984 NIV translation reads), but, literally, that the "first things" (*prota*) passed away.

That same contrast between first and second creations, rather than between sin and redemption, appears, but is often unnoticed, in 1 Corinthians 15:42–58, on the resurrection. There the contrast is not between the fallen and the redeemed body as such, but between the "natural" (*psuchikos*) and the "spiritual" (*pneumatikos*), between the "living soul" of Genesis 2:7 and the "life-giving spirit," and between the first man from the dust of the earth and the second man from heaven, the perishable and the imperishable.

This is a perspective that also makes more sense of a tricky passage like Romans 8:18–22, which is about the good, but corruptible, creation longing to put on incorruption through the stalled "Adam project" rather than its being a creation rendered evil by the fall—something that Scripture never asserts.

The theological weight that the Bible is therefore seen to place on the new creation, from the formation of Adam to the final kingdom of Christ, seems to shrink the old creation almost to nothing—practically speaking, almost to just the first chapter of Genesis. This is only a problem if the Bible is believed to be about "life, the universe and everything." However, if it is deliberately intended as the history, primarily, of the new creation, then the reason for such an emphasis is clear and logical. In the next chapter, I will try to show how Genesis 1 acts, in literary terms, as the theological prologue to the Bible.

Conclusion Relative to Genealogical Adam

I note that the Genealogical Adam hypothesis—which is primarily to do with placing Genesis into world history, rather than with adding anything to the Bible's theological agenda—restores a balance between old and new creations. It shows how the old creation, largely outside the purview of the Bible's concerns about the new, relates to those concerns.

It suggests that the Bible writers were quite aware of that original world, but chose to look forward, rather than backward, and concentrate their efforts on chronicling the birth of the new world.

15.

A TALE OF THREE TESTAMENTS

Third Time Lucky

GREG BEALE, IN HIS *New Testament Biblical Theology*, draws numerous typological parallels between Adam and Christ from the characters in Scripture. For example, he points out that Noah and Abraham both received versions of the commission given to Adam,[1] and that David's kingship also mirrors elements of Adam's.[2]

These parallels are valid both in their literary links to Genesis, and also in their being New Testament types. Noah and the flood are compared to Christ and baptism in 1 Peter 3:20–22. Abraham's promised seed is said to be Christ in Galatians 3:16. And of course it is David on whom the teaching about Messiah is modelled.

However, most such parallels are only very partial. Noah's role was more one of simple survival, or perhaps of the rebooting of the old creation, than its transformation to a new one. Abraham, though an important figure and the "father of faith," was only to bring about God's purposes, including the land promise, through his distant offspring.[3] And the rule of David's line was limited to Israel, apart from far-off promises of a future Messiah who would rule the nations.

1. Beale, *New Testament,* 46–47.
2. Ibid., 70–71.
3. Gen 15:13–21.

Most of the heavy lifting of Beale's narrative comes from the parallels between Adam, Israel, and Christ. It is the same in John Sailhamer's work on the Pentateuch, whose author, he argues, sees in Adam the forerunner of Israel's apostasy, and prophetically glimpses a Savior in the distant future. Seth Postell, likewise concentrating on Adam, sees him as the forerunner primarily of Israel, and Israel as the forerunner of Christ. This emphasis is present in the New Testament writings too, in which Jesus is the new, or second, Adam[4] and also the true Israel (partly by being the true Davidic king and the true temple[5]), but in which he is not described as the new Noah or the second Abraham.

I have found it helpful, as a tool for understanding the overall narrative structure of the Bible, to concentrate attention on these three major "phases" of new creation history, by dividing the Bible into three, not two, Testaments. This division occurred to me through an off-the-cuff comment by N. T. Wright in an online interview, in which he described Genesis 1—11 as "The Old Testament of the Old Testament," a phrase taken from R. W. L. Moberly.[6]

The call of Adam is linked thematically and in literary terms with the Mosaic Covenant with Israel, and that of Israel in turn with the New Covenant in Christ. All turn out, on examination, to be initiated with the goal of uniting humankind to God, and through that to bringing about a renewing of the whole creation in which God's glory will fill all things— the same eschatological goal that grounds the Christian hope.

The central thrust of the biblical narrative (as a narrative, that is) therefore becomes a drama in three distinct acts, corresponding to these three "Testaments," the first being the protohistory of Genesis 2—11, the second the remainder of the Old Testament, and the third the New Testament. This pattern quite neatly matches Reformed covenant theology: the covenant in Adam[7] leads to catastrophic failure; the covenant in Israel

---

4. Rom 5; 1 Cor 13.

5. E.g. Matt 2:15; John 11:50.

6. Moberly, *Old Testament of the Old Testament,* 159–66.

7. The existence of a covenant in Genesis 2–3 is disputed, but it would not be expected to resemble the Mosaic covenant apparently based on Hittite treaty covenants. Beale writes: ". . . it is probable that God's covenant with Adam is referred to as a covenant elsewhere in the OT (Hos 6:7). The essential elements of a covenant are found in the Gen 1–3 narrative: (1) two parties are named; (2) a condition of obedience is set forth; (3) a curse for transgression is threatened; (4) a clear implication of blessing is promised for obedience." *New Testament Biblical Theology,* 42–43. Seth Postell also writes to the same effect, from the intertextuality with Mosaic covenant texts, in *Adam*

recapitulates that failure; and lastly the covenant in Christ succeeds, to the glory of God, and yet also redeems the former failures because Jesus is both the second Adam and the true Israel. In this way the Bible narrative has three principal, parallel movements.

In the first movement, God's original plan to transform the cosmos through mankind is stymied by the serpent's malicious deception and Adam's sin, leading to the latter's exile and to the blighting of creation, ending in the episode of Babel.

In the second, Israel is called as a remedy, through the patriarchs Abraham, Isaac, and Jacob, to know God personally at Sinai, and so become the "kingdom of priests" that will restore the knowledge of God to the nations and so achieve his original goal. But Israel fails even at that first encounter,[8] and the Old Testament records Israel's slow spiritual and social deterioration leading to the exile in Babylon, and to Yahweh's name being held in contempt among the nations.

The third movement is, of course, the incarnation of God's own Son as both the faithful Adam and the true Israel, who succeeds where the others failed through the scandal of the cross and the victory of resurrection. He defeats Satan, and saves humankind, as the church, to transform the world in and through him, so that God's whole initial purpose is finally vindicated and accomplished.

What is somewhat interesting is that, seen as a story, that three-movement narrative fits the classic storytelling pattern known as the *Rule of Three*.[9] One of the most ubiquitous folk-story plots, if not *the* most ubiquitous, is this: a good hero has a legitimate goal in mind, but an evil enemy puts some impediment in the way to prevent it. The hero, through many, but commonly three, heroic and difficult endeavors (and perhaps with the aid of some helper),[10] not only manages to achieve the goal at last, but also gives the enemy his due reward.

Think of the Three Little Pigs, concerned only to make their way in the world by building houses and living quietly, apart from grunts. But a big bad wolf blows down the lazy straw-builder's house and eats him

---

as Israel, 126–35.

8. John Sailhamer's analysis of this in *Meaning of the Pentateuch* is thorough and persuasive. I will return to it in discussing the temple imagery of Genesis in chapter 16.

9. "Rule of three (writing)," *Wikipedia*. https://en.wikipedia.org/wiki/Rule_of_three_(writing).

10. See the discussion of narrative forms in Wright, *New Testament and People of God*, 69–80.

(in the original!), and then blows down the almost-as-lazy stick builder's house, equally fatally. But the wise and industrious third pig's stone house resists the wolf, who tries to enter by the chimney, and has the tables turned on him by landing in a cauldron and being cooked and eaten, enabling the surviving pig, or him and his refugee brothers in the sanitized versions, to live safely as originally planned.

The Three Billy Goats Gruff is not dissimilar: a legitimate desire for nice new pasture just over the bridge is thwarted by a troll. Two small but cunning goats sneak past the being-eaten-for-supper threat by pointing to their fat big brother, who turns the tables on the troll through courage and horn power. Result: the pasture is reached as originally planned, and a drowned troll floats off downstream into the sunset.

A similar triple pattern is found in one of the earliest recorded folk tales, the somewhat comic Akkadian *Poor Man of Nippur*, from the early first millennium BCE.[11] In this, a poor man cheated out of a goat by the corrupt mayor of Nippur gets threefold revenge, in increasingly cunning (and violently slapstick) ways.

The same even occurs in several of Jesus' stories. The first character in the Good Samaritan only wants to get from Jerusalem to Jericho. Bandits prevent that, and then we have rescues that fail (through moral deficiency and fear) on the part of a priest and a Levite. An unlikely Sir Galahad, in the form of a third traveller, the Samaritan, bravely and lovingly risks the bandits and saves the day and (by implication) enables the injured man eventually to reach his desired destination.

There is a certain neatness to such plot lines: three is the minimum number of episodes necessary to give the requisite sense of repetition and persistent endeavor without becoming tedious. It seems to me that the form is highly appropriate for the story that is of the most importance to all the ordinary people of the world—the drama of God's transformation of the cosmos. If such a pattern in the Bible is deliberate, of course, then it is not a device of the human authors, but of the divine author, of Scripture, for it is only visible across a disparate body of literature that took shape over several millennia. Intentional or not, it is a memorable and accurate overview.

Not only does this pattern provide a simple shape to the overarching metanarrative of Scripture, but it provides a basis for finding where in the narrative where each part of the Bible fits, as well as enabling us to

11. See a description at http://cdli.ox.ac.uk/wiki/doku.php?id=tale_poor_man_nippur.

find our *own* place in it as participants. Thus the Bible narrative begins to interpret itself as an example of *omne trium perfectum*.[12] The Adam story, the Israel story, and the Christ story all fit together as parallel episodes in the bigger overall narrative of God's intended completion of his creation. The garden narrative is both God's first "goal-seeking" attempt and the "obstruction" to his plan that turns the Bible into a true story at all. The call of Israel, the "second attempt," appears to be a large-scale solution to the problem that has emerged, calling an entire nation rather than one fallible couple. But as we have seen, the story recapitulates the story of Adam and things end up looking worse than ever.

In this structure, the coming of Jesus is shown to be no accident, or whim, or *ad hoc* solution, but the third and final movement of God's remedy for evil—or more precisely the third movement of his plan to recreate the world—through the "champion" helper, his own Son, for whose glory, as the New Testament finally reveals, the whole drama was planned before time.[13] The Lamb, it turns out, was actually slain from the creation of the world.[14]

This threefold pattern ought not to be controversial, really, since the stories of Adam and Israel screamed out their parallels to every exilic Jew who heard them. And the coming of Messiah was, of course, presented from the very start in the prophets as a New Covenant to replace that made through Moses (and to fulfill that made through Abraham).[15]

Perceiving this pattern, I suggest, helps us to interpret the origins narratives more accurately too. In the first place, if the Adam story is indeed an intentional parallel both to the history of Israel and to the gospel of Jesus, then we must give full weight to that fact. It is not simply a folk explanation for evil, or even just for human sin or for death. Rather it is a crucial world event whose human characters are a foundational couple who failed in an appointed, and fundamentally cosmic, role. Thereby they became both agents of a failure that needs to be corrected, and bearers of a guilt that needs to be dealt with in order to correct the failure and reach God's intended goal.

Satan's role as deceiver in the garden, and the remedy for it, both also need to be accounted for fully, since that aspect of Christ's work

---

12. "Everything that comes in threes is perfect."

13. Eph 1:3–12; Col 2:19–20.

14. Rev 13:8.

15. Isa 42:6; 61:8; Jer 31:31–37; Ezek 16:59–60; 34:23–31.

remains of major importance in the New Testament. It is more than the defeat of "evil forces," but a clear case of the punishment needing to fit the original crime.

The current state of the world, and the "groaning of creation" described in Romans 8, become explicable in terms of the (subjectively—but see chapter 3) long delay in the consummation of the new creation, as well as the corruption of sin, both of which are the fault of Adam through his succumbing to Satan, yet both of which are remedied, as first intended, through "the glorious freedom of the sons of God," a freedom that was offered to Adam, but lost.

The role of Israel is also cast in its proper cosmic light, as of course was always intended by the divine author, whose purpose for Israel was that they should see themselves called to complete what Adam did not, and not merely to be the followers of a particular national god, nor even simply to be the favorites of the true God. When God first addressed Moses, as Israel assembled at Mount Sinai (shortly before their rebellion), he said they were to be "a kingdom of priests and a holy nation" to "all the peoples."[16]

The Non-Story of Genesis 1

Another use of this threefold narrative framework is in drawing a sharper distinction between Genesis 1 and Genesis 2 than is often done, and this is highly relevant in distinguishing Adam from those I have suggested to dwell in "the old creation" outside the garden. The two accounts are *not* simply alternative creation stories, because chapter 1 is not a "story" in the proper sense at all, but some other kind of account. On its own it is rather like N. T. Wright's example of a non-story:

> Little Red Riding-Hood was sent by her mother to take some food to her grandmother; she did so, and they were all happy.[17]

Genesis 1 simply describes what God did, completely unopposed. The Babylonian *Enuma elish* is a creation *story*—plenty of drama and conflict there. But not Genesis 1.

In narrative terms, this means that the creation account of Genesis 1:1–2:3 should not be seen as part of the narrative at all, but rather as

16. Exod 19:5–6.
17. Wright, *New Testament and People of God*, 71.

the *setting* in which the real drama will take place. The creation account, although containing key truths, does not have the characteristics of story. Biblical scholars such as Richard Middleton, Walter Brueggemann, and Francis Watson, have all noted this lack of "story" in Genesis 1, and used it to assert, as I do, that the creation account is the *background* to the drama that then begins in chapter 2. Middleton, in *The Liberating Image*, quotes Walter Brueggemann as saying that Gen 1

> . . . is the presupposition for everything that follows in the Bible.[18]

He also quotes Francis Watson, that it

> . . . must determine the theme and scope of the story that follows. The "beginning" referred to at the outset is *also* the beginning of a book, and engenders in the reader's mind the expectation . . . of a coherent plot.[19]

Middleton himself notes the unopposed ease of God's creation, concluding that this is

> . . . reflected even in the gentle, repetitive cadences of the text, which progressively builds to a climax, but unlike a genuine narrative contains not a trace of plot tension or resolution (that is, there is no evil to be resisted or overcome).[20]

It is tempting, in the light of this, to speculate that the actual protohistory received as a tradition by the author of Genesis, "the Old Testament of the Old Testament," began at Genesis 2:4, and that the creation account—so unlike others in ANE literature—was added as a theological preface for the larger work. Be that as it may, what Genesis 1 does *narratively* within the Bible (ignoring its brilliant role in establishing the creation as God's temple) is to set the scene for the beginning of the real story, whose action begins in chapter 2—the story of the new creation. It quite literally describes the "resting state" before the story, *as a story*, begins.[21] Genesis 1 sets out the Bible's "storefront," in the way that "Once

---

18. Middleton, *Liberating Image*, 293n68.

19. Ibid.

20. Ibid., 265.

21. See the discussion in Beale, *Temple*, 61–66, on how God's "sabbath rest" represents God's settled rule over the "very good" Genesis 1 creation. The change comes only at 3:1.

upon a time there was a good king who lived in a forest" might in some generic fairy tale.

Only in chapter 2 does the real action begin, by describing the intention God has for *change* from this initial situation. In the first place, that intention is to call a representative human into fellowship, and into royal and priestly service. Ultimately, as I have already described, it is to transform creation by filling it with divine glory. As Richard Middleton writes:

> The human race was created to extend the presence of God from heaven (the cosmic holy of holies) to earth (the holy place) until the earth is filled with the glory of God as the waters cover the sea (combining Numbers 14:21; Isaiah 11:9; Habakkuk 2:14); or, to use Pauline language, when God will be all in all (1 Corinthians 15:28).[22]

The Eden account introduces the villain and his mischief. Chapters 2—3 are the equivalent of "One day the king sent his son off to marry a beautiful princess in the next kingdom. But an evil giant, who was jealous, captured the prince and put him in a deep dungeon . . ." *Now* we have the beginnings of a story.

The purpose of the Eden story, when Genesis 1 is not taken as part of the narrative, is far more like a commissioning narrative than a creation story, as traditionally thought. Another passage in Genesis is, unquestionably, a covenant commissioning narrative: the call of Abram in Genesis 12. You will remember that this begins:

> 12 Now the Lord said to Abram,

> "Go forth from your country, And from your relatives And from your father's house, To the land which I will show you; . . ."[23]

It goes on to describe God's promise to Abram to bless him and make him a great nation, and also to become a blessing to all peoples on earth.

Now, if one were to delete *everything* in Genesis from God's appointment of the Sabbath at the end of his work of creation in 2:4, right up until the passage I have just quoted about Abram (that is, the entire protohistory), it would still make perfect sense as a narrative. God is shown in Genesis 1 to be the sole Creator and at the end to be the owner and ruler

22. Middleton, "Further Thoughts on the Imago Dei."

23. Gen 12:1.

of a world full of all that we see today, including humanity. And then, in Genesis 12, one man is called out from that race for a new and special role in relationship to God—now described using his covenant name of "Yahweh." The sense of God's doing new business with the human race he has created is perfectly logical and clear, even without chapters 2—11.

In fact, the features of the transition between the two accounts, thus brought together, which is so coherent and logical, is pretty much identical to that between the creation account and what is *actually* next in the Genesis text—the Eden account. There are significant differences, of course, but the narrative flows just as it did in my expurgated version: God makes the world, and calls a man from it to special relationship—even the change to the covenant name *Yahweh* is the same.

That is not to suggest that the intervening text is irrelevant, or still less that it has been inserted at some later stage in the text's history (it is more likely to predate the Abram account as an ancient tradition). What the exercise above does achieve is to demonstrate the similarity of *function* of Genesis 2 and Genesis 12: both are about commissioning individuals to bless the humanity created in Genesis 1.

The exercise also enables us to see better exactly what would be *lost* if Genesis did jump straight from 2:4 to 12:1, omitting the protohistory. That is the story of a failed commission and the progressive unravelling of human society and religion that result. Its omission would make the purpose of Abram's commission rather hard to explain. As it is, the protohistory enables us to see the call of Abram not simply as God's attempt to relate to man (as in Adam's story), but such an attempt with the *added* problem of dealing with human sin and its effects. Cue the rest of the Bible.

Suppose, on the other hand, that we regard the story of Eden in the traditional way, as an "alternative creation account." I suggest that if we were to test that by another deletion—that is, by expunging the Genesis 1 creation account from the text, together with the story of Adam's descendants (which, in the real text, creates a genealogical bridge between Adam and Abraham)—we would end up with a pretty nonsensical and disjointed story. If Genesis started at 2:5, making the Eden narrative the sole "creation account," and then after the exile of 3:24 the text jumped straight to the call of Abraham, it would be extremely difficult to work out how, if at all, they are connected, what is going on, and why.

Even if we allowed the ensuing chapters to remain in place, we'd find out that Adam had many descendants of which Abram was one, but it would still (I suggest) be pretty hard to make sense of why Abram was called, and how he might be a help to anyone by his wanderings into Canaan. We end up with no clear picture of what the world means, or how God relates to it. The Eden account on its own makes a poor introduction to Genesis, that is, it makes a poor creation narrative.

It is only Genesis 1, setting up the background for the very specific events of Eden, which turns the book into such a powerful story. It becomes a narrative of one divine calling, that of Adam, which failed and brought disaster, and one calling, that of the patriarchs, which succeeded and holds promise (as we reach the end in Genesis 50) for the future.

My conclusion is that there is only one, non-narrative, creation account in Genesis, that of 1:1–2:3. But it paves the way wonderfully for something new, within history, in the account of the garden.

If this is correct, and Genesis 1, for all its importance for the theology of creation, is narratively only describing the "initial conditions" ("Once upon a time there was a good king . . .") then its chronology becomes very much irrelevant to the story. We never ask, of a fairy tale, how long the king had been reigning in his forest, or what that reign had been like. For all we know it could have involved half a century of social reform, or the king might have been crowned only the week before. Those things are simply assumed. It is what happens *next* that matters. The "initial state" of God's reign "in rest" in Genesis 1—2:4 might, therefore, have been just as long as modern science suggests. Humankind, even, could have been living in that state of God's settled rule for tens of millennia before God decided to move creation along to something new. What is more, such a long time scale would be highly appropriate.

The spoof English history book *1066 and All That*[24] commences,

> The first date in English history is 55 BC, in which year Julius Caesar (the *memorable* Roman Emperor) landed, like all other successful invaders of these islands, at Thanet.

Its authors' "compulsory preface" says humorously, but actually rather profoundly,

> History is not what you thought. *It is what you can remember.*
> All other history defeats itself.

History is what you can remember—or perhaps, what you *choose* to remember. Although the writer of Genesis chooses not to remember any

24. Seller and Yeatman, *1066 and All That*.

history before Adam, he doesn't leave us entirely ignorant of what was in the world as Adam's tale began to unfold. It contained all that is mentioned in the creation account—the heavens and the earth and all their hosts, all (importantly) the uncontested, good work of God created by and for his good pleasure. It included, as it describes, humanity, male and female, created in the image and likeness of God, just as the Genealogical Adam hypothesis suggests.

Metanarrative and Missio Dei

The theme of "mission" in the repetitive stages of God's new creation initiatives within Scripture also provides soft support for the Genealogical Adam thesis. This has more to do with the detailed sweep of the narrative than with the simplified, three-stage version I have just outlined.

For such a "metanarrative" view also places Adam and Eve in the mainstream of the Bible's *missiological* message, as opposed to their being a purely ontological preface to that overarching scriptural theme. To clarify that, by "missiological" I refer to what is called *missio dei*, the mission (i.e. "sending") by God into the world in order to bring it into relationship with himself.

If we start with Abraham, usually seen as the beachhead of God's salvific mission to the world, we see God calling one man who, through learning from God in faith and receiving his blessing, is given the promise that he will become a blessing for the whole world. Genesis 12:1–3 can be seen as a literal "mission statement" for the salvation history through Israel, which is to say the whole Bible.

The promise is kept alive despite various challenges during the patriarchal period of Genesis, in the first place through individuals chosen from each generation, until in Exodus Israel is called as a nation—but again through one man, Moses, once more to bring blessing to mankind by embodying Yahweh's blessing through their faith relationship with him and their subsequent righteous behavior. Both Israel's ongoing relationship and their failures lead to other acts of mission by God—such as the sending of the prophets and anointed kings—to try and keep Israel on track and, through them (as we read particularly in Isaiah) to bring the rest of the world into faithful obedience to God.

Even the religious disaster of the exile plays its part in the unfolding plan of Yahweh, leading as it does to the announcement of the New

Covenant of grace, to be implemented through Messiah, as we particularly find in the later chapters of all three Major Prophets and Daniel. John the Baptist is the final messenger sent by God before that occurs, like all his predecessors an individual sent in order to call all the people back to obedient relationship with God, so that (in the angel's words to John's father Zechariah) the disobedient would be turned to "the wisdom of the righteous"[25]—that is, to the kind of wisdom that ought to have been gained in Eden for humankind's service of God on earth.

The last to be sent from God is, of course, the Son, and his message is primarily the kingdom of God, that is, salvation from sin as the portal to participating in the original intention for Adam, of reigning as God's vice-regents in the fruition of his final purposes for the cosmos.

We can easily push that missiological role back to the story of Noah. Second Peter describes Noah as a preacher of righteousness,[26] not merely saving himself, his family and their pets from destruction, but sent first by God to try to turn corrupt mankind from their evil ways back to Yahweh's purpose.

Now, if we view Adam too as a man called from his race into relationship with Yahweh, the parallel is close. He is a representative who would receive the blessing of eternal life, and wisdom through the wisdom of his personal instruction, and then be sent to spread it through the world. We can see that he stands in exactly the same tradition as all the prophets and saints, and latterly Jesus the Son, who is so crucial as to be called the second Adam. In all cases God calls by grace (not works), teaches by revelation (not human insight), trains into righteousness (not conformity to human ways), sends by command, and blesses eternally (not temporally).

In every case, too, God calls an *individual* to represent his word to the many. It is, of course, possible that Adam is an exception because he is the first human. It is far less likely that he is an exception to the rule because he did not exist. But as discussed in chapter 2, Genesis 4:26 describes how "men began to call on the name of the Lord." Adam does not appear to be an exception to the missiological pattern.

Within the almost cyclical nature of the Bible narrative, it is at least plausible that Adam, like every other biblical hero, was a prophetic (as

25. Luke 1:17.
26. 2 Pet 2:5.

well as priestly and kingly) individual called *from* the people *for* the people.

There are also parallels between Adam and other key biblical figures in the contrast between the land outside the garden, where Adam had been formed from the dust of the earth, and the garden itself, where he encounters Yahweh. This call from "the world" into God's presence is equivalent typologically to Abram's coming *out* of Ur in order to begin to receive the promise *in* Canaan (though in his case, of course, the fulfilment had to wait 400 years for the exodus as his descendants spent generations in Egypt), and to Moses coming out of Egypt to Horeb, to which he also leads Israel for their commissioning.

Not only, then, can we in this way appreciate Adam as the first of God's "missionaries" to the world, but we see that his appointed message of faith and obedience, his work of serving God freely and "without fear in holiness and righteousness all [his] days," [27] and his reward of eternal life in God's presence in a transformed cosmos are all of a piece with the gospel we have now received through Christ. The continuity is complete, except that where Adam and his successors failed, Christ overcame.

The gospel, then, truly is eternal[28]—it was what Adam heard from God himself, even before he sinned against it. It was the good news of the kingdom of God. If, as Irenaeus insisted, Adam is redeemed, then for all his historical distance from us, his testimony will be familiar to us when we meet him. For Jesus Christ, contrary to certain recent teaching, is the same yesterday, today, and forever.

Conclusion Relative to Genealogical Adam

Under Genealogical Adam, the people outside the garden are those for whose sake Adam is called, in parallel with every other example of such a vocation in Scripture. The literary function of Genesis 1, rather than the recency and immediate spoiling of the old creation, accounts for the brevity of the creation account.

27. Luke 1:75.
28. Rev 14:6.

16

A TALE OF TWO TEMPLES

The Cosmic Temple of Genesis 1

AN INCREASING TREND IN biblical scholarship has been to recognize the Genesis creation account as representing a "cosmic[1] temple," and the seven-day creation as a temple inauguration text. This is not a new insight, and was in fact recognized in the sixth century by the Alexandrian monk Cosmas Indicopleustes.[2] Additionally a possibly fifth-century Jewish midrash, *Tanhuma Yelammedenu Exodus* 11:2, says "The Temple is equal to the creation of the world" and goes on to compare the various furnishings with the creation account.[3]

But amongst its current proponents are Greg Beale,[4] Richard Middleton,[5] and John Walton,[6] who writes:

1. I personally dislike the description "cosmic," for the reason that the whole concept of a "cosmos" arose in Greek thought centuries after Genesis was written, and gives a misleading impression of the Hebrew worldview.

2. His own rather eccentric, and *illustrated*, book, *The Christian Topography*, is worth examining and is available online. His work is also summarized in my blog post of 2014, "The cosmos of Cosmas." I think I may have been the first to alert the biblical studies community to Cosmas's anticipation of their work—see Middleton, "The Ancient Universe and the Cosmic Temple."

3. Beale, *Temple*, 61n.

4. Beale, *Temple*.

5. Middleton, *New Heaven and New Earth*.

6. Walton, *Genesis 1 as Ancient Cosmology*.

As in a temple inauguration which in its core elements is the initiating of sacred space and its commensurate ritual functions, the creation account at its core is a narrative of the initiation of the functioning of the cosmos by recounting the primary purposes for which the elements have been put in place and by officially installing the appropriate functionaries in their place. The entire cosmos is viewed as a temple designed to function on behalf of humanity; and when God takes up his rest in this cosmic temple, it "comes into functional existence" (real existence in ancient thinking) by virtue of his presence . . .

Many of these points were already made by M. Weinfeld three decades ago [in "Sabbath, Temple and the Enthronement of the Lord"], so they are not new, though they have only gradually been making their way into the mainstream of biblical scholarship.[7]

Seth Postell also follows John Sailhamer in seeing Genesis 1 as similarly typological of both the Mosaic tabernacle and Solomon's temple, and of the promised land of Israel itself as sacred space.[8]

Part of the case for such temple imagery in the creation account is the linguistic parallelism with the account of the building of the tabernacle in Exodus 25—40. Part are the parallels with ANE temple ritual, including the existence of temples built, or dedicated, over seven days, like the week of creation. Part is the installation of humankind as an image of God as the final act of creation. Part is the cosmic imagery of both the tabernacle and temple, which show them to represent a microcosmic version of the universe

Incidentally, note once again the presence of "representational" or "participatory" imagery here: both the heavens and the temple holy of holies are made sacred by the presence of God, but neither is, in fact, considered to be his "literal" dwelling in Scripture, but rather the setting for his representational presence.[9]

This is actually a considerable change in the perception of reality from the representational world of the surrounding nations. For example, Egyptian coffin paintings that represent the sky-goddess Nut arching over the earth, which is the god Geb, whilst she is supported by her brother, the air god Shu, tend to be taken as evidence that the Egyptians "really"

7. Walton, *Genesis 1 as Ancient Cosmology*, 190–91.

8. Postell, *Adam as Israel*, 110–14.

9. 2 Chr 6:18–20.

considered the sky to be a solid arch. In fact, they show the reverse: that they really considered the sky to be a goddess, *representing herself* in the form of the blue heavens, the stars and so on. In turn the Egyptians *represented* her in human form in a sacred painting. The air god Shu, of course, represented the empty space under the sky, and nobody has suggested that air is therefore solid. The Egyptians did not clearly separate the various concepts, and it caused them no difficulty.

In contrast one, usually neglected, aspect of the uniqueness of Genesis amongst ANE literature is that what God creates is, literally, separate from himself. Like a temple, the cosmos is his dwelling, not his body.

A large part of the case for Genesis 1 as a temple inauguration account is the tripartite nature of the "creation temple," reminiscent of the strict divisions within the tabernacle and, subsequently, the Jerusalem temple. John Walton has possibly done most to popularize the cosmic temple understanding in *The Lost World of Genesis One*.[10] Unfortunately (in my view) he is a little too influenced by nineteenth-century conceptions of "ANE cosmology" in which a flat earth floats in an infinite cosmic ocean, protected from inundation by a solid "firmament" or *raqia* forming a vaulted roof.

There are various reasons why these representations are anachronistic. For example, Assyriologist Wayne Horowitz in his authoritative work on Babylonian cosmology writes:

> . . . no surviving text presents clear evidence for the bounds of the physical universe or explains what might be found beyond the limits of the universe. Such problems are endemic to this study, since no single surviving ancient Mesopotamian source or set of sources presents a comprehensive view of the physical universe.[11]

As for the solid dome assumed by many to be ubiquitous through the ANE, he writes:

> Although the clear sky seems to us to be shaped like a dome, rather than a flat circle, there is no direct evidence that ancient Mesopotamians thought the visible heavens to be a dome. Akkadian *kippatu* are always flat, circular objects such as geometric circles or hoops, rather than three dimensional domes.[12]

10. Walton, *Lost World of Genesis* 1.
11. Horowitz, *Cosmic Geography*, xiv.
12. Ibid., 265.

Hoops, of course, do not keep out infinite oceans: the whole traditional picture must be wrong. It is certainly oversimplified, and over-
generalized across a number of disparate, and often contradictory, ANE
cosmologies, none of which had a concept of a bounded cosmos at all.[13]
There is much work still to be done in freeing our understanding of ancient worldviews from modern materialistic presuppositions. But I wish
to present an alternative here simply to suggest that the tripartite nature
of the Genesis 1 "heavens and earth" is much clearer in the text than is
often understood, and also that the natural world it describes is based
entirely on phenomenology, and not on ancient, erroneous, scientific
theories.

This will enable us to see that, just as the ancient Egyptians saw their
world as consisting of real deities manifesting as material things, so it is
best to understand Genesis as showing a universe that is a *real* temple,
manifesting as the material world of experience.

A Phenomenological Temple Account

A two-part article by Andrew Perry suggests that in Genesis 1 the narra-
tor is shown as viewing events as it were from the earth's surface, looking
across at the horizon, rather than looking up at the apparent "vault" of
heaven.[14] Consider this in what follows, together with my suggestion that
"air" has no word in Hebrew (because air only became a material substance through later Greek thought: see the Introduction to this book).
Thus we start with an ocean deep (*tehom*) that has a *surface*, above which
is "a space not needing creation" because, air not having been discovered, it contained nothing except (in Genesis 1:2) both the active wind,
or breath (*ruach*), of God and, of course, thick darkness. If God's breath
were in the deep water of a cosmic ocean, it would simply bubble up, as
any Israelite child drinking from a pottery beaker knew! And so:

13. Cachão, "Earth-Sky Cosmologies."
14. Perry, *Myth of the Solid Dome, Parts 1 & 2.*

1 In the beginning God created the heavens and the earth. 2 The **earth** (*eretz*) was formless and void, and **darkness** was over the **surface** of the **deep**, and the Spirit (*ruach* - **breath/wind**) of God was moving over the **surface of the waters**.

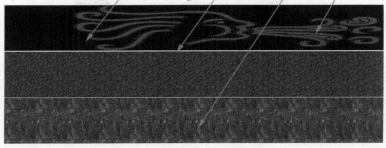

This is the primordial "heavens and the earth" of Genesis 1:1–2, a term that is a merism meaning "heavens, earth, and all in between." The earth already exists as the seabed, but is for that reason functionless (*tohu wabohu*). Hence it is named formally only on Day 3, when its scope becomes restricted to the "dry" revealed by the gathering of the sea. The deep (*tehom*) is by no means infinite: it has both a bed, and a surface. Next:

3 Then God said, "Let there be **light**"; and there was light. 4 God saw that the light was good; and God separated the light from the darkness. 5 God called the light day, and the darkness He called night. And there was evening and there was morning, one day.

Profound theological reasons are often suggested for the existence of light before the heavenly bodies. But it is actually a phenomenological necessity for the period. With no concept of air to scatter light, there was simply no phenomenological reason to associate light only with the sun, or with any material thing (just as there was no reason not to call the moon "a light"). The blue sky *is* the light (though the *meaning* of the text has more to do with the function of time, the *alternation* of light and dark).[15]

> 6 Then God said, "Let there be an **expanse** (something stretched out) in the midst of the waters, and let it separate the waters from the waters." 7 God made the expanse, and separated the waters which were below the expanse from the waters which were above the expanse (cloud); and it was so. 8 God called the expanse heaven. And there was evening and there was morning a second day.

This "expanse" is named "heavens" (*shemayim*) and contains . . . nothing, for the Hebrews had no concept of "air," still less of "atmosphere." It is the physical separation—the gap—that is the essence of what is made, just as the Egyptian air god Shu represents, or *is*, the *realm* of air, rather than a physical substance.[16] The upper waters are simply clouds,[17] and the lower waters become seas. But for this separation to happen, the upper waters must be lifted up (since the solid earth cannot sink) into the empty space that was always above the waters, in which God's spirit "hovered" from the beginning. Nevertheless the "face" of the upper waters is retained, as it is on the upper surface of the clouds.

The translation "vault of the sky" (as in the New International Version) is plain wrong: *raqia* is derived from a root for "stretch," which might indicate a metal sheet—but never a vault. That word is derived from the nineteenth-century mistranslation of the Babylonian *Enuma elish*, transferred across language and culture for a different word root and a different concept! Vaults or domes larger than a small room were architecturally unknown in ancient times.

15. Note that the derivation of the Greek *aether* for the upper air is from a root meaning "light."

16. We still retain this sense when we describe an "aerial display" or a "radio aerial," denoting *where* these are, rather than the material medium they occupy.

17. See Poythress, "Rain Water Versus a Heavenly Sea."

9 Then God said, "Let the waters below the heavens be gathered into one place, and let the dry land appear"; and it was so. 10 God called the dry land **earth**, and the gathering of the waters He called seas; and God saw that it was good. 11 Then God said, "Let the earth sprout vegetation, plants yielding seed, and fruit trees on the earth bearing fruit after their kind with seed in them"; and it was so. 12 The earth brought forth vegetation, plants yielding seed after their kind, and trees bearing fruit with seed in them, after their kind; and God saw that it was good. 13 There was evening and there was morning, a third day.

From here onwards things are conceptually easier. The lower waters are gathered to reveal the land, whose crowning glory is vegetation.

14 Then God said, "Let there be lights in the expanse of the heavens to separate the day from the night, and let them be for signs and for seasons and for days and years; 15 and let them be for lights in the expanse of the heavens to give light on the earth"; and it was so. 16 God made the two great lights, the greater light to govern the day, and the lesser light to govern the night; He made the stars also. 17 God placed them in the expanse of the heavens to give light on the earth, 18 and to govern the day and the night, and to separate the light from the darkness; and God saw that it was good. 19 There was evening and there was morning, a fourth day.

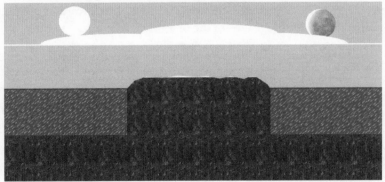

You will see that here there is an apparent fudge, in that the heavenly bodies are above the upper waters. Yet we have seen that the clouds *are* the upper waters, open above to the original place where darkness and God's *ruach* already was. Yet phenomenologically the sun and moon *are*

above the clouds—it is an obvious, and always observed, fact. It is only a *problem* if we believe the Israelites *must* have thought the upper waters were an ocean, and did not know clouds were water, even though many Scriptures show they did.[18] If clouds *are not* the upper waters, then where is such an essential feature of creation in Genesis 1? In fact, they serve the function of a veil, like that of the holy place in the tabernacle.

20 Then God said, "Let the waters teem with swarms of living creatures, and let birds fly above the earth in the open expanse of the heavens." 21 God created the great sea monsters and every living creature that moves, with which the waters swarmed after their kind, and every winged bird after its kind; and God saw that it was good. 22 God blessed them, saying, "Be fruitful and multiply, and fill the waters in the seas, and let birds multiply on the earth." 23 There was evening and there was morning, a fifth day.

The fish and birds appear logically together because the former are denizens of the waters below, and the birds of those above. Thus the heavenly lights belong to the highest heavens, the birds to the upper waters/lower heavens, and the fish to the seas. In this way the creatures not only occupy, but clarify, the realms of the first three days.

24 Then God said, "Let the earth bring forth living creatures after their kind: cattle and creeping things and beasts of the earth after their kind"; and it was so. 25 God made the beasts of the earth after their kind, and the cattle after their kind, and everything that creeps on the ground after its kind; and God saw that it was good.

18. E.g., Job 36:27–28; 38:24, 37; Prov 3:19.

Everything is now complete except for humankind, which I leave you to imagine. The above scheme explains why God is called "Most High" from Genesis 14 on, and descends from, speaks from, dwells in heaven as the highest part of creation, not meaning either "in the air" or "under a cosmic ocean." This agrees with the Hebrew use of the intensive "heaven of heavens," i.e. "highest heaven," for God's dwelling. It involves no speculative ancient science whatsoever: just a theological (functional and cultic) explanation of what the author saw as he looked at the horizon.

It shows a world of three distinct layers, with no definite extent (matching other ANE concepts which lacked the Greek idea of a spatially defined "cosmos"). These layers divide the "heavens and the earth" into three parts, corresponding to the divisions of the Israelite tabernacle and temple, and on a larger scale, to Israel as a holy land. Note that, although the Hebrews believed in some kind of underworld, *sheol*, it is not included in the creation account. The best explanation for this is that *sheol* is irrelevant to the tripartite temple theme.[19]

This is the significance of the language of *separation* that marks the first three days, when the various "realms" are created. Just as the humanly built tabernacle was set up by separating the tent from the courtyard with curtains, and the holy of holies from the tent with the veil, so God does the same. The sea is included because, as we have already seen, it represents that which is not yet sacred space. This is tabulated below:

GENESIS "COSMIC TEMPLE"	HEBREW TEMPLE	LAND OF ISRAEL
Heavens	Holy of Holies	Jerusalem Temple
Firmament	Curtain of the Temple	Wall of the Temple
Sky (and mountains)	Sanctuary of Priests	Jerusalem
Land	Court of Worshippers	Land of Israel
Sea	Outside World	Lands of the Gentiles

The Garden as a Temple

The recognition of temple imagery in Genesis 2—3 is somewhat independent of that in Genesis 1. Gordon Wenham wrote an important paper

19. Sheol's absence might also reflect an absence of human death, but immortality is not a concern of Genesis 1, whereas temple imagery is.

in 1986, which was reprinted in a book of 1994.[20] But as in the case of Genesis 1 he finds that there are early Jewish sources noting the same thing: *Genesis Rabbah* 16:5 suggests that "till and keep"[21] may mean sacrifice (Exodus 3:12; Numbers 28:2), and *Genesis Rabbah* 21:8 that the expulsion from the garden is parallel to the exile from Jerusalem (that is from the temple worship).

Wenham also acknowledges his debt to David Chilton,[22] who identified, as analogous to the tabernacle, the entrance to the garden from the east, jewels and gold like those in the temple (in Ezekiel 28), and the trees symbolized by the *menorah*. Wenham adds further parallels: God walking in Eden as he walked in the tabernacle; the cherubim which elsewhere are always temple guardians; fullness of life in the sanctuary (including the menorah as a probable stylized tree of life in the tabernacle); the fact that the words for "tilling" and "keeping" are only used *together* with reference to Levitical guarding of the tabernacle;[23] God clothing Adam and Eve in tunics, like Levitical priests; a sacred river like that flowing from the temple in prophetic oracles; and the tree of wisdom representing the tablets of the law kept in ark of the covenant in the temple.

Wenham suggests that the move from the "long-noted" Genesis 1 temple-building imagery (with many parallels in Exodus 25—40) to the imagery of Genesis 2—3 forms a "smooth transition."[24] He summarizes his case thus:

> The Garden of Eden is not viewed by the author of Genesis simply as a piece of Mesopotamian farmland, but as an archetypal sanctuary, that is a place where God dwells and where man should worship him. Many of the features of the garden may also be found in later sanctuaries particularly the tabernacle or Jerusalem temple. These parallels suggest that the garden itself is understood as a sanctuary.[25]

Greg Beale, in a much longer treatment of the temple imagery of the whole Bible, restates much the same case,[26] but adds Eden as a unique

20. Wenham, "Sanctuary Symbolism." (Originally in *Proceedings of the Ninth World Congress of Jewish Studies, Division A: The Period of the Bible*. Jerusalem: World Union of Jewish Studies, 1986, 19–25.)

21. Gen 2:15.

22. Chilton, *Paradise Restored*, 29

23. Num 3:7–8, 8:2, 18:5–6.

24. Wenham, "Sanctuary Symbolism," 403.

25. Ibid., 399.

26. Beale, *Temple*, 66–80.

place of God's presence, Adam as the first priest, the garden imagery of
the tabernacle and temple decoration, and the presence of a holy mountain, at least in Ezekiel's description of Eden.[27]

It is relevant to the position I am building that the temple imagery in
Genesis, particularly in the garden narrative, has been disputed. A number of the specific connections have been challenged as, at best, tenuous,
which is a fair criticism. More important are larger issues like the lack of
a clear tripartite structure to the garden. But the most general criticism
is of most significance. For example, Brian Collins questions primarily
what is symbolizing what:

> But to argue that God's presence in Eden makes Eden a temple
> is to mistake the reality for the symbol. The temple is needed as
> a symbol of God's presence because the reality of God's presence
> has been withdrawn due to sin. . . .
>
> Since the cherubim are placed to guard the garden only after
> Adam and Eve were expelled from the garden, their presence on
> the tabernacle curtains is probably an indication that the way to
> God is still barred for sinful humans rather than an indication
> that Eden was a temple. . . .
>
> While it may be true that the lampstand symbolized the tree of
> life (I am inclined to think so), and while the lampstand and
> other parts of the tabernacle make use of garden imagery, this
> only demonstrates that the tabernacle and temple looked back
> to Eden. It does not demonstrate that Eden was a temple. [28]

The key claim here is that temples only became necessary because
of the failure of Adam and Eve in the Garden to live in the reality. In
a recent *Festschrift* in Beale's honour, Daniel Block casts doubt on the
temple imagery in *both* passages:

> In my response to reading Gen 1—3 as temple-building texts,
> I have hinted at the fundamental hermeneutical problem in-
> volved in this approach. The question is, should we read Gen
> 1—3 in the light of later texts, or should we read later texts in
> light of these? If we read the accounts of the order given, then
> the creation account provides essential background to primeval
> history, which provides background for the patriarchal, exodus,
> and tabernacle narratives. By themselves and by this reading
> the accounts of Gen 1—3 offer no clues that a cosmic or Edenic

27. Ezek 28:11–17.

28. Collins, "Was Eden a Temple?"

temple might be involved. However, as noted above, the Edenic features of the tabernacle, the Jerusalem temple, and the temple envisioned by Ezekiel are obvious. Apparently their design and function intended to capture something of the original environment in which human beings were placed. However, the fact that Israel's sanctuaries were Edenic does not make Eden into a sacred shrine. At best this is a non-reciprocating equation.[29]

So the response to those who see temple imagery in Genesis is largely that the later tabernacle and temple sought to echo the "primeval situations" of both the cosmos (as created in Genesis 1) and the Garden of Eden, now lost because of sin, rather than the reverse.

This insight is important. But it seems to neglect the fact that the Genesis 1 account is not "the creation of the world," but an *interpretation* of the creation for Israel, with some particular theological purpose. Furthermore, creation and the fall did not simply *happen* sequentially—they were *recorded* in some order, and at least in the final form we have them, by the same author. If we accept a Mosaic core to the *Torah* (or even if we don't, but we allow a final editorial hand for all five of its books), then the same author who placed these two narratives at the beginning of Genesis also placed the tabernacle-construction narrative at the end of Exodus.

Quite possibly the account of the Exodus was written down before that of Genesis. If that author was Moses, then long before he wrote anything down at all, he had received his instructions to build the tabernacle "after the pattern . . . , which was shown to you on the mountain."[30]

So it is utterly plausible that Moses was *simultaneously* made aware both of a cosmic pattern of creation, and of an architectural plan that was to imitate it in the form of the tabernacle. Or else it is possible that later, his inspired reflection on the divinely appointed structure of the tabernacle led him to the understanding of the cosmos that inspired Genesis 1 (which, as I argued in the last chapter, may well be his prologue to the older, traditionally transmitted protohistory). So whichever insight came first, it is likely to be the same prophetic mind that gave us *both* the pattern of the tabernacle, *and* the temple imagery of the creation narrative.

Each therefore informs the other, making it foolish to ask if the tabernacle is a representation of the cosmos, or that the description of the cosmos is derived from the tabernacle. As described in the *Torah*, they

29. Block, "Eden," 20–21.
30. Exod 25:40.

are *both* simply macrocosmic and microcosmic representations of God's relationship to the world.

But that raises an interesting, and crucial, question about the Eden account, which is, as it stands, only a *partial* representation of the tabernacle. A number of its elements, as the critics point out, do not correspond to "the pattern shown on the mountain," and although set immediately next to Genesis 1, these have not been edited into compliance with its imagery, nor that of the Exodus tabernacle account. On the other hand, some elements of Eden *are* incorporated not only into the tabernacle, but into prophetic temple representations up to and including the last chapters of Revelation, as fully documented by Beale in his book.

It is as if there are actually *two* distinct, though partially overlapping, patterns of sacred space in Genesis. I suggest that distinguishing these two patterns is crucial to understanding the two-creation model I have been following in this book, and I believe that the separation is maintained throughout Scripture.

Temples of the Old and New Creations

Richard Middleton has pointed out the odd fact that despite the temple imagery in Genesis 1, the text nowhere speaks of God's glory coming to fill it. This is despite the *shekinah* being a significant culmination of the building of the tabernacle,[31] and of the later building of the temple by Solomon,[32] as well as its absence being theologically significant in the second temple.[33] The significance of the latter is that the Mosaic covenant had been abrogated and Israel awaited the promised New Covenant from a state of theological exile. Middleton explains its absence from the creation account thus:

> If we read canonically, this Spirit filling is delayed until the garden narrative of Genesis 2.[34]

The story of Adam explains the absence of the glory, because only through the endowment of God's spirit, through Yahweh's inbreathing of Adam in Middleton's understanding, would God's glory come to fill all

31. Exod 40:34–38.
32. 2 Chr 7:1–3.
33. Ezek 10:18–19; Ezra 6:16–18.
34. Middleton, *New Heaven and New Earth,* 48.

things—in the same way that Christ's gospel promises the same, through the same Spirit, after Adam's failure.

In Genesis 2, then, the garden was a place full of the glory of God, and more significantly, a place in which humankind *shared* that glory. This, I suggest, explains the discontinuities between the Eden "sacred space" and the imagery of the tabernacle, not least the tripartite creation of Genesis 1. In my view, these discontinuities show that the Garden of Eden is to be understood as a different *kind* of sacred space from either the tabernacle, or the Genesis 1 "cosmic temple," as I shall now explain.

First, remember what a temple actually *is*. It is not simply a place for worship—altars were built at many places on Israel's journey to Canaan, to sacrifice to God in heaven. Instead, a temple is a place where God is represented as *dwelling* amongst his people, which is why Exodus 40, the coming of God's glory to the tabernacle, is the climax and finale of the book.

But because of the rebellion and faithlessness of Israel the tabernacle, Solomon's temple, and the second temple were all designed to emphasize the holiness and *separation* of God from an unholy people. Only duly sanctified Levitical priests might enter the house within the courtyard, and only the High Priest, once annually, was permitted to enter the holy of holies to make atonement. Moses was fully aware of this, as the one who, alone apart from Joshua, met God face to face both at Sinai and in the "tent of meeting" on the journey, so that his face shone and had to be veiled.[35]

So it is no accident that the "architecture" of the cosmic temple of Genesis 1 is like that of the tabernacle, and it confirms, though with reservations, the criticisms of those who say that temples are only necessary because of the fall. For the creation account, of course, precedes the fall, just as God's heavenly temple in Revelation is unaffected by it.[36]

The emphasis in the creation account is on God's dwelling, in glory, *in heaven*. For him to fill the whole *earth* with his glory too (which does not happen in the text), would be a step *beyond* the tabernacle, equivalent to his glory filling not just the holy of holies, nor even the house, but the courtyard containing Israel as worshippers.

35. Exod 34:29–35. Second Corinthians 3:7–18 puts this passage in a new *v.* old creation context.

36. Rev 4; 7:15; 11:19; 14:15–17; 15:5–8; 16:1, 17. The heavenly temple has no divisions either: it is, essentially, a "holy of holies."

In the New Testament, such a bursting of holy bounds occurs as a major theme, and is represented by the tearing of the temple curtain at the death of Jesus, revealing the holy of holies. It is usually taken as Christ's victory over sin, but it is actually more than that—it is his inauguration of the new creation, which sin had prevented, in which God is seen face to face by his people, and dwells among them.

Contrast the situation at the close of the creation account—God in his heaven, humankind on earth—with that of a spirit-filled Adam in the garden, in Genesis 2. Here no boundaries or barriers are mentioned. Adam and Eve are free to walk in the midst of the garden, where Yahweh also walks. When they seek to evade God, they hide among the trees, for there are no structural divisions.

And so, after the fall, when cherubim are sent to guard the way to the garden, it is the *whole* garden, not just an especially holy part of it, that they guard. Contrast that with the guardian cherubim flanking the Ark of the Covenant *within the holy of holies* in the tabernacle. In Eden, then, the whole emphasis is on free and open access to God, not on separation. This profound contrast provides a strong argument from the narrative itself that the story of Adam *follows on* from the creation account, rather than duplicating it.

It is a contrast that continues throughout the Bible. In the patriarchal narratives, it is sometimes hard to distinguish worship, from prophetic revelation, from theophany. But it is the last that is the equivalent to the concept of "temple" in the sense of God's presence. We see that Abraham, the man of faith, meets God personally, as for example, when visited by the three men prior to the destruction of Sodom, [37] and also when he enters into an inviolable oath[38] and covenant with him.[39] Similarly, Jacob meets God in actual combat as he returns home.[40] What is important is that, in all such theophanies, no temple architecture intervenes. The encounters are face to face, as they were in the garden of God.

The same is true of Moses, who first meets God in open country by the bush at Sinai, returns there after the exodus, and continues to meet God face to face to receive further revelation. The contrast is even more obvious because Israel was offered the chance for such an unmediated

---

37. Gen 18.
38. Gen 15.
39. Gen 17.
40. Gen 32:24–32.

encounter when they first arrived at Sinai, but disobeyed through fear, insisting instead that Moses be their mediator.[41] Thereafter, direct access to God was lost, and the whole priestly apparatus, together with a tripartite tabernacle modelled after the *old* creation, not after the garden sanctuary, replaced it for Israel, actually *restricting* Israel's access to God.[42]

Subsequent to Sinai, in the desert wanderings, the same separation is seen. In Exodus 33, and to a lesser extent elsewhere, there are confusing mentions of a "tent of meeting" that appears to be different from the tabernacle that is, frequently, referred to by the same name (and by the same Hebrew words):

> 7 Now Moses used to take the tent and pitch it outside the camp, a good distance from the camp, and he called it the tent of meeting. And everyone who sought the Lord would go out to the tent of meeting which was outside the camp. 8 And it came about, whenever Moses went out to the tent, that all the people would arise and stand, each at the entrance of his tent, and gaze after Moses until he entered the tent. 9 Whenever Moses entered the tent, the pillar of cloud would descend and stand at the entrance of the tent; and the Lord would speak with Moses. 10 When all the people saw the pillar of cloud standing at the entrance of the tent, all the people would arise and worship, each at the entrance of his tent. 11 Thus the Lord used to speak to Moses face to face, just as a man speaks to his friend. When Moses returned to the camp, his servant Joshua, the son of Nun, a young man, would not depart from the tent.[43]

Even the mini-concordance in the *New American Standard Bible* notes this confusion, without explanation:

> TENT OF MEETING: perhaps the same as the Tabernacle or at certain periods a separate meeting place.

The description in Exodus 33 is of a simple tent taken from the camp by Moses and pitched some distance outside, perhaps for simple seclusion or, as one source suggests, because at this time Yahweh refused to associate with his disobedient people until Moses interceded for them in this very tent. The official tabernacle, in contrast, was placed at the *center* of the camp, with the tribes marshalled around it. This is an irreconcilable

---

41. Exod 19:13, 16–18, 20:18–21.
42. Sailhamer, *Meaning of the Pentateuch,* 378–87, 392–98.
43. Exod 33:7–11.

difference requiring two, quite separate, tents[44]. It suggests an Eden-type sanctuary to which Moses, the man of God, had access—but not the rebellious people.

Moses is said to stay within this tent until the Lord descends to its doorway to speak to him, as it were, face to face, in a pillar of cloud (compare Genesis 18:1–2). Not only that, but his young assistant Joshua, an Ephraimite and not a Levite, is permanently stationed within the tent. In contrast, the Tabernacle was a place where God's glory dwelt permanently, from which all but Levitical priests in the course of their duties were excluded, and of course only the High Priest could enter the holy of holies and encounter Yahweh in his glory during his annual act of atonement.

I suggest that there is a running theme in the *Torah* of the contrast between the old creation of the Genesis 1 "cosmic temple," and the new creation of the Genesis 2 Garden of Eden sanctuary. This contrast, as I have already mentioned, continues in the direct encounters with Yahweh of the patriarchs and Moses, comparable to the garden; and with the worship of the Tabernacle and Temple, in which the worshipper is separated from God by curtains and walls comparable to the cosmic divisions of the creation story.

If that is a genuine concern of the writer, then the placing of the description of Moses's tent of meeting in Exodus 33 is deliberate and significant, because it is sandwiched between two detailed descriptions of the *other* tent of meeting, the tabernacle. For after the giving of the plans for the tabernacle on the mountain, Moses descends to find Israel in the midst of the rebellion of the golden calf, and smashes the tablets of the covenant. Yahweh makes as if to destroy Israel and continue his purposes only through Moses, but the latter, interceding "face to face" in this non-partitioned tent, speaks Christ-like words about his willingness to be blotted out of God's book rather than God's not remaining with Israel along with himself. Moses is a blessing to Israel through his intimacy with Yahweh, a theme to be found from Adam to Jesus. Yet Israel never shares that intimacy, because of their rebellion, though it had been offered to them.

---

44. This geography is, perhaps, reflected in the attention drawn in Hebrews 13:10–14 to the contrast between the tabernacle inside the camp, and the effective sacrifice of Christ outside it, providing access to the "lasting city" to come.

The *Torah* even contrasts Israel's apostasy with the hope of future glory, at what John Sailhamer regards as a "compositional seam":[45]

> 20 So the Lord said, "I have pardoned *them* according to your word; 21 but indeed, as I live, all the earth will be filled with the glory of the Lord. 22 Surely all the men who have seen My glory and My signs which I performed in Egypt and in the wilderness, yet have put Me to the test these ten times and have not listened to My voice, 23 shall by no means see the land which I swore to their fathers, nor shall any of those who spurned Me see it. [46]

Finally I need not, I hope, dwell on the great emphasis of the New Testament on direct access to God through Christ. Not only the tearing of the curtain, but the idea that believers become living stones in the temple that is Christ's body, resemble an Edenic kind of temple, rather than a Mosaic one. The giving of the Holy Spirit at Pentecost is the *shekinah* glory of that temple, though it is only a deposit guaranteeing the final consummation—the coming together of heaven and earth when God will dwell with his people (as he did in the garden), and there is no longer any need for a temple in the Mosaic sense.[47]

Such a vision is *not* simply a return to the original order of things, though it *is* a return to Eden, because the garden was intended to inaugurate a *new* order of things. It is, however, as Scripture explicitly states, a new creation, in which the old temple architecture of Genesis 1—where heaven is the holy of holies, the skies the holy house, and the earth the temple court—is replaced with a universal version of the Garden of Eden, where there is free access for all creation to the tree of knowledge and the tree of life. This means no less than to dwell eternally in the glory of God.

That is my principal reason, rather than considerations from science or anthropology, for seeing the first two chapters of Genesis as sequential. Genesis 1 is about the old creation, which is still represented in the "weak" covenant of rebellious Israel with its tabernacle and temple.[48] But Genesis 2 is about the new creation, and the free worship of the patriarchs, Moses, and the saints both before and after Christ, who finally succeeds in completing that new creation, as the New Adam and the True Israel.

---

45. Sailhamer, *Meaning of the Pentateuch,* 40, 243, 347–48.

46. Num 14:20–22.

47. Rev 21:22.

48. Gal 4:21–31.

The science and anthropology, and notably the Genealogical Adam hypothesis, tell us that there was a time before this new kind of worship became available, when the temple cosmology, which divides heaven off so fully from earth, was appropriate and good. After Adam, though, the tripartite temple is a sign of regression. And that is why it is abolished in Christ, in whom we meet God face to face.

Conclusion Relative to Genealogical Adam

Genealogical Adam recognizes an old creation humanity, which in this book I suggest to be worshippers of God by nature, from afar off, and a new creation humanity, in the form of Adam and Eve in the Garden of Eden, brought into a new covenant relationship with God, whose covenant name of Yahweh is used in the text.

I find this division reflected in two quite distinct types of sanctuary found in the Bible. The first, tripartite sanctuary reflects old creation cosmology, and so is suitable and good for the "Sabbath reign" of God in his old creation, where his human worshippers, by nature, acknowledge him as the high God, or sky Father (see chapter 10). This pattern becomes, in the *Torah,* representative of the fall-back tabernacle of Israel's failure to embrace intimacy with God by faith, through fear. Fallen Israel is unholy, and so remains separated from God by the institutions of the tabernacle and temple.

The second type of sanctuary, marked by a lack of any internal divisions and open access to Yahweh, is first seen in the Garden of Eden, and recurs in the worship of those who exhibit new-creation faith: the patriarchs in their informal worship, Moses on Sinai and in the special "tent of meeting," and finally Jesus in his abolition of Jewish temple worship, his tearing of the veil, the new temple centered on his body, and eschatologically in the new heavens and the new earth, where there is no temple apart from the living presence of God amongst his people, his glory filling all things.

17

THE DEVIL AND ALL HIS WORKS

Revisiting the Ransom Theory

SATAN HAS TRADITIONALLY BEEN seen as a fallen angel, whose fall occurred even before creation. For example, the 1668 gloss to the start of Milton's *Paradise Lost* tells us that:

> The poem hastes into the midst of things, presenting Satan and his Angels now fallen into Hell , describ'd here, not in the Center (for Heaven and Earth may be suppos'd as yet not made, certainly not yet accurst) but in a place of utter darkness, fitliest call'd Chaos . . .[1]

This poses contradictions with the biblical account, for the angels are part of creation, though not mentioned in Genesis 1 unless in the first-person plural of verse 26, and after the creation of humanity, creation was "very good."[2] It poses even greater problems in this regard for any old earth scenario, including the Genealogical Adam concept being defended in this book, for man would be created within a fallen, not a pristine, cosmos.

There has been a tendency to merge Satan's evil into old earth schemes in the form of natural evil or chaos, including of course the supposed evils of evolution, which God has perpetually to limit, or finally to

1. Milton, *Paradise Lost*, 4.
2. Gen 1:31.

overcome. But as I argued at length in my book *God's Good Earth,* there are several reasons why this is untenable. And among the strongest is this same black and white assertion in Genesis 1, that at the time humankind was created, the whole creation was good, not corrupted.

In chapter 14 I described Irenaeus's account of the creation narratives, which portrays Satan in Genesis 1 as an archangel appointed to oversee the various tasks angels were given, and not at all consigned to the abyss. But in commenting on Genesis 2 Irenaeus begins to introduce this steward as Eve's deceiver. I went on to show that Irenaeus must have drawn his argument from Psalm 8, and from the Hebrews 2 exposition of the psalm. Consider the meaning of Hebrews 2:14–15:

> 14 Therefore, since the children share in flesh and blood, He Himself likewise also partook of the same, that through death He might render powerless him who had the power of death, that is, the devil, 15 and might free those who through fear of death were subject to slavery all their lives.

The writer here introduces Satan into the picture of humankind's temporary subordination to the angels, and its glorification by the work of Christ. This mention of Satan suggests that he has some particular relevance to the relationship between mankind, angels, and divine glory.

I want to deal with that in the context of the Eden story, and in the light of the oldest popular theory of the atonement—the Ransom Theory—which although now probably virtually extinct in the Western church, actually has some traction in explaining the several New Testament passages in which Christ's defeat of the "spiritual powers and authorities" is at the forefront. It can also help account for Satan's place in the created order of an inhabited old earth, for which this book argues.

In the Ransom Theory, Christ rescues humans from Satan's bondage by paying a ransom to him of his own death, but outwits him (thus turning the tables on Satan's deception) by his unexpected resurrection. Origen, Gregory of Nyssa, and Augustine all spoke of God actually deceiving Satan (fittingly, the devil being the arch-deceiver himself), the last even using the analogy of Jesus as bait in an animal trap (an image to which Gregory of Nazianzus objected, so beginning the eventual eclipse of Ransom Theory).[3]

---

3. Stott, *Cross of Christ,* 113.

The theory was revisited by Gustav Aulén, whose academically, though not popularly, influential 1931 book *Christus Victor*[4] greatly affected the thinking of C. S. Lewis, amongst others. To summarize, he re-examined the main theories of atonement, casting the earliest explanations of Christ's work in a more positive light, and reinstating the importance of seeing the cross as a victory over the powers of evil enslaving mankind. Starting with the old "Ransom Theory" he removed some elements he found objectionable, and arrived at what is known as the "Christus Victor" theory of atonement. The victory over evil is indeed a prominent New Testament theme, especially in Paul, a theme which often gets strangely sidelined in our thinking.

The theory appears today mainly in a changed form in which the defeat of Satan is replaced with a demythologized defeat of "evil." Since it does not appear to mesh with other themes found in Scripture and theology, notably substitutionary punishment and propitiatory sacrifice, these tend to be simply jettisoned when it is adopted. It has to be said that Aulén himself also treated his "Classical Approach" as an either/or choice intended to displace other aspects of atonement.[5]

In my view the victory of Christ hinges on the personal nature of the "powers and authorities," because it arises from the Eden narrative in which the serpent's personal temptation and deception are central. Without such a personal understanding, the evil to be defeated would necessarily be something in God's own direct work of creation, making God the author of sin.

In the New Testament's own authentic Christus Victor theology, the victory is essentially, and specifically, said to be over the wiles of the devil and his angelic followers ("powers and authorities in the heavenly realms")[6] in causing sin, in order to destroy humanity. It *needs* a personal devil as the locus of the evil that Christ conquers by death and resurrection. Also, it is wrong to emphasize it over against other aspects of the atonement, for it depends on them, which I will attempt to show.

---

4. Aulén, *Christus Victor*.

5. Stott, *Cross of Christ*, 229–30.

6. Eph 3:10.

The Psychology of Satan

It may help, at this stage, to see what is said in Scripture about Satan's primary motivations. Starting with the deutero-canonical *Wisdom*, from (it is thought) just before the New Testament period, we read:

> . . . for God created man for incorruption, and made him in the image of his own eternity, but through the devil's envy death entered the world, and those who belong to his party experience it.[7]

The question then is of whom the Jews considered Satan to be envious. Jesus says:

> 44 ". . . He was a murderer from the beginning, and does not stand in the truth because there is no truth in him. Whenever he speaks a lie, he speaks from his own *nature*, for he is a liar and the father of lies."[8]

"In the beginning" usually seems to carry the implication of "as Scripture describes the beginning," so that Jesus is here alluding to the garden, where the serpent first appears, in the first place confirming that the serpent is indeed to be identified as Satan, and secondly that his deception had as its motive "murder." Putting that together with the *Book of Wisdom's* "envy," we get the picture of a divine being consumed with envy of Adam and Eve,[9] and using lies and deception with murderous intent. The "murder" would, of course, be achieved by the knowledge that God had ordained death as the penalty for eating from the tree of knowledge: it is comparable to how hatred might cause someone to frame a man of a capital offense, so that the judicial system itself becomes the murder weapon.

This seems to endorse the common "demonological" interpretation of Ezekiel's lament over the king of Tyre (Ezek 28:11–19), in which the prophet is using an expansion of the Eden narrative as a metaphor for

---

7. Wis 2.23–24.

8. John 8:44.

9. Popular preaching often pictures Satan as envious of *God*, and desirous of displacing him. But that is not realistic. Some humans may see themselves as, literally, challenging God's rule, but that is only a result of delusional ignorance of who, and what, God is. The Bible affirms that Satan was part of the divine council that sees God face to face. He would know from the start that God is God, and that even angels are not. "You believe that God is one. You do well; the demons also believe, and shudder." (Jas 2:18.)

an earthly king's sin, suggesting that the serpent was actually a guardian cherub, i.e. one of the *elohim*, and so had a legitimate reason for being in the garden as a member of the divine council, and also that his sin only arose *within* the garden in relation to Adam, of whom he became jealous.[10]

The exposition Hebrews 2 gives of Psalm 8 provides a good motivation for this envy: a proud and glorious divine being, foremost amongst God's creation, realizes that lowly man is also to be granted access to wisdom and eternal life. Satan already has the former,[11] and assumes he has the latter by inalienable right.[12] Now, a mere creature of dust is to be "promoted over his head."

One might compare this to the story in Esther of Haman, who pathologically resents Mordecai's preferment, his jealousy resembling Satan's jealousy of Adam. One might also compare the story of Daniel and Darius in Daniel 6, in which courtiers, jealous of the "upstart Jew" Daniel, persuade the king to make a law that they know will entrap Daniel, through his religious observance. The edict Darius makes (in this case by cunning inducement) gives Daniel's enemies a legal right over his death, because of the immutability of "the law of the Medes and the Persians."

Darius could not simply punish the accusers for their malice, since Daniel was legally guilty. And he could not, without impugning his own justice, simply let Daniel off. Consequently Daniel paid the judicial penalty of exposure in the lions' den, but was spared from the lions by God, and Darius was then free to punish the accusers for their own wrongs in like manner.

Analogously, Satan had the power over human death described in Hebrews 2 only because God had decreed death to Adam in case of disobedience. His power lay only in his ability to accuse humankind before God ("*satan*," of course, means "accuser") though of course he also remained a tempter of those already held under the sway of inherent sin.

Satan could not be justly and finally punished for his malice whilst humankind was not justly and finally punished for its disobedience. God was in "moral debt," as it were, to punish humanity, not because Satan was owed anything whatsoever, but because the devil and the other "powers"

10. Others interpret the figure in the garden as Adam, who would be called a "cherub" on the basis of his intended appointment over the angels of God. I marginally prefer this interpretation.

11. Ezek 28:12; Gen 3:5, taking *elohim* as generic.

12. But see Ps 82.

were witnesses to God's just sentence on Adam's seed. This understanding overcomes the greatest objection to the "Ransom Theory," which is that God surely could not be in any debt to Satan.

When Christ, truly representing the human race, died, Satan no longer had any accusation against the race that they had sinned but not been justly punished. At the same time his own defense—the outstanding penalty of mankind—collapsed, so that his fate was sealed.

Loosely, this might be seen as Christ's paying the ransom of a slave—and *ransom* is certainly one of the words used of the atonement in Scripture. Satan gets what he has long desired—but discovers through the resurrection (in experience, if he had not already had some sense of foreboding!) that the cross condemns *him*, and not sinful mankind. That sounds awfully like the Ransom Theory, and moreover appears the perfect narrative *denouement* of the fall story in Genesis.

However, to pay such a ransom and defeat Satan, everything hinges on God's finding a way for his *own* justice to be seen to be preserved. Only that could defeat Satan's malevolence towards man, which depended on God's inflexible justice. Unlike Darius's foolish law, God's command and warning to Adam were just and righteous, and the devil could only be defeated if God's just sentence were actually, and publically, fulfilled in the death of Christ. So Christus Victor, in the form of the Ransom Theory, is incomplete without an account in terms of God's retributive justice, lest God himself be undermining the divine moral order underlying Creation.

This condition is met through the other key theme of atonement—substitutionary punishment. The death of Christ prevents death coming to us. God's judicial sentence in the garden is death for Adam's race, and Christ in the gospels "tastes death for everyone."[13] That is penal substitution, or propitiatory sacrifice.

So there are *two* separate but related problems to be solved by the atonement: the meeting of God's justice, and the defeat of evil spiritual powers. *Three* problems, if we also include how these can bring forgiveness and reconciliation to sinful individuals.

The last is solved only by a true spiritual union of the sinner with Christ, through faith, achieving solidarity both with his death, and with his glorified life. What is his becomes ours, and ours his: we are in Christ, as we were formerly in Adam. And that, of course, is the other key Pauline

13. Heb 2:9.

theme that has been so seldom understood, even by the New Testament scholars, if N. T. Wright is to be believed: that our salvation depends primarily on being "in Christ," just as our condemnation depended on being in a historical Adam.[14]

So God's own justice must be served because God is just, and because he himself set the penalty for breaking the command in the garden. Satan's hold over man is only God's own justice, and so that *must* be satisfied not only for God's own righteousness's sake, but to demonstrate his justice to the powers and principalities, as Paul writes, so disarming them. Christ's death is therefore substitutionary (because in our place), penal (because fulfilling God's righteous edict), and a ransom (because it looses Satan's hold over us, and liberates God's justice over Satan and the other corrupt powers).

One might even wave a small flag for the Moral Influence Theory here, in that the self-sacrifice of Jesus is the model on which the redeemed should live, and on which the power structures in the New Creation are founded. It does not, however, redeem—that is something far more direct and potent in Christ's work.

I hope you see how thinking along these lines makes the whole of "salvation history," from Genesis 3 to the gospel, one interwoven tapestry. And it also makes that salvation history part of the even bigger narrative that the Bible gives us about the new creation. *Contra* Galileo, the Bible does *not* simply tell us how to go to heaven—it tells us how the fullness of all creation was achieved by, through, and for Christ, on behalf of that ambiguously brutish and angelic creature, our own race.

Satan and Humanity Before Adam

If this is a true understanding of Scripture, then it makes the whole question of creaturely rebellion against God, and therefore evil itself, a relatively short-lived episode in the scheme of things. We do not have to look for clues of Satan's wicked activity in evolutionary history, nor even in human life before Adam. We may not be looking at moral perfection then, but that is because we are looking at lower created natures, not because we are looking at sin.

---

14. Some writers say that Wright is *not* to be believed on the neglect of union with Christ by the tradition: see particularly the response by Chester, *Reading Paul.*

Satan and his angels were either employed about some business in God's first creation or, in the light of Hebrews 1:14, were possibly only created as "powers and principalities" to assist humankind, which would explain their virtual absence from scriptural passages on the old creation.[15] In the latter case, sin would have come into the world through one man because Satan himself had only come into the world for the sake of that one man's race.

It would therefore appear that Satan's goal is specifically to disrupt God's plan for the new creation, which appeared to reduce his own glory by giving it to the rest of creation too. This was, indeed, a rebellion against God's will, but in the same way that Joab's murder of Abner, against King David's will,[16] was a rebellion not in order to usurp the kingdom, but to serve the king under his own crooked terms and maintain the status quo to his advantage.

The direct activity of the devil against Jesus in the New Testament too, mostly fits that pattern of seeking to derail his mission, rather than to destroy his (divine) life and so "replace God." The temptations in the wilderness centered on getting him to follow the easy path to earthly power, rather than the chosen way of suffering. Jesus' rebuke of Peter as "Satan" was the result of Peter's attempt to turn him away from the cross. And, if we accept a role for Satan as tempter in Gethsemane (which isn't stated, but which may be implied by the garden setting), that temptation was to avoid the cup of suffering.

At the same time, of course, Satan entered Judas in order to betray Jesus. If it were a purely human story one would suspect that Satan lacked a coherent plan by this stage. Perhaps, as I have seen suggested, his failure to avoid the death of Jesus was replaced by an idea to make it as disgraceful, and so ineffective, as possible.

If there *was* a surprise for him, apart from the resurrection (though the general resurrection of the righteous was a near-universal Jewish hope), it was the left-field matter of the incarnation itself, a plan that Scripture suggests to be a mystery hidden within the Trinitarian Godhead alone since the creation, to which even the angels were not privy.[17]

Perhaps that is the point at which Satan's own character made him blind. His vendetta against humankind was based on the unacceptability

15. Garvey, *God's Good Earth*, ch. 5, 60–68.

16. 2 Sam 3:20–39.

17. Col 1:19–27; 1 Tim 3:16; 1 Pet 1:10–12.

to him of the disruption of "proper hierarchy" by humanity's "promotion." From the role of God in relation to the divine council and its operations (whatever they are in the universe), he knew all about status, power, and responsibility—and must have known, as I have already said, the infinite power and majesty of God at first hand.

Yet the selflessness of God is indeed the key to the divine nature—and that, without controversy, was exhibited by the generosity of the very act of creation from the highest guardian cherubim to the lowliest earthly creature. God did not have to give us being, but delighted to do so for our own sakes. Yet, for whatever reason, Satan remained strangely unaware of that, seeing in God's desire to elevate Adam's race not an opportunity for his own more generous service of God, but rather a threat to his dignity and power.

With a blind spot like that, it is not hard to imagine that for God himself, as the Son, to step down not only into the lowly physical creation, but to dishonor and disgrace,[18] would be seen by Satan as anything but what it was—the subversion of his truncated concept of power by the Author of Power himself. Perhaps Satan truly failed to realize that "loss of face" may demonstrate true power, not weakness. It is a rare perception even amongst humans apart from those who have learned it from Christ.

And so there is a wonderfully apt response to the Genesis Eden narrative in the work of Christ, as the destruction not only of Satan's malicious work against mankind, but also the discrediting of all his supposed dignity and power by the demonstration to all creation, in Christ, of just what true dignity and power are. The lesson of the incarnation was, in God's great scheme, a lesson not only for mankind, but for the glorious angels, as well as being the template for the nature of the eternal spiritual creation.

The Devil as a Personal Being

The depopulation of heaven in the last few centuries of Western culture was, at least in part, a product of the same Promethean forces that gave us the "mechanical universe" of Baconian science, exacerbated by the Enlightenment and Deism.[19] It has nowadays, amongst "educated" Westerners, reached the end stage where any discussion is usually about

18. Phil 2:5–11.

19. See McGrath, *Re-Enchantment*, especially chapters 3–5.

the difficulty of believing in "a personal devil," rather than accounting for the numberless host of divine, but created, beings that the Bible describes (and on which Paul took his own stand, in an unusual strategic collaboration with the Pharisees, Acts 23:6–9).

I suppose the historical motivation for the abolition of "*elohim*," "sons of God," "powers and principalities," and so on initially follows much the same line that early modern science took in denying Aristotelian final causes to nature—so that God would be the sole supernatural power, thus avoiding perceived or actual idolatry. By the time eighteenth-century Deism arrived, even the Trinity became an embarrassment to the idea of the utterly transcendent and aloof Clockmaker God, dwelling in distant solitude.

How much more untidy even than the Trinity is a multitude of the heavenly host not only existing in some sort of governing capacity under God's control, but presumably serving actual functions within the created universe! Reason left no space for such busybodies interfering in human affairs (including the controlled world of science), so therefore they could not exist. Eventually of course, the invisibility of God put even *his* existence in doubt—which was not the end of the story, as eliminative materialists concluded that even human consciousness and will must be illusory epiphenomena of matter.

But against that is the testimony not only of Scripture, but of Jesus himself. As we have seen, it is a significant strand of the core narrative framework of the Bible, which begins at Genesis 3:1 with a serpent "more subtle" than any beast (subtlety not really being a characteristic of *any* of the animals, including snakes), and ends with "the dragon, the serpent of old, who is the devil and Satan," consigned to a lake of fire in Revelation 20:1.

John Chrysostom (349–407AD) comments on what seems to us a particularly "difficult" passage, Colossians 2:14–15, largely because we have abolished "the powers":

> Having forgiven us all sins, having wiped out by the doctrines
> the handwriting which was against us, which was contrary to us,
> He took it out of the way, having nailed it to His cross. Having
> disarmed principalities and powers, He made a public spectacle
> of them, having triumphed over them in it.

In interpreting the meaning of this handwriting that, somehow, gives the spiritual powers and authorities a hold over us, Chrysostom includes this:

> . . . the devil held possession of the handwriting which God
> set down against Adam—"In the day you eat from the tree of
> knowledge, you will die" (Gen. 2:17). This handwriting, then,
> which the devil held in his possession, Christ did not hand to
> us, but Himself tore it in pieces, as One who joyfully forgives.[20]

The view of Michael Heiser, which I mentioned in chapter 1, is, I think, illuminating here. He suggests that, since the garden is described as Yahweh's sacred space, it would to any ancient Israelite imply that God was not alone there, but he would be assumed to be surrounded and assisted by his divine council. Adam and Eve would then be seen as being newly privileged to live and serve within God's own "seat of government." Heiser argues that this, by the original readership of Genesis, would be taken as a matter of course. Not only would this justify Eve's encounter with a powerful spiritual being, who would have a good reason to be there in the garden, but such a figure would appear, to her, to have sufficient authority to "explain away" the motives of Yahweh in forbidding the couple access to the tree of knowledge. Eve was in that case deceived plausibly (but should still have obeyed God's word, not the creature's).

If this view is correct, it gives Paul's words in Colossians a new clarity. It would mean that God's original command to Adam was made in the full knowledge—in the hearing, if you like—of his own "divine council," and hence that Adam's succumbing to the serpent's temptation would have been soon known to the appointed spiritual rulers within creation. Not only that, but as the garden was then God's dwelling on earth, that act of disobedience actually took place in the very place from which God's rule of justice over the world emanated. For God to fail to carry out the penalty of death for this act of rebellion within his own "administration" would be seen by all those spiritual beings to convict God of injustice.

All this gives a poetic justice to the atoning role of Jesus, for he himself is the ontologically divine superior of all the powers, who himself (as the *Logos* of God) issued the command to Adam not to eat the tree of knowledge. But he is also, through the incarnation, a perishable "animal" from the seed of Adam who, though innocent, fulfills the penalty of death in his own body, and thereby receives an undeniable place at the Father's right hand.

What divine being is going to dare, now, to say that man in unworthy to sit in God's council? Or to deny that divine power is a sign of

---

20. John Chrysostom, "Commentary on Col 2:14–15." In Needham, *Daily Readings,* January 10.

self-giving love, rather than of self-assertion? Whether or not St. Paul had that particular part of Scripture, and Heiser's supernaturalist understanding, in view in Colossians is impossible to say with certainty. But it certainly gives an illuminating biblical background for what Paul says of the work of Christ on the Cross.

Conclusion Relative to Genealogical Adam

Genealogical Adam enables Adam and Eve to exist within real history. Consequently it also places Satan's involvement within human history, and not an ill-defined and ahistorical dualistic conflict of good and evil.

Thus angelic evil, like sin itself, is seen to be a temporary aberration spanning the short interval between the end of the old creation, and the fulfillment of the new. The powers were not evil before Adam, and so we need not look for their destructive role either in earth's prehistory, or in the religious lives of early humans living before Adam.

Since I argued the case, in my book *God's Good Earth*, that "natural evil" and a "cosmic fall" are not taught in Scripture (nor in early Christianity, nor by nature itself), the old earth presuppositions of Genealogical Adam are quite consistent with this whole picture.

18.

ALTERNATIVE VIEWS

Genealogical Adam: A Versatile Paradigm

IN THE INTRODUCTION I suggested that Genealogical Adam is a *paradigm* more than it is a *theory*. By drawing attention to newly realized scientific truths about genealogy, it demonstrates that there is no longer a scientific argument against the existence of the biblical Adam and Eve, provided we are willing to embrace the evidence that other, fully human, people existed "outside the garden" before and alongside Adam. Joshua Swamidass has made the scientific case compellingly in *The Genealogical Adam and Eve*. This means that Genealogical Adam is compatible with most theological positions affirming a historical Adam, and with virtually any historical setting for him for which evidence may be adduced.

In this book I have attempted more than that, by seeking to integrate such a genealogical Adam and Eve into a coherent biblical theology. I have also suggested that the biblical metanarrative, as understood by the Bible writers themselves, is quite likely to *assume* the existence of people outside the garden. There is little or nothing in the text itself, or in the cultural milieu of the ANE, that requires that Adam and Eve be the sole, single precursor couple for the entire human race.

This chapter will seek to explore how Genealogical Adam interacts with other prevalent views on Adam and Eve both positively and negatively, and draw some final conclusions.

Ahistorical Views of Adam

Self-evidently a view such as Genealogical Adam, arguing that a historical Adam is possible, might conceivably be held together with a belief that he did *not* in fact exist, but the possibility tends to weaken the need for such ahistorical beliefs. Allegorical and mythological views of Adam have mainly arisen in contexts in which the biblical narrative seemed implausible, formerly because of the Enlightenment bias against the supernatural and against the reliability of traditional authorities, and latterly because of the discovery of deep time and evolutionary science.

Genealogical Adam completely disarms the latter, and in Chapter 1 I showed that there is actually very little, once genre is taken into account, that appears fabulous in the Genesis account. In any case, the trend of the last half century or more, within the Western church, has been towards a greater acceptance of the supernatural.

In previous chapters I presented evidence that the genre of the protohistory is neither mythological nor allegorical. For most of church history these accounts have been treated as history, and there seem few serious writers who doubt that Jesus and the New Testament writers assumed their basic historicity. Those who argue otherwise usually have to implicate Paul, in particular, in understandable or unimportant error, which naturally assumes, and encourages, a more limited view of Scriptural reliability than that embraced by most traditions since apostolic times.

Perhaps the main problem, though, is that efforts to reinterpret the account of Adam, in order to dehistoricize it, inevitably leave sin not only unexplained, but the responsibility of God rather than humanity. I have argued this in previous chapters, so I need say no more on it here.

I would just note that the kinds of reinterpretation that are proposed—and that have usually taken very similar forms since nineteenth-century liberals began to give "evolutionary" accounts of sin—largely depend on collapsing biblical inspiration down into fallible authorial belief. Thus Paul's discussion of Adam, which undoubtedly depends on the latter's individual existence, is held to reflect the errors of Paul's own culture, or his misrepresentation of the original figurative intent of the author(s) of Genesis. The only important truth, it is said, is the undeniable fact that sin exists. However sin is a "fact" that is *routinely* denied by many of those skeptics who do not accept the biblical account of humanity but do accept the evolutionary account. So a biblical account of sin is actually necessary to convince many of the need for forgiveness, if the Bible is to be a sufficient means for salvation.

Many modern ahistoric theories tend to exclude almost entirely any real engagement with the divine authorship of Scripture. This is crucial, as I have yet to see an account of what is called the "incarnational approach" to inspiration that isn't *in practice* psilanthropic, reducing what is divine in the Bible to the merely human.

Not only do these theories leave us without an *explanation* of sin, so that we must assume it is a natural consequence of the process of evolution, "red in tooth and claw," even though that process was created by a good God. They also leave us without a Christian understanding of the *nature* of sin. We see this in the common practice, in these discussions, of taking sin to be *selfishness*, making connections with the self-preservation (or sometimes, the "selfish-gene" metaphor) behind evolution, and so making God's salvation entirely to do with showing us a new way of unselfishness, bucking the natural process ("evolutionary creation") that produced us.

But Genesis teaches us that sin came into the world by one act of disobedience to a specific command. It was the direct denial of the Lordship of Yahweh, the preference for seizing our own kind of wisdom instead of learning from our true Teacher. Paul, in Romans 1, develops the relationship of this to the more general manifestation of evil, and it is a historical, as well as a personal, process. The roots of this process are religious and relational: sidelining the God men knew led them into idolatry, and idolatry led to sexual perversion and all the other moral perversions, in themselves an act of reprobation by God. Note the repeated phrase, *"God gave them over . . ."* in Romans 1.

It is only because the root of sin is the historic event of breaking existing fellowship with God that we can know that the *solution* to sin must also begin in a historical restoration of that fellowship. Attempts at moral reformation cannot succeed because it is God himself who has, for both chastisement and to spur repentance, *"given us over"* to sin. And so the gospel order is repentance that leads to obedience as well as forgiveness, which breaks the idols in our hearts, which opens the way to our moral reformation and our ability to return to the role Adam was given in God's kingdom.

Mention of that kingdom, and humanity's role in it, demonstrates another thing that is lost by ahistoric reinterpretations of Genesis. Evolution gives mankind *no* role except that of survival, a role inherited not only by humans but by animals, plants, and the lowliest protists. The creation ordinance to rule and subdue the earth—and Adam's more specific priestly role—are over and beyond that, and must have become so at some point in time, at least as far as linking whatever "natural" royal endowments of mind and will we have with the conscious service of Yahweh, the only true and living God.

This cannot be divorced from the question of God's image in man. The existence of this image seems to be one of those fundamentals that is seldom questioned, even when its sole source, Genesis 1, is otherwise regarded as a primitive attempt at ancient science. The Son, the second Person of the Trinity, is the eternal image of God: humanity was created in that image, to represent Christ on earth. That can only happen by a creative process over which God is sovereign, and whilst one might, at a pinch, conceive of it as some kind of emergent process, it cannot possibly be ahistoric, or entirely natural (in the sense of "unguided").

In ahistorical schemes Adam is usual regarded as an explanation for sin to be reinterpreted, or replaced, in the light of science. But to focus on the origin of sin alone is to neglect the total context of Genesis 2—3: the gifts of command, and of conscience, are what make both sin and conscious obedience possible. Conscience is a unique spiritual dignity. In Romans Paul integrates conscience into his whole theology of sin, which is entirely based on the Genesis narrative.[1] Conscience is the flip side of sin, but it too must have a historical origin, for no animal has it. In relation to the biblical concept of sin, it must also encompass an original command, for Paul also says "sin is not taken into account where there is no law."[2]

In short, to remove the question of sin from history entails removing the *whole* of human origins from history, as far as any truly theological account of humanity goes, and Christianity is nothing if it is not a theological account of humankind. In effect it is to render humankind itself ahistorical, in the same sense that the vagaries of an unguided evolution would be ahistorical because they would be meaningless. But, as I have endeavored to maintain, God's dealings with us indeed are a story—a *history*. No story makes sense without an ending. And no ending makes sense unless it resolves an actual beginning.

1. Rom 2:12–16.
2. Rom 5:13.

Not all "ahistorical" views dispense with the "core" of the Eden narrative altogether. Usually in an attempt to accommodate to the supposed genetic or paleontological impossibility of a single original couple, the story of a divine command and an act of disobedience is sometimes transferred to a group of which Adam and Eve are considered symbolic— perhaps the first human population.

For example, famously C. S. Lewis toyed with the possibility that, in the mists of time, God by an evolutionary process formed humanity, who fell corporately from a state of innocence, as the Bible says.[3] But,

> we do not know how many of these creatures God made, nor how long they continued in the Paradisal state.[4]

But like the more "allegorical" views most of these ideas still divorce Adam from history, and at some stage the apparently chronological narrative of the Bible has to *become* history, whether that be at the tower of Babel, the call of Abraham, the exodus under Moses, or the descent of Jesus from King David, from Abraham and from Adam, as the genealogies describe. Wherever one places the division between history and allegory, the structure of the edifice of the biblical meta-history is traced down from the present reality through the saving death of Jesus, only to find, at some point, that it is not connected to a foundation—or that the foundation is, in fact, mythological.

Such considerations are, of course, why a historical Adam is still considered non-negotiable by so many. Fortunately, Genealogical Adam does not negotiate him, but embraces him.

Young Earth Views of Adam

It may surprise some to learn that I consider the modern Young Earth views of serious Evangelical thinkers to be as much a threat to a historical Adam as the ahistorical views considered above.

The historicity of the faith is important to such people, for the same reasons that I described in chapter 1. We are real people, and need a Savior for causes that arose in history. Our Savior too came in history, and even arose *from the dead* in history: ahistorical, spiritualized, accounts

---

3. This proposal was "Socratic": his real views were probably far closer to the biblical picture. See West, "Darwin in the Dock," 109–51.

4. Lewis, *Problem of Pain*, 76–79.

of the resurrection have proven to be both historically and theologically inadequate.

Some Young Earth Creationists have been amongst those who, like me, have seen the importance of a consistent biblical theology, in the sense of a historical narrative that runs through the Bible. Indeed it is that very commitment to biblical historicity that leads to young earth views in the first place, because the narrative traced through the Bible, including of course the genealogies, severely constrains the time span available for a historical Adam. In turn, he, as the first man, if made on the sixth day of creation, determines the age of the universe.

The much-discussed question of biblical inerrancy works itself out, in this instance, in the question of historicity. For this reason, biblical history ends up being pitched against secular history, leading to the rejection of, for example, historical sciences that all agree that the earth is much older than 6,000 years.

And herein I find the historical problem. Our faith is historical not because it tells an internally consistent story, but because it is true within real history. It is important not only that the Bible says Jesus was born at the time of Herod the Great and Caesar Augustus, but that he *was*, and moreover that those kings really existed too. It matters not only that Jesus is the true Israel and the true Davidic king, but that there really was a nation of Israel with a king called David.

One of my bugbears, teaching in church, is what I call the "Flannelgraph Bible," in which we conceive of heroes dressed in blankets and tea towels having extraordinary encounters with angels or God, in a wonderful biblical world that bears no relationship to the one that we inhabit. But it is *history* that enables our faith to be real. That is, we can check out that Abraham plausibly matches a historical setting where they wore something quite different from tea towels. We can discover that the Israelite prophets' view of religious experience reflects those of their neighbors. We can find, from archaeological estimates of the size of Israel at the Canaan settlement, that when Moses reminds them that they were the "fewest of all peoples" when they left Egypt[5] we must revise our interpretation that that means 600,000 men plus women and children.[6]

---

5. Deut 7:7.

6. Exod 12:37. The *total* population of Canaan at that time is estimated at around 600,000—and Canaan was not a single nation, but a cluster of tribal entities, as Exodus shows. Fortunately there are solutions to the apparent grossly exaggerated population. See Kitchen, *Reliability*, 264–65.

The Bible is, apart from anything else, a historical source—not a source in *opposition* to history. Where it is historical, it demonstrates God's significant actions within the world of history we discover from other sources. Remove that setting, and it is just a story. An Adam living alone in the world in 4004, or even 10,000 BCE, is not a historical Adam at all, but a Flannel-graph Adam, and therefore as ahistorical as a mythical Adam would be.

But under Genealogical Adam, by contrast, a historical Adam might indeed live in 4004 BCE, or any other biblically plausible date, and do all the things that Genesis attributes to him. If my contention that Genesis 1 is a preface to Adam's story, in the genre of a phenomenological temple inauguration account, is also accepted, then that historical Adam will be an Adam unobjectionable to the physical sciences, too. We no longer have to squeeze his entire life, and his fall, and God's Sabbath reign of creation, into the first week of the universe's existence. Genealogical Adam offers us a real person, in our own world.

Older Alternatives

In this section I examine views on creation which only tangentially affect the nature of Adam, but do affect a biblical theology that takes note of Genealogical Adam theory.

One prominent Evangelical, R. C. Sproul, explains his own return to Six-Day Recent Creationism in terms of his rejection of three other theories: the Framework Theory, the Day Age Theory, and the Gap Theory.[7] As "accommodationist" theories, these are actually rather old, the "Day Age" Theory having, in one shape or another, been around since the Second Temple period, and the Gap Theory since the Renaissance. In their more modern forms, however, they developed as nineteenth- and twentieth-century Western responses to nineteenth- and twentieth-century Western science, rather than arising either from the text or from rigorous historical studies. As such they do not really engage that well with current issues. Nevertheless, there is some benefit to be gained by viewing them in the light of Genealogical Adam.

---

7. Schlehr, "What Is R. C. Sproul's Position on Creation?"

The Framework Hypothesis

Sproul names Nicholas Ridderbos (1909–2007) as the originator of this theory, which is a deduction from the wider study of style and genre in the early chapters of Genesis. In particular, the structure of the creation narrative of Genesis 1:1—2:3 presents an account that is orderly in a formal, rather than a historical way. Meredith Kline noted the division into domains and their respective denizens, and J. D. Levenson was among the first to relate this order to temple imagery.[8]

Ultimately Sproul rejects it, though he once favored it, because he cannot get around the assertion that God created the world in six days.[9] However, he also describes the theory in accommodationist terms, hinting that it is intended to subordinate Scripture to science:

> The author of Genesis, then, is trying to show that God's work of creation took place in seven distinct stages, which incidentally fit remarkably well into the stages identified by the modern theories of cosmic evolution.

> Therefore, the framework hypothesis allows one to step into a Big Bang cosmology while maintaining the credibility and inspiration of Genesis 1—2. This is not history, but drama. The days are simply artistic literary devices to create a framework for a lengthy period of development.[10]

However, this is scarcely fair on Ridderbos, who was not concerned with Big Bang cosmology in the 1950s (it only became the main cosmological contender after 1964). The Framework theory is a literary theory, not an accommodationist one, and really does not match modern cosmic evolution at all well. It is, therefore, a good match to what we know from temple imagery and phenomenology, but a poor match to modern science. Six day creation, on the other hand, forces one to make a stand for an understanding of Scripture that contradicts many sciences, including the evidence of many millennia of human culture, without gaining much understanding of the positive purpose of the text's particular form.

8. Beale, *Erosion of Inerrancy,* 184.

9. This is only explicitly stated in Exodus 20:11, and if the genre of Genesis 1 is other than literal (for example, a temple inauguration account), one would expect the commandments on Sinai to express the same literary sense, especially if Moses was the original author of both books. This can scarcely, therefore, be seen as a separate scriptural claim.

10. Schlehr, "What Is R. C. Sproul's Position on Creation?"

The Day Age Theory

This theory too began life as a theological interpretation of the text. The division of the world's history into six one-thousand-year periods, culminating in God's final Sabbath, existed in Second Temple times, perhaps based on the lack of an evening to the seventh day in Genesis. Augustine, noting this and reasoning that the almighty God would surely create the world instantly, similarly avoided the literal understanding.

But geologist Arnold Guyot in the nineteenth century recycled the idea specifically to deal with deep time, postulating six epochs in the history of the earth. The first problem with this is that, as stated for the Framework Theory, the structure does not, in fact, match the science at all well. Sproul spends many words arguing against the science of evolution and deep time that are supposed to be the reason theistic evolutionists accept it (perhaps some do). But no thorough understanding of the origins sciences supports it anyway.

More importantly, this not-really-scientific insight on the order of creation could only have come to the author of Genesis by direct dictation, and for no very clear purpose. As we saw in chapter 1 regarding Adam, biblical inspiration simply does not work that way.

The Gap Theory

Sproul condemns this last theory by its association with the Dispensationalist *Scofield Reference Bible*, but it actually predates that by a century or more, being popularized by Thomas Chalmers in 1814. As a response to the geological discovery of deep time, it was suggested that the gap between the creation of heaven and earth in Genesis 1:1, and the beginning of its organization in 1:2, might be a place to "hide" a previous creation, or even several, now evidenced by sedimentary rocks, bizarre fossils, and so on.

Sproul attributes the gap to a cosmic fall—perhaps the fall of Satan—but there is nothing intrinsic to the theory that necessitates this flat denial of the goodness of the Genesis creation. What the geological record, and therefore the theory, *does* suggest is that catastrophes have occurred in the past. To attribute these to evil is to go beyond Scripture. To deny they occurred is simply to ignore pervasive evidence from geology.

Once again, to suggest that God is hiding current scientific knowledge in Genesis—in this case literally between the lines—is poor exegesis and poor theology. In this way the Gap Theory fails. But interestingly, if we take the literary and theological approach I have attempted in this book, suggesting that the creation account is the preface to the traditional protohistory that forms "the Old Testament of the Old Testament," then the *whole* of Genesis 1 becomes a "gap filler," hiding not a previous, fallen creation, but abbreviating the original good one, setting the scene for the drama of the new creation to come.

R. C. Sproul begins the explanation of his return to Creationism with a commentary on a passage of the Westminster Confession that reads:

> It pleased God the Father, Son and Holy Ghost, for the manifestation of the glory of the eternal power, wisdom and goodness, in the beginning, to create, or make of nothing, the world, and all things therein, whether visible or invisible, in the space of six days, and all very good.[11]

One of my copies of the Confession is a reprint of an edition of 1845, with a commentary by Dr. Robert Shaw (1795–1863), who was a Scottish "Original Secession" Presbyterian theologian and minister at Whitburn (halfway between Edinburgh and Glasgow). His other, long out of print, work was a critique of a "New Theology" of that time, that had softened the Calvinist doctrine of atonement and provoked a strong and very typically Scottish Presbyterian response of synods and libel suits, much of which quoted Shaw's analysis. In other words, Shaw was a Calvinist of Calvinists.

Apart from the important general theological truths in the passage from the *Confession*, upon which Shaw principally enlarges, he explains the received 4004 BC date of creation, but then mentions the fly in the ointment in the form of modern geology (remember that he wrote fourteen years before Darwin's theory was published). He then mentions Christian responses to this science, including the Victorian equivalent of Flood Geology held by "some" ("all the changes which have taken place in the materials of the earth occurred either during the six days of the Mosaic creation, or since that time"), but adds that "most" think that "the facts which geology establishes prove this view to be utterly untenable." He then discusses the Day Age Theory, and its weaknesses, and goes on at last to the Gap Theory, which is based on the observation that Genesis 1:1

---

11. Shaw, *Exposition*, ch. IV.1.60.

"leaves the time before the six day creation altogether indefinite." Shaw concludes:

> This explanation, which leaves room for a long succession of geological events before the creation of the existing races, seems now to be the generally received mode of reconciling geological discoveries with the Mosaic account of the creation [for which he gives several citations, including one from the biologist Louis Agassiz].[12]

This commentary accords fully with what historian of science Ted Davis said about the Evangelical response to deep time geology in an essay on BioLogos a few years ago: recent creationism was then a minority view amongst thinking Evangelicals, and the Gap Theory was the most favored option.[13] Shaw's words confirm that this was true in Britain as well as America, amongst the most conservative of conservative Calvinists. It would appear possible that Reformed opposition to such theories arose not with the discovery of deep time back in the eighteenth century, but with the evolutionary culture wars, and the rise of "Creation Science" in the 1960s.

Whilst those like Robert Shaw were happy to hide the distant geological past within the first verse of Genesis, but had to account for the whole modern world in a six-day "makeover," the task for modern Reformed conservatives is easier: simply to recognize that the genre of the account is all about God's constituting the world of humankind as the sacred space for his worship. It is simply not concerned about material origins in terms of cosmology, geology, or biology before that situation of worship came to be. The "gap" is not hidden after Genesis 1:1, but in what the author has no interest in teaching. Note that this conclusion arises not from a desire to accommodate the Bible to science, but from the text itself.

Of course, Genealogical Adam fits this perfectly well. It allows for there to be the kind of world described by non-biblical sources in history, archaeology, geology, biology, and so on, and it even allows evolution to be a part, at least, of the story, without jeopardizing the possibility of special creation. When I look at Robert Shaw's acceptance of the somewhat crude and undeveloped Gap Theory, which was clearly favored by a large number of conservative Reformed theologians and ministers then,

12. Ibid., 61–62.
13. Davis, "Concordism, Part 1."

it is hard to believe he would not have been willing to recognize temple inauguration imagery and genealogical science as a better option, had the knowledge been available. After all, one motto of Reformed theology is *Semper reformans*, and adjusting to new light on Scripture is the very least threatening kind of reformation.

Concluding Thoughts on the Historical Adam

This book has attempted no radical revisions of traditional Christian theological doctrine, though it has attempted to build on, and strengthen, current themes in biblical theology. Rather than reconfiguring theology, the Genealogical Adam paradigm is a powerful discovery in *restoring* the plausibility of older teaching, after a long period when it has either been maintained against the intellectual tide, or made to give ground progressively in the light of the "assured results" of science.

The first position has made Evangelical theology a ghetto pursuit, except in those few places where it is culturally dominant, in which case it is the rest of human knowledge that has had to retreat to the ghetto. The second has tended to chip away at core Christian teaching—or even more seriously, to set off its collapse like a line of dominoes.

It is rightly said (as Joshua Swamidass states from the start of his book, *The Genealogical Adam and Eve*) that our faith is in Jesus, not in Adam. Yet the Fundamentalists are by no means entirely wrong to claim that demolishing the foundational narrative on which the Bible, and hence the gospel, is built cannot but jeopardize the superstructure.

There is evidence aplenty in our times that doing away with the historical Adam produces an entirely new doctrine of sin, or even the denial of sin as our real theological problem. A new doctrine of sin necessarily leads to reformulation of the doctrines of atonement, at which point our understanding of, and faith in, what Jesus has done is directly impacted. Since these reworked teachings are not to be found in the Bible, then that can no longer be relied on as a fully sufficient authoritative source. And when ones view of Scripture becomes that of fallible human efforts, only imperfectly and subjectively "indwelt" by God, then it is inevitable that comparisons with the incarnation of Christ be made, and that the human Word of God become as prone to error as his written word. And so on.

This is not a slippery slope argument, because all the doctrinal revisions I have mentioned are current, even within Evangelicalism. It may be instructive to look at specific ways in which rejection, or marginalization, of the Eden account as history has affected religious life at various times in the past.

In Jesus' own time, two schools of rabbis had created a small "culture war" over the business of marriage and divorce in the Law of Moses. Jesus had to cut through that by treating the pattern of the marriage of Adam and Eve as determinative of kingdom marriage values.[14] But we also saw in chapter 12 that Judaism had not really stressed the impact of Adam's sin, until first St. Paul, and then 2 *Baruch* and 4 *Ezra*, began to appreciate how central Adam is to understanding why the world is as seriously deranged as it is, and why God must act, in Jesus, as he has. It is no coincidence that the crucifixion of the Son of God was accompanied by a much blacker doctrine of sin.

During the European Renaissance, as I have described in detail elsewhere,[15] the story of Adam was reinterpreted to endorse the growing hubristic glorification of humanity, and especially its supposed wisdom. The eating of the tree of knowledge became an act of self-liberation from the unfair constraints of God upon the human spirit. Before too long, Adam was no longer necessary at all, his civilizing role being transferred to the Greek Prometheus, whose cult remains our society's "creation myth" to this day.

During the Enlightenment this process continued, and Adam, along with the whole concept of "traditional authority," was relegated to the realm of primitive fable. The result of this was the modernist myth of progress, of the moral power of "pure reason," and of humanity's ability to abolish evil by taking careful thought and improving its biological and political structures. As N. T. Wright wryly observes,

> It would be difficult to maintain that this biopolitical process has done what it said on the tin.[16]

Evolutionism, off the back of biological evolutionary theory, brought its own particular guns to bear on Adam. First of all, Adam became lost in deep time, as the origins of the human race appeared to be earlier and earlier in the rocks. Even old earth believers in a historical Adam have been caught up in this, looking for a genetic bottleneck where Adam and Eve might be placed, and finding it to be so far back, if it exists at all, that

14. Matt 19:8.

15. Garvey, *God's Good Earth*, ch. 8, 103–15.

16. Wright, "Christ and the Cosmos," 104.

the only part of the Genesis protohistory that remains is "single original couple." Noah built his ark ten generations after the first *Homo erectus*, and Abraham (if we were to follow the genealogies) made crude stone tools in Africa before the last ice age. Such an Adam is not historical, because it even contradicts the biblical account, taken in its entirety.

In the last century genetics seemed to eliminate any possibility of Adam, as an intellectually respectable belief. But here, of course, Genealogical Adam appears, and suddenly the Bronze Age fairy tale turns out to have been scientifically legitimate all along.

Then again evolutionism, as described in chapter 10, ridiculed the very possibility that the first man would be a monotheist, since the developmental pathway of religion from animism was self-evident to all right-thinking intellectuals. Except that this, too, proved mistaken.

In our own time, the historicity of the Genesis protohistory is as important as ever, and one of the reasons returns us to the use Jesus made of it in Matthew 19. Modernist positivism and rationalism have been, within the intellectual structures that produce our politicians, journalists, and artists, replaced with postmodern philosophical theories in which all evils derive from patriarchy and binary polarization.[17] If the Adam story is ahistoric, then within a worldview community like ours such views seem plausible for now.

It is true that it is in Genesis 1 that God creates '*ādām* male and female, rather than fluidly gendered. But it is in Genesis 2, within the new-creation covenant shared by the whole of humankind in Adam, that these relational issues are made normative.

Genesis 2 teaches that our sexual and family relationships, and what we are by our creation, are all determined by God, not by us. We are dependent on him for who we are, and what is more, we can rely on his word as being for our good. And we *must* so rely on it, because covenant involves penalty, and our race is lost because of that very fact. The Garden of Eden necessarily involved a binary power relationship, not between Adam and Eve, but between humanity and Yahweh.

It is ironic that, this late on in history, key issues should still hinge on the original question of the serpent to Eve, "Did God say . . . ?" We may choose to rebel against that exercise of divine authority, and the binary distinction behind it. Or, we may accept that the Eden narrative is true history rather than patriarchal machination. In that case, by perceiving

17. Cox, "Susan Cox."

the biblical metanarrative that shows that power of Yahweh in Eden to have been that of the divine Son, exercised in the same way he exercised it in the incarnate Christ on the cross, we may make peace with our Creator through repentance and faith.

That is an excellent role for us to take within such an ancient story. It is a role that will endure until the generations of the heaven and the earth are fully revealed as a new heaven, and a new earth, the home of righteousness, in which God is all in all.[18]

Soli Deo Gloria.

---

18. 2 Pet 3:13.

BIBLIOGRAPHY

Online bibliography available at http://generations.jongarvey.co.uk.

Alexander, Andrew C. J. "Human Origins and Genetics." *Clergy Review* 49 (1964) 344–53.

Andreasen, Niels-Erik. "Adam and Adapa: Two Anthropological Characters." *Andrews University Seminary Studies* 19.3 (1981) 179–94. https://faculty.gordon.edu/hu/bi/ted_hildebrandt/otesources/01-genesis/text/articles-books/andreasen_adamadapa_auss.htm.

Applegate, Kathryn. "Why I Think Adam was a Real Person in History." *BioLogos* (2018). https://biologos.org/blogs/kathryn-applegate-endless-forms-most-beautiful/why-i-think-adam-was-a-real-person-in-history.

Aristotle. "De anima (On the Soul)." Translated by J. A Smith. *Internet Classics Archive.* http://classics.mit.edu/Aristotle/soul.html.

———. *Nicomachean Ethics.* Translated by J. A. K. Thompson. London: Penguin,1976.

Arnold, Bill T., and Brian E. Beyer. *Readings from the Ancient Near East: Primary Sources for Old Testament Study.* Grand Rapids: Baker Academic, 2002.

Athanasius. "On the Incarnation of the Word." *Christian Classics Ethereal Library.* https://www.ccel.org/ccel/athanasius/incarnation.ii.html.

Attwater, Donald, and Rachel Attwater, trans. *The Book Concerning Piers the Plowman.* New York: Dutton, 1957.

Augustine, Aurelius. *Confessions, City of God, On Christian Doctrine.* Great Books of the Western World 18. Chicago, IL: Benton, 1989.

———. "A Treatise on the Merits and Forgiveness of Sins, and on the Baptism of Infants." *New Advent.* http://www.newadvent.org/fathers/15011.htm.

Aulén, Gustav. *Christus Victor: An Historical Study of the Three Main Types of the Idea of the Atonement.* London: SPCK Classics, 2010.

Bacon, Francis. *The New Atlantis.* Kindle Amazon Media EU S.à r. l. version.

Barfield, Owen. *Saving the Appearances.* Middletown, CT: Wesleyan University Press, 1988.

Bauckham, Richard. "Gospel Narratives and the Psychology of Eyewitness Memory." In *Christ and the Created Order*, edited by Andrew Torrance and Thomas McCall, 111–27. Grand Rapids: Zondervan, 2018.

———. "Reading Scripture as a Coherent Story." In *The Art of Reading Scripture*, edited by Ellen Davis and Richard Hays, 38–53. Grand Rapids: Eerdmans, 2003.

Beale, Gregory K. *The Erosion of Inerrancy in Evangelicalism: Responding to New Challenges to Biblical Authority*. Wheaton, IL: Crossway, 2008.

———. *A New Testament Biblical Theology: The Unfolding of the Old Testament in the New*. Grand Rapids: Baker, 2011.

———. *The Temple and the Church's Mission: A Biblical Theology of the Dwelling Place of God*. Downers Grove, IL: InterVarsity, 2004.

Berkhof, Louis. *Systematic Theology*. Edinburgh: Banner of Truth, 1976.

Best, Robert M. *Analysis of the Numbers in Genesis 5* (2009). https://measureoffaith. blog/wp-content/uploads/2017/08/Genesis5analysis.pdf.

BioLogos Staff. "Genealogical is not Genetic." *BioLogos*. https://discourse.biologos. org/t/genealogical-is-not-genetic/35659.

Bird, Michael. *The Saving Righteousness of God*. Eugene, OR: Wipf & Stock, 2007.

Block, Daniel I. "Eden: A Temple? A Reassessment of the Biblical Evidence." In *From Creation to New Creation: Biblical Theology and Exegesis: Essays in Honor of G. K. Beale*, edited by Daniel M Gurtner and Benjamin L Gladd, 3–30. Peabody, MA: Hendrickson, 2013.

Brock, Brian. "Jesus Christ the Divine Animal? The Human Distinctive Reconsidered." In *Christ and the Created Order*, edited by Andrew Torrance and Thomas McCall, 55–75. Grand Rapids: Zondervan, 2018.

Broushaki, F., Mark G. Thomas, et al. "Early Neolithic genomes from the eastern Fertile Crescent." *Science*, Vol. 353, No. 6298, 2016. 499–50: DOI: 10.1126/science.aaf7943. http://science.sciencemag.org/content/early/2016/07/13/science.aaf7943. full.

Brown, Francis. "A Recent Theory of the Garden of Eden." *The Old Testament Student* IV.1 (1884). https://www.jstor.org/stable/pdf/3156297.pdf.

Cachão, Rita. "Earth-Sky Cosmologies: A Reflection on Cosmology Through Human Practices (Part 1)." *Transtechnology Research*, 2012. http://www.trans-techresearch. net/wp-content/uploads/2015/05/TTReader2011_004_Cachao.pdf.

Cardinal, Harold, and Walter Hildebrandt. *Treaty Elders of Saskatchewan: Our Dream is That Our Peoples Will One Day be Clearly Recognized as Nations*. University of Calgary, 2000.

Carson, D. A. *Matthew 1—12*. Expositor's Bible Commentary. Grand Rapids: Zondervan, 1995.

Chang, Joseph T. "Recent Common Ancestors of All Present-Day Individuals." *Advances in Applied Probability* 31.4 (1999) 1002–26.

Charles, R. H., trans. "The Book of Enoch." *Sacred Texts*. https://www.sacred-texts. com/bib/boe/index.htm.

Chester, Stephen J. *Reading Paul with the Reformers: Reconciling Old and New Perspectives*. Grand Rapids: Eerdmans, 2017.

Chilton, David. *Paradise Restored*. Tyler, TX: Reconstruction, 1985.

Church, Leslie F., ed. *Matthew Henry's Commentary on the Whole Bible in One Volume*. London: Marshall, Morgan, & Scott, 1973.

Clines, David J. A. "Response to Rolf Rendtorff's 'What Happened to the Yahwist?' Reflections after Thirty Years." *SBL Forum*, n.p. [cited June 2006]. http://sbl-site. org/Article.aspx?ArticleID=551.

Cole, Graham A. "The Peril of a 'Historyless' Systematic Theology." In *Do Historical Matters Matter to Faith? A Critical Appraisal of Modern and Postmodern*

Approaches to Scripture, edited by James K. Hoffmeier and Dennis R. Magary, 55–69. Wheaton, IL: Crossway, 2012.

Collins, Brian. "Was Eden a Temple?" *Exegesis and Theology* 08/22/2016. https://www.exegesisandtheology.com/2016/08/22/was-eden-a-temple/.

Collins, C. John. *Did Adam and Eve Really Exist? Who They Were and Why It Matters*. Nottingham: Inter-Varsity, 2011.

———. "The Theology of the Old Testament." In *The ESV Study Bible*, edited by Lane T. Dennis and Wayne Grudem, 29–31. Wheaton, IL: Crossway, 2008.

Collins, Steven, and Latayne C. Scott. *Discovering the City of Sodom: The Fascinating, True Account of the Discovery of the Old Testament's Most Infamous City*. New York: Howard, 2016.

Cosmas Indicopleustes. "The Christian Topography." *Tertullian.org*. http://www.tertullian.org/fathers/cosmas_01_book1.htm.

Couenhoven, Jesse. "St Augustine's Doctrine of Original Sin." *Augustinian Studies* 36.2 (2005) 359–96.

Cox, Susan. "Susan Cox 01.29.17." *Resistance Radio*, 2017. https://resistanceradio transcripts.wordpress.com/2018/03/11/susan-cox-01–29-17/.

Cunningham, Conor. *Darwin's Pious Idea*. Grand Rapids: Eerdmans, 2010.

Custance, Arthur C. *Noah's Three Sons: Human History in Three Dimensions*. Grand Rapids: Zondervan, 1984. II.1.23. http://www.custance.org/Library/Volume1/Part_II/Chapter1.html.

Cyprian. "Epistle LVIII to Fidus." In *Ante-Nicene Christian Library*, vol. 8, edited by Alexander Roberts and James Donaldson, 195–99. Edinburgh: T&T Clark, 1867–1885.

Dalley, Stephanie, trans. *Myths from Mesopotamia: Creation, The Flood, Gilgamesh, and Others*. Oxford: Oxford University Press, 2000.

Davis, Edward. "The Heart of a Great Scientist." *BioLogos*, 2013. https://biologos.org/blogs/ted-davis-reading-the-book-of-nature/the-faith-of-a-great-scientist.

———. "Science and the Bible: Concordism, Part 1." *BioLogos*, 2012. https://biologos.org/blogs/ted-davis-reading-the-book-of-nature/science-and-the-bible-concordism-part-1.

Delitzsch, Friedrich. *Wo Lag das Paradies*. Leipzig: Hinrichs'sche Buchhandlung, 1881.

Doyle, Robert C. *Eschatology and the Shape of Christian Belief*. Carlisle: Paternoster, 1999.

Eusebius. *The History of the Church*. Translated by G. A. Williamson. London: Penguin, 1989.

Evans-Pritchard, E. E. *Theories of Primitive Religion*. Oxford: Clarendon, 1965.

Feser, Edward. "Monkey in your soul?" 2011. http://edwardfeser.blogspot.com/2011/09/monkey-in-your-soul.html.

———. *Scholastic Metaphysics: A Contemporary Introduction*. Heusenstamm: Editiones Scholasticae, 2014.

Finkel, Irving. *The Ark Before Noah: Decoding the Story of the Flood*. London: Hodder, 2014.

Fischer, Richard James. *Historical Genesis: From Adam to Abraham*. Lanham, MD: University Press of America, 2008.

Fretheim, Terence E. *God and World in the Old Testament: a Relational Theology of Creation*. Nashville: Abingdon, 2005.

Gangai K., G. Sarson, and A. Shukurov. *The Near-Eastern Roots of the Neolithic in South Asia.* PLos ONE, May 2014. DOI: 10.1371/journal.pone.0095714. Source: PubMed.

Garvey, Jon. *Adam and MRCA Studies*, 2010. https://zenodo.org/record/1336742.

————. "Flood Geography." *The Hump of the Camel*, 2015. http://potiphar.jongarvey.co.uk/2015/10/30/flood-geography/.

————. *God's Good Earth: The Case for an Unfallen Creation.* Eugene, OR: Cascade, 2019.

————. "A Short History of Air." *The Hump of the Camel*, 2016. DOI: 10.5281/zenodo.1837053.

————. "The cosmos of Cosmas." *The Hump of the Camel*, 2014. http://potiphar.jongarvey.co.uk/2014/08/22/the-cosmos-of-cosmas/.

Goldsworthy, Graeme. *Gospel and Kingdom: A Christian Interpretation of the Old Testament.* Carlisle: Paternoster, 1994.

Gould, Steven Jay. *Dinosaur in a Haystack: Reflections in Natural History.* New York: Three Rivers, 1995.

————. *Ever Since Darwin.* London: Norton, 1977.

Hardin, Jeff. "On Geniality and Genealogy." *BioLogos*, 2017. https://biologos.org/blogs/deborah-haarsma-the-presidents-notebook/on-geniality-and-genealogy.

Harris, R. Laird. "The Bible and Cosmology." *Journal of the Evangelical Theological Society* 5 (1962) 11–17. http://www.etsjets.org/files/JETS-PDFs/5/5–1/BETS_5–1_11–17_Harris.pdf.

Heim, Erin M. "In Him and Through Him from the Foundation of the World." In *Christ and the Created Order*, edited by Andrew Torrance and Thomas McCall, 129–49. Grand Rapids: Zondervan, 2018.

Heiser, Michael S. *The Nachash and His Seed*, 2012. https://www.pidradio.com/wp-content/uploads/2007/02/nachashnotes.pdf.

Hill, Carol A. "Making Sense of the Numbers of Genesis." *Perspectives on Science and Christian Faith* 5.4 (2003) 239–51. https://asa3.org/ASA/PSCF/2003/PSCF12–03Hill.pdf.

————. "A Time and a Place for Noah." *Perspectives on Science and Christian Faith* 53.1 (2001) 24–40. https://www.asa3.org/ASA/PSCF/2001/PSCF9–01Nelson.html#Eden%20and%20Noah.

Hogenboom, Melissa. "Clothes are not a necessity for everyone, so why do we bother wearing clothes at all?" *BBC Earth*, 2016. http://www.bbc.co.uk/earth/story/20160919-the-real-origin-of-clothes.

Horowitz, Wayne. *Mesopotamian Cosmic Geography.* Winona Lake, IN: Eisenbrauns, 1998.

Hughes, Philip Edgcumbe. *The True Image: The Origin and Destiny of Man in Christ.* Grand Rapids: Eerdmans, 1989.

Hurtado, Larry W. *Destroyer of the gods: Early Christian Distinctiveness in the Roman World.* Waco, TX: Baylor University Press, 2016.

Irenaeus. "Against Heresies." In *Ante-Nicene Christian Library* vol. 1, edited by Alexander Roberts and James Donaldson, 309–367. Edinburgh: T&T Clark, 1867–1885.

————. "The Proof of the Apostolic Preaching." *Tertullian.org.* http://www.tertullian.org/fathers/irenaeus_02_proof.htm.

Ishiguro, Kazuo. *The Remains of the Day.* London: Faber & Faber, 1990.

Jablonka, Eva. *Evolution in Four Dimensions: Genetic, Epigenetic, Behavioral, and Symbolic Variation in the History of Life.* Cambridge, MA: MIT Press, 2014.

Jeffreys, M. D. W. "The Batwa: Who Are They?" *Africa* 23.1 (1953) 45–54. DOI:10. 2307/1156032.

Josephus, Flavius. *The Antiquities of the Jews. Documenta Catholica Omnia.* http://www.documentacatholicaomnia.eu/o3d/0037–0103,_Flavius_Josephus,_The_Antiquities_Of_The_Jews,_EN.pdf.

Keller, Tim. "Creation, Evolution, and Christian Laypeople." *BioLogos*, 2012. https://biologos.org/uploads/projects/Keller_white_paper.pdf.

———. "Keller, Moore, and Duncan on the Non-Negotiable Beliefs about Creation." *The Gospel Coalition* (2017). https://www.thegospelcoalition.org/article/keller-moore-duncan-non-negotiable-beliefs-about-creation/.

Kemp, Kenneth W. Science, "Theology, and Monogenesis." *American Catholic Philosophical Quarterly* 85.2 (2011) 217–36. DOI: 10.5840/acpq201185213. https://www3.nd.edu/~afreddos/papers/kemp-monogenism.pdf.

Kenoyer, Mark. *Meluhha: the Indus Civilization and Its Contacts with Mesopotamia.* 2010. https://www.youtube.com/watch?v=8zcGLlLEbmI.

Kidner, Derek. *Genesis.* London: Tyndale, 1967.

King, Martin Luther, Jr. *What is Man?* Dexter Avenue Baptist Church, Montgomery, AL, 07/11/1954. https://kinginstitute.stanford.edu/king-papers/documents/what-man-sermon-dexter-avenue-baptist-church.

Kitchen, A., C. Ehret, S. Assefa, and C. J. Mulligan. "Bayesian phylogenetic analysis of Semitic languages identifies an Early Bronze Age origin of Semitic in the Near East." *Proceedings: Biological sciences Royal Society (Great Britain)* 276.1668 (August 7, 2009) 2703–10. https://www.ncbi.nlm.nih.gov/pmc/articles/PMC2839953/.

Kitchen, Kenneth A. *On the Reliability of the Old Testament.* Cambridge: Eerdmans, 2006.

Lang, Andrew. *The Making of Religion.* 2d ed. London: Longman, Green & Co, 1900. Kindle Edition.

Levin, Michael. "Morphogenetic fields in embryogenesis, regeneration, and cancer: Non-local control of complex patterning." *Biosystems* 109.3 (September 2012) 243–61. DOI: 10.1016/j.biosystems.2012.04.005.

Lewis, C. S. *The Problem of Pain.* New York: MacMillan, 1962.

———. *Studies in Words.* Cambridge: Cambridge University Press, 2013.

———. *Till We Have Faces.* San Francisco, CA: HarperOne, 2017.

Livingstone, David N. *Adam's Ancestors: Race, Religion and the Politics of Human Origins.* Baltimore: John Hopkins, 2008.

Loke, Andrew T. "Reconciling Evolution with Biblical literalism: a proposed research program." *Theology and Science* 14 (2016) 160–74.

———. *The Origin of Humanity: Science and Scripture in Conversation.* Forthcoming.

Mann, Charles C. "The Birth of Religion." *National Geographic,* June 2011. https://www.nationalgeographic.com/magazine/2011/06/gobeki-tepe/.

McGrath, Alister. *The Re-Enchantment of Nature.* London: Hodder & Stoughton, 2002.

Middleton, J. Richard. "The Ancient Universe and the Cosmic Temple." *BioLogos*, 2016. https://biologos.org/blogs/jim-stump-faith-and-science-seeking-understanding/the-ancient-universe-and-the-cosmic-temple/.

————. "Further Thoughts on the Imago Dei: After *The Liberating Image*." *Creation to Eschaton*, 2014. https://jrichardmiddleton.wordpress.com/2014/08/05/further-thoughts-on-the-imago-dei-after-the-liberating-image/.

————. *The Liberating Image: The* Imago Dei *in Genesis 1*. Grand Rapids: Brazos, 2005.

————. *A New Heaven and a New Earth: Reclaiming Biblical Eschatology*. Grand Rapids: Baker Academic, 2014.

Milton, John. *Paradise Lost*. Edited by Christopher Ricks. London: Penguin, 1989.

Mitchell, T. C. "Nations, Table of." In *The New Bible Dictionary*, edited by J. D. Douglas, 865–69. London: Inter-Varsity, 1974.

Mithen, Steven. *After the Ice: A Global Human History 20,000–5000 BC*. London: Phoenix, 2004.

Moberly, R. W. L. *The Old Testament of the Old Testament: Patriarchal Narratives and Mosaic Yahwism*. Overtures to Biblical Theology. Minneapolis: Fortress, 1992.

Mörner, Nils-Axel. "The Flooding of Ur in Mesopotamia in New Perspectives." *Archaeological Discovery* 3.1 (2015) 26–31. http://file.scirp.org/Html/3–1140038_52979.htm.

Needham, Nick. *Daily Readings from the Early Church Fathers*. Fearn: Christian Heritage, 2017.

Newbigin, Lesslie. *The Gospel in a Pluralist Society*. London: SPCK, 1997.

New English Bible. Oxford: Oxford University Press, 1970.

Noble, Denis. *The Music of Life: Biology Beyond Genes*. Oxford: Oxford University Press, 2006.

Noll, Mark A., and David N. Livingstone. *B. B. Warfield: Evolution, Science, and Scripture*. Grand Rapids: Baker, 2000.

Olson, Steve. *Mapping Human History*. London: Bloomsbury, 2002.

Opderbeck, David. "Behold, the Man." *BioLogos*, 2012. https://biologos.org/blogs/archive/behold-the-man.

————. "A 'Historical' Adam?" *Biologos*, 2010. https://biologos.org/articles/a-historical-adam.

————. "Origen on Adam." *Through a Glass Darkly*, 2016. https://davidopderbeck.com/tgdarkly/2016/08/31/origen-on-adam.

Oppenheim, Leo A. *"Man and Nature in Mesopotamian Civilization."* Detroit: Scribner, 1978. *Encyclopedia.com*. https://www.encyclopedia.com/science/dictionaries-thesauruses-pictures-and-press-releases/man-and-nature-mesopotamian-civilization.

Origen. *"Contra Celsum."* Ante-Nicene Christian Library vol. XXIII, edited by Alexander Roberts and James Donaldson. Edinburgh: T&T Clark, 1867–1885.

————. *"De Principiis."* In *Ante-Nicene Christian Library*, Vol. X, edited by Alexander Roberts and James Donaldson, 1–368. Edinburgh: T&T Clark, 1867–1885.

Oxford University. "The Debate between Sheep and Grain." *The Electronic Text Corpus of Sumerian Literature*. http://etcsl.orinst.ox.ac.uk/section5/tr532.htm.

————. "Enki and Ninhursaja." *The Electronic Text Corpus of Sumerian Literature*. http://etcsl.orinst.ox.ac.uk/cgi-bin/etcsl.cgi?text=t.1.1.1&charenc=j#.

Penley, Paul T. "A Historical Reading of Genesis 11:1–9: The Sumerian Demise And Dispersion Under The Ur III Dynasty." *Journal of the Evangelical Theological Society* 50.4 (December 2007) 693–714. https://www.etsjets.org/files/JETS-PDFs/50/50/-4/JETS_50-4_693-714_Penley.pdf.

Penman, James. "The Place of Adam—2." *The Hump of the Camel* 2012. http://potiphar. jongarvey.co.uk/2012/05/30/guest-post-by-a-penman-the-place-of-adam-pt-2-of-2/.

Perry, Andrew. *The Myth of the Solid Dome, Parts 1 & 2.* https://www.academia. edu/5247294/The_Myth_of_the_Solid_Dome_Part_1_; https://www.academia. edu/5255903/The_Myth_of_the_Solid_Dome_Part_2_-_Concluded.

Plantinga, Alvin. *Where the Conflict Really Lies: Science, Religion and Naturalism.* New York: Oxford University Press, 2011.

Postell, Seth D. *Adam as Israel: Genesis 1—3 as the Introduction to the Torah and Tanakh.* Eugene, OR: Pickwick, 2011.

Poythress, Vern S. "Rain Water Versus a Heavenly Sea in Genesis 1:6–8." *Westminster Theological Journal* 77 (2015) 181–91.

———. "Three Modern Myths in Interpreting Genesis 1." *Westminster Theological Journal* 76 (2014) 321–50.

Pringle, Peter. "The Epic Of Gilgamesh In Sumerian." *YouTube*, 2014. https://www. youtube.com/watch?v=QUcTsFe1PVs.

Quammen, David. *The Tangled Tree: A Radical New History of Life.* London: Collins, 2018.

Rae, Murray. "Jesus Christ, the Order of Creation." In *Christ and the Created Order*, edited by A. B. Torrance and T. H. McCall, 23–34. Grand Rapids: Zondervan, 2018.

Rao, Rajesh. "Computing a Rosetta Stone for the Indus Script." 2011. https://www. youtube.com/watch?v=kwYxHPXIaao.

Richardson, Don. *Eternity in Their Hearts.* Ventura, CA: Regal, 1981.

Richardson, Ken. "It's the End of the Gene as We Know It: we are not nearly as determined by our genes as once thought." *Nautilus*, 2019. http://nautil.us/ issue/68/context/its-the-end-of-the-gene-as-we-know-it.

Riches, Aaron. "The Mystery of Adam 1: The Reduction of Reason in the Debate." *The Colossian Forum* (2015). https://colossianforum.org/2015/02/25/the-mystery-of-adam-1-the-reduction-of-reason-in-the-debate/.

Rochberg, Francesca. *Before Nature: Cuneiform Knowledge and the History of Science.* Chicago: University of Chicago Press, 2016.

Rogers, R. W. "Adapa and the Food of Life." In *Cuneiform Parallels to the Old Testament.* At *Sacred Texts.* http://www.sacred-texts.com/ane/adapa.htm.

Rohde, D. L. T. "On the common ancestors of all living humans." (2005) Submitted to *American Journal of Physical Anthropology.* http://citeseerx.ist.psu.edu/viewdoc/ download?doi=10.1.1.67.9110&rep=rep1&type=pdf.

Rohde D. L. T., S. Olson, and J. T. Chang. "Modelling the recent common ancestry of all living humans." *Nature* 431 (2004) 562–66.

Roux, Georges. *Ancient Iraq.* London: Penguin, 1992.

Sailhamer, John H. *The Meaning of the Pentateuch.* Downers Grove, IL: IVP Academic, 2009.

Sarna, Nathan M. *Genesis.* JPS Torah Commentary. Philadelphia: Jewish Publication Society, 1989.

Schlehr, Karisa. "What is R. C. Sproul's Position on Creation?" *Ligonier Ministries*, 2011. https://www.ligonier.org/blog/what-rc-sprouls-position-creation/.

Schmidt, W. *The Origin and Growth of Religion.* London: Methuen, 1935.

Scruton, Roger. *Modern Philosophy.* London: Mandarin. 1994.

Seller W. C., and R. J. Yeatman. *1066 and All That*. London: Methuen, 1930.

Shapiro, James A. *Evolution: A View from the 21st Century*. Upper Saddle River, NJ: FT Press Science, 2011.

Shaw, Robert. *An Exposition of the Westminster Confession of Faith*. Fearn: Christian Focus, 1992.

Sherratt, Andrew. "Environmental Change: The Evolution of Mesopotamia." *Archatlas* 4.1 (2004). https://www.archatlas.org/EnvironmentalChange/EnvironmentalChange.php.

Sidky, Homayun. "On the Antiquity of Shamanism and its Role in Human Religiosity." *Method and Theory in the Study of Religion* 22 (2010) 68–92.

Staniforth, Maxwell, trans. *Early Christian Writings: The Apostolic Fathers*. Harmondsworth: Penguin, 1988.

Stockton, Angela. "What do Native Americans call themselves?" *Quora*. https://www.quora.com/What-do-Native-Americans-call-themselves-Ive-read-that-even-tribal-names-like-Apache-and-Sioux-are-not-what-these-tribes-call-themselves-but-rather-they-are-what-their-enemies-called-them.

Stott, John. *The Cross of Christ*. Leicester: Inter-Varsity, 1989.

Sunkar, Murat, and Saadettin Tonbull. "Paleoflood Analyses in Southeastern Turkey: Batman Case." *Austin Journal of Hydrology* 2.1 (2015) 1012–9. http://austinpublishinggroup.com/hydrology/fulltext/ajh-v2-id1012.php.

Swamidass, S. Joshua. *The Genealogical Adam and Eve: The Surprising Science of Universal Ancestry*. Downers Grove, IL: IVP Academic, 2019.

————. "A Genealogical Rapprochement on Adam?" *Peaceful Science*, 2017. http://peacefulscience.org/genealogical-rapprochement/.

Swamidass, S. Joshua, Richard Buggs, et al. "Adam, Eve and Population Genetics: A Reply to Dr. Richard Buggs (Part 1)." *BioLogos*, 2017. https://zenodo.org/record/1323939.

Trent, Council of. Fifth Session (1546). *Christian Classics Ethereal Library*. http://www.ccel.org/ccel/schaff/creeds2.v.i.i.iii.html.

Tylor, Edward Burnett. *Researches into the Early History of Mankind and the Development of Civilisation*. London: John Murray, 1865.

Tyndale, William. *The Obedience of the Christian Man*. Edited by Thomas Russell. London, 1831. https://www.richard-2782.net/obediencechristianman.pdf.

Van der Toorn, Karel. "The Nature of the Biblical 'Teraphim' in the Light of the Cuneiform Evidence." *Catholic Biblical Quarterly* 52.2 (1990) 203–22.

Walsingham, Thomas. *Historia Anglicana*, vol II. Edited by H. T. Riley. London: Longman, 1864.

Walton, John H. *Ancient Israelite Literature in its Cultural Context*. Grand Rapids: Regency, 1989.

————. *Genesis 1 as Ancient Cosmology*. Winona Lake, IN: Eisenbrauns, 2011.

————. *Genesis (NIV Application Commentary)*. Grand Rapids: Zondervan, 2001.

————. *The Lost World of Adam and Eve*. Downers Grove, IL: InterVarsity, 2015.

————. *The Lost World of Genesis One: Ancient Cosmology and the Origins Debate*. Downers Grove, IL: IVP Academic, 2010.

Wenham, Gordon J. *Genesis 1—15*. Word Biblical Commentary. Nashville: Nelson, 1987.

————. *Rethinking Genesis 1—11: Gateway to the Bible*. Eugene, OR: Cascade, 2015.

————. "Sanctuary Symbolism in the Garden of Eden Story." In *I Studied Inscriptions from Before the Flood*, edited by Richard S. Hess and David Toshio Tsumura, 399–404. Winona Lake, IN: Eisenbrauns, 1994.

Wesley Center Online. *2 Baruch*. http://wesley.nnu.edu/sermons-essays-books/noncan onical-literature/noncanonical-literature-ot-pseudepigrapha/the-book-of-the-apocalypse-of-baruch-the-son-of-neriah-or-2-baruch/.

West, John G. "Darwin in the Dock." In *The Magician's Twin: C. S. Lewis on Science, Scientism, and Society,* edited by John G. West, 109–51. Seattle, WA: Discovery Institute, 2012.

Westermann, Claus. *Creation.* Translated by John J. Scullion. Philadelphia: Fortress, 1974.

White, Carolinne, trans. *Early Christian Lives.* London: Penguin, 1998.

Wright, Christopher J. H. *The Mission of God: Unlocking the Bible's Grand Narrative.* Downers Grove, IL: IVP Academic, 2006.

Wright N. T. "Christ and the Cosmos: Kingdom and Creation in Gospel Perspective." In *Christ and the Created Order*, edited by Andrew Torrance and Thomas McCall, 97–109. Grand Rapids: Zondervan, 2018.

————. "Justification: Yesterday, Today and Forever." *Journal of the Evangelical Theological Society* 54.1 (March 2011) 49–63.

————. *The New Testament and the People of God.* London: SPCK, 2002.

————. *Paul and the Faithfulness of God.* 2 vols. Minneapolis: Fortress, 2013.

Wright, Nigel Goring. *A Theology of the Dark Side.* Downers Grove, IL: InterVarsity, 2003.

Wright, Tom. *Surprised by Hope.* London: SPCK, 2007.

Younker, Randall W. "Crucial Questions of Interpretation in Genesis 1." *Biblical Research Institute,* 2009. https://adventistbiblicalresearch.org/sites/default/files/pdf/Crucial%20Questions%20of%20Interpretation%20in%20Genesis%201.pdf.

Younker, Randall W., and Richard M. Davidson. "The Myth of the Solid Heavenly Dome: Another Look at the Hebrew (rāqîaʿ)."*Andrews University Seminary Studies* 1 (2011) 125–47. https://digitalcommons.andrews.edu/cgi/viewcontent.cgi?article=3130&context=auss.

GENERAL INDEX

INDEX OF ANCIENT SOURCES